Transmitting Inequality

Transmitting Inequality

Wealth and the American Family

Yuval Elmelech

ROWMAN & LITTLEFIELD PUBLISHERS, INC.
Lanham • Boulder • New York • Toronto • Plymouth, UK

ROWMAN & LITTLEFIELD PUBLISHERS, INC.

Published in the United States of America
by Rowman & Littlefield Publishers, Inc.
A wholly owned subsidary of The Rowman & Littlefield Publishing Group, Inc.
4501 Forbes Boulevard, Suite 200, Lanham, Maryland 20706
www.rowmanlittlefield.com

Estover Road
Plymouth PL6 7PY
United Kingdom

British Library Cataloguing in Publication Information Available

Library of Congress Cataloging-in-Publication Data

Elmelech, Yuval, 1965–
    Transmitting inequality : wealth and the American family / Yuval Elmelech.
        p. cm.
    ISBN-13: 978-0-7425-4584-7 (cloth : alk. paper)
    ISBN-10: 0-7425-4584-9 (cloth : alk. paper)
    ISBN-13: 978-0-7425-4585-4 (pbk. : alk. paper)
    ISBN-10: 0-7425-4585-7 (pbk. : alk. paper)
    1. Inheritance and succession—United States. 2. Social stratification—United
States. 3. Wealth—Social aspects—United States. I. Title.
HB715.E46 2008
305.5'120973—dc22   2007040962

Printed in the United States of America

∞™ The paper used in this publication meets the minimum requirements of
American National Standard for Information Sciences—Permanence of Paper
for Printed Library Materials, ANSI/NISO Z39.48-1992.

To my parents,
Naomi and Clement R. Elmelech

Contents

~

Tables and Figures

Tables

Figures

Acknowledgments

This book is based upon my Ph.D. dissertation in sociology, earned from Columbia University in 2002. I would like first to thank the members of my dissertation committee: I am grateful to Sy Spilerman, whose work on social stratification and wealth inequality sparked my interest in the topic; I have benefited greatly from his excellent guidance, knowledge, and support over the years. Conversations with Charles Tilly and Peter Berman led me to broaden the theoretical framework and to study the historical and institutional context that underlies wealth accumulation processes. I thank Melvin Oliver, who served as an external reader on my board and whose work inspired and motivated my interest in racial inequality in asset holdings and wealth. My research has greatly benefited from suggestions and technical advice I received from my colleague and dear friend Hsien-Hen Lu, who died at a young age; it was a privilege and an honor to know him and work with him. The research and writing of the dissertation was supported by a doctoral dissertation research grant from the National Science Foundation (SES-9906969) and by Ford Foundation grants to the Center for the Study of Wealth and Inequality at the Institute for Social and Economic Research and Policy (ISERP) at Columbia University. During my studies at Columbia, I also benefited from the generous support of the Lazarsfeld Fellowship, the Public Policy Consortium Fellowship (2000–2001), and Dissertation Fellowship, Department of Sociology (2000–2001).

I appreciate the opportunities I had to present my work and to exchange ideas with the fellows of ISERP, Columbia University. Chapters from this book have been presented at the Annual Meetings of the Eastern Sociological Society (2000, 2006), the Annual Meetings of the American Sociological Association (2000, 2002) and at the Symposium on Public Policy and The Academy at Columbia University (February 2004). I benefited from comments and suggestions received from participants in these meetings. Parts of this book, sometimes in different forms, have appeared in *Sociological Inquiry*, and as a chapter in *Wealth Accumulation and Communities of Color in the United States: Current Issues*, edited by J. G. Nembhard and N. Chiteji (University of Michigan Press, 2006). I am grateful for the permission to reprint. I would also like to thank the various organizations and institutions that provided me the survey data used in my analyses: the RAND Corporation for making the RAND HRS 2000/2 data file available and for the technical support from the RAND staff members; the Institute of Social Research at the University of Michigan for making the HRS-92 data available; and the International Social Survey Programme (ISSP) for providing me with the ISSP datasets.

I thank everyone at Rowman & Littlefield who helped make this book possible, especially Alan McClare, who believed in this project from the beginning, and Michael McGandy, Nancy Driver, Catherine Forrest Getzie, and Ariel Giraldi, who were very professional and exceptionally patient even as deadlines passed. The reviewer's report was very helpful and I am grateful for the careful reading of, and thoughtful suggestions on, an earlier verion of the book.

I thank my students and colleagues at Bard College:
   To the many students who took my classes over the past few years and whose questions have led me to sharpen my undeveloped ideas. To Sarah (Jo) Brand for library research, to Margaret Dobbins and Cynthia Werthamer for editing, and to Bethany Lord and Emma McGowan, who proofread and offered helpful comments on an earlier draft of the manuscript.
   To my colleagues in the Sociology and Economics Departments—Amy Ansell, Sanjaya DeSilva, Michael Donnelly, Kijong Kim, Andrew Pearlman, Gautem Sethi, and Tsu-Yu Tsao—for the numerous informal conversations over lingering lunches and dinners. These discussions have greatly benefited and improved my work. To Tamar Khitarishvili for explaining to a sociologist how financial markets and macroeconomic variables interact; to Youngwhan Song, for his helpful suggestions on data analysis; and to Joel Perlmann, for his invaluable comments relating to both content and presentation.

I dedicate this book to my family, near and far. To my parents, who have always given us everything we needed and expected nothing in return, and to my brother and sister for their great sense of humor and genuine interest in me and my work. To my wife and best friend, Beate, for her kindness, generosity, and unlimited patience and love. To Idan and Liad, who forgave me for not spending more time playing with them while working on this book—and for being the kindest, funniest, and most loving kids. This family's unconditional love and unfailing support have been my greatest assets.

Introduction:
Beyond Income

As one digs deeper into the national character of the Americans, one sees that they have sought the value of everything in this world only in the answer to this single question: how much money will it bring in?

—A. de Tocqueville, *Democracy in America*

Dams and Rivers

The United States is the richest nation in the world, with mean wealth per individual that substantially exceeds levels in other industrial countries.[1] In the past two decades, the rate of home ownership has reached its highest level in history, stock ownership has risen dramatically, and the proportion of households that own shares in at least one mutual fund has increased four-fold. Between 1992 and 2001, the average net worth (the value of real estate, stocks, bonds, and other assets minus outstanding debts) of the American family has grown from $230,500 to $395,500, reflecting an increase of 71 percent in real terms (U.S. Census Bureau 2006a, table 702: 476).[2] However, these indicators of economic prosperity and high living standards mask persistent and extreme inequality. In 2001, more than half (57.7 percent) of the total net worth in the United States was owned by the wealthiest 5 percent of the population, whereas the bottom 50 percent held less than 3 percent of the country's net worth (Kennickell 2003).

Some social scientists view the unequal distribution of economic resources as inevitable, even functional. According to this literature, socioeconomic inequality reflects disparities in talent, skills, and effort; in a free market, differential rewards motivate people to acquire education and skills—a process that contributes to economic growth and prosperity. Millions of Americans seem to share this view. When asked whether they agree with the statement "People should be allowed to accumulate as much wealth as they can, even if some make millions while others live in poverty," the majority (58.2 percent) of the respondents in a nationally representative sample of the American adult population either agreed or strongly agreed with the statement. About one quarter disagreed with the statement and only 5.8 percent chose the category "strongly disagree."[3]

In contrast to the public tolerance of wealth disparities, scholars and policymakers have warned that the recent growth in economic inequality is unhealthy and unsustainable. Economist Paul Krugman cautions that wealth inequality today is reaching levels not seen since the late nineteenth century and early twentieth century, a period known as the golden age of American capitalism, when Rockefeller, Morgan, Vanderbilt, Carnegie, and others amassed massive personal wealth in iron, steel, railroads, and finance (Hamnett 2004). In one of his last testimonies before the U.S. Senate Committee on Banking, Housing, and Urban Affairs, Alan Greenspan (2005), chairman of the Federal Reserve Board, warned that the extreme income and wealth bifurcation among large sectors of the population could stimulate public resentment and political polarization, and that these social developments could lead to political clashes and misguided economic policies that work to the detriment of the economy and society as a whole.

Notwithstanding the growing wealth gulf and the potential risks posed by such economic gaps, measures of economic well-being and inequality are based almost exclusively on earnings and income. In the United States, the official measurement of poverty is based on the government's estimate of the minimum amount of income required to sustain a family.[4] The assumption underlying the official poverty line is that annual income is the best indicator of a family's economic well-being, and its ability to acquire necessary goods and services. With the exception of some minor changes made in 1981, the official U.S. poverty measure has not been revised since the Bureau of the Budget (the predecessor of the Office of Management and Budget) issued it in 1969; it has several limitations, which lead scholars and policymakers alike to call for thorough review of the measure (Fisher 1992). One of the main shortcomings of the poverty measure as an indicator of economic status is that, in contrast to wealth, income poverty may be brief (due to unemployment or illness, for example) and does not reflect a long-term record of either success or hardship.[5] Indeed, contrary to common belief, wealth and income are not strongly correlated; empirical research has produced estimates of the correlation between income and wealth that range from a low of 0.26 to a high of 0.50 (Keister and Moller 2000) and the correlation between the two measures is substantially weaker among the higher and lower income brackets (Inhaber and Carroll 1992, figure 5.3: 91).[6]

For property owners, particularly those at the upper end of the wealth distribution, control over tangible assets more often determines income than the reverse. Income can be likened to the flow of a river; the water stream can be massive in some rivers and small in others, especially during dry seasons (unemployment, disability). Wealth, on the other hand, is akin to a dam that holds a substantial volume of water, storing some of the flow and generating currents during dry seasons. "So to be wealthy implies at least the potential for high income. On the other hand, having a high income does not always imply wealth" (Inhaber and Carroll 1992: 5). Moreover, whereas labor income is a flow of financial resources received as payment or *compensation* for work, and thus requires effort, time, and good health, the wealth accumulated in private property represents *control over* capital and goods (Turner and Starnes 1976). For millions of American families whose wealth is small or modest, compensation received in the form of wages and earnings is viewed purely as a means to acquire assets, accumulate wealth, gain control over financial resources, and reduce reliance on both work and welfare. A case in point is lottery winning; data colleted from interviews with small samples of lottery winners who won large sums of money reveal that the vast majority of those who were employed full time prior to their winning quit their jobs; although the proportion of those quitting their jobs upon winning the lottery tended to decrease as earnings and occupational level increased, a majority of workers in every occupational category, including professionals, quit their jobs (Kaplan 1978: 29). Drawing on the fundamental relationships between income and wealth, Haslett (1986: 123) concludes:

> A family's financial well-being does not depend upon its income nearly as much as it does upon its wealth, just as the strength of an army does not depend upon how many people joined it during the year as much as it does upon how many people are in it altogether. So if we really want to know how unevenly economic well-being is distributed in the United States today, we must look at the distribution not of income, but of wealth.

The tendency to rely on annual income rather than on accumulated wealth guides not only policymakers but also the majority of scholarly works on social inequality. The academic literature on social stratification, class formation, and economic mobility has been characterized by an almost exclusive emphasis on the labor market as the main arena in which socioeconomic inequalities are produced and reproduced, while giving education and labor market remuneration a major role in the stratification processes. Shared by the vast majority of research on inequality is the treatment of individual's position in the production process as the key component of the stratification system. Most of the explanatory, or independent, variables in contemporary analyses of class structure and formation have been operationalized and interpreted as individual characteristics—such as educational attainment, age, seniority—and their relations to labor market remuneration. This emphasis on labor market differentials emanating from individual characteristics often leads to the dismissal of extra-individual and structural constraints and invokes a neoclassical, free-market conception of placement in the stratification system (Horan 1978). Under these assumptions, ascribed processes of economic advantage contradict the principle of equal opportunity and are viewed as an obstacle to socioeconomic mobility. The prominent sociologist Talcott Parsons expresses this view by stating that stratification research needs to "divorce the concept of social class from its historic relation to both kinship and property as such" (Parsons 1970: 24).

Individuals, Families, and Individuals as Members of Families

The emphasis on economic attainment based on a universalistic definition of merit necessitates the adoption of the individual as the unit of analysis and promotes the view that human capital and effort are the only keys to the gates of fortune. In contrast to the meritocratic model, theoretical writings on inequality acknowledge that the family is a social institution that plays a critical role in determining the cultural, social, and economic status of its members, and conclude that the family is the appropriate unit in stratification analysis (Barber 1957: 73; Parkin 1971: 14–15, in Spilerman 2000: 497–98; Schumpeter 1966). Why should we treat the family, not the individual, as the unit of analysis within the stratification system?

> This is because in every society, the family, despite variations in its internal structuring, tends to be a solidarity unit based on marriage, sharing a common residence, and caring for dependent children. In order to maintain its solidarity and effectively perform its several different social functions, the family is composed of members all of whom share the same prestige and the same degree of social privilege. (Barber 1957: 73)

Indeed, theories and research regarding aggregate phenomena such as inequality along class, race, or ethnic lines will be more valuable and practical if their theoretical units are families and households instead of individuals (Curtis 1986: 168), particularly when the focus of the analysis shifts from differences in labor market outcomes to variations in asset holdings, consumption patterns, saving behavior, and wealth accumulation processes. For most of human history, the stratification structure was based on systems of family property, and inequality in wealth, status, and power depended primarily on control of land. In that sense, families and individuals—as members of families, not individuals per se—have been the classic property owners (McDermott 1991: 6–7). Families continue to be the unit of analysis in the property system. Family-owned businesses constitute a large proportion of businesses in the United States (the estimates range from 42 to 95 percent) and account for a significant share of the economy;[7] most Americans expect that married couples would share ownership of cars and a main residence and pool their financial resources (checking and saving accounts, stocks and bonds); community property laws in some states consider virtually all property procured by a husband and wife during their marriage (except for gifts or inheritances) to be jointly owned, even if that property was originally acquired in the name of only one partner (Blumstein and Schwartz 1983; Weitzman 1985 in Treas 1993).

What is the source of the discrepancy between the empirical emphasis on the individual in production processes and the theoretical emphasis on family property as the key building block in the stratification literature? The answer to this question partly lies in the enormity of asset-based inequality. Since property tends to be more heavily concentrated in the hands of the few, it is rarely seen as a primary source of reward for the vast majority of the population. Accordingly, earlier works on wealth focused exclusively on a small number of the wealthiest families and the elite (Sorokin 1925; Mills 1956; see Jaher 1980: 224). Gradually, with industrialization, urbanization, and, later on, the increasing number of the adult population—women in particular—who entered the labor market in the second part of the twentieth century, occupational rank has become the dominant factor shaping the reward system for the average American family (Parkin 1971; Sorensen 2000: 139).

Paradoxically, the importance of earnings as a primary source of remuneration for the majority of the population in the post–World War II era has contributed to the growing importance of property ownership in contemporary U.S. society. First, because a growing number of individuals in well-rewarded occupations were able to increase their personal wealth through savings and investment of surplus earnings in desirable assets such as homes, pension plans, and liquid assets, the occupational order became more closely associated with property ownership (Parkin 1971: 24). Second, with the emergence of the two-earner family—from 12 percent in 1960 to 30 percent in the mid-1990s (Farley 1996, figure 4–1: 109)—and the rise in the share of women's income and capital income as important components of total household income, the need to rely on families and households as units of observation in stratification research has become more apparent. Third, the financial resources accumulated by individuals who entered the labor market during the booming post–World War II years are now being transferred to their children. In that sense, intergenerational transfers of wealth are a secondary source of inequality, but that is not to say that they are of secondary importance; family transfers in the form of inter-vivos gifts and bequests perpetuate and potentially intensify economic inequalities arising originally from labor market remuneration (Wedgwood 1929: 60). According to some educated predictions, Americans are embarking on the largest intergenerational transfers of wealth in history, and studies estimate that members of the post–World War II baby boom generation and their children will inherit trillions of dollars from parents and grandparents. Estimates suggest that between 1998 and 2017, Americans' future estates will total between $11.6 trillion and $17.5 trillion, and between 2018 and 2052—a period covering the transfers of the baby boom assets—the amount will be even larger (Samuelson 2000). Using simulation models to predict a low-, medium-, and high-growth scenario of intergenerational wealth transfers, Havens and Schervish (1999) estimate that during the 55-year period from 1998 to 2052, transfers of wealth will total between $41 trillion and $136 trillion. Responding to criticisms that these estimates are too high, the authors have recently reiterated that despite the depressed stock market, recessionary growth, increasing life expectancy, and several other criticisms "the $41 trillion estimate remains valid as a 2% low-growth estimate" (Havens and Schervish 2003), and added that $25 trillion of the $45 trillion will pass directly from descendents to heirs.

Bringing Property and Family Back In

The significance of accumulated wealth to the life chances and living standards of individuals and families, and the changing relationships between one's position in the labor market and the economic well-being of her or his family members and relatives, necessitates a new approach to stratification. This book advances a conceptual framework that contemplates the causes and socioeconomic consequences of social inequality, and brings property and kinship back into the model. One of the critical premises of this book is that private property and its value (net worth) encompass a concept of socioeconomic status that transcends the boundaries of human capital and labor market attainment and is more closely related to the classical concepts of life chances, economic security, and living standards. In this formulation, socioeconomic inequality is measured by assets and net worth rather than by income; focuses on families, households, and generations rather than on individuals; and calls for the consideration of other social factors that have been regarded as "exogenous" by the vast majority of stratification literature.

First, capital accumulation and labor market remuneration are analytically distinct processes, generated by distinct sociodemographic factors, and embedded in different markets. As such, they must be understood as two distinct phenomena of the allocation of status and power (Saunders 1978, 1984; see Burrows and Marsh 1992: 3). Specifically, the study of asset inequality sharpens the notion that labor market remuneration is not an end in itself but is primarily a means by which people achieve economic and social independence and security. Thus, not only has the study of wealth inequality and its determinants been overlooked, but the literature also has given little attention to the complex link between production and capital accumulation processes. Second, asset-based analysis brings back the role that ascription mechanisms play in the stratification system and emphasizes the need to distinguish between ascription and achievement as two distinct (though related) trajectories to wealth. Consequently, disparity in accumulated assets is more critical to the understanding of economic inequality and its cross-generational replication than the more common measures of inequality (for example, poverty, earnings, and occupational status). Third, asset-based analysis explores the increasingly important role that social transactions between and within generations play in the replication of socioeconomic inequality—an issue with critical implications for social inequality in aging societies. Fourth, wealth analysis better unveils the extent to which exogenous factors—such as state redistributive policies, demographic transitions, property rights, and investment opportunities—shape the living standards and life chances of individuals and families.

Overview of the Book

Using data from several national surveys—including the Health and Retirement Study (HRS-92), Generations Survey, Current Population Survey, and 1999 Social Inequality and 2001 Social Networks modules of the International Social Survey Program (ISSP)—as well as publicly available data from other sources, this book's arguments unfold in four parts.

The first part proposes a theoretical framework for the study of socioeconomic inequality. In chapter 1, I describe the historical development and institutionalization of the *commodity market*—a term I use to describe the arena in which individuals, social groups, and financial intermediaries engage in exchange of, and competition over, tangible assets and property rights. The chapter outlines the institutional and structural changes in the United States economy that began in the early 1970s, the impact of deindustrialization and economic restructuring on the labor market outcomes, the deregulation of large segments of the economy, the growing segmentation of the commodity market, and the proliferation of financial assets. As labor income stagnated and the list of things considered to be property expanded to include various financial and income-producing assets such as stocks, bonds, bank deposits, and mutual fund shares, wealth and income inequality increased.

The key thesis presented in chapter 2 is that the historical development of the commodity market coincided with changes in the functions of the family and the role that family and kin relations play in determining the allocation and redistribution of material resources. The analysis focuses on the effects that aging and changing family patterns over the past 50 years have had on the distribution of wealth and asset holdings. By showing that inequalities in control over material resources have an impact on people's life chances, and that these property-based divisions are not a simple product of human capital and labor market disparities, this chapter establishes a conceptual ground for stratification analysis, which highlights the critical role that kinship-based transactions of material resources play in shaping socioeconomic disparities. Whereas the correlation between parental wealth and children's attainment is well documented, what is missing in many of the studies of socioeconomic mobility is the social *mechanism* that links the two variables. This chapter emphasizes the importance of the "pivot" generation—middle-aged Americans on the verge of retirement—as a concept tying younger and older generations, and concludes by proposing the Family Transactions Model (FTM), a theoretical model that links labor and commodity market processes through two social-based mechanisms: marriage and inheritance.

In chapter 3, I argue that the analysis of asset-based inequality is relevant both to the study of class structure and life chances (through the measurement of the level and type of asset holdings in the market) and to the analysis of social status and lifestyle as measured by consumption behavior. Chapter 3 also presents a new scheme of class typology, based on asset holdings rather than labor market remuneration. The essence of this formulation is a broadening of the concept of social class to include considerations of asset type and net worth. This is not an extension of productive property, such as appears in neo-

Marxian formulations. Instead, it views life chances and lifestyles as factors increasingly linked to capital accumulation potential, which encompasses the store of wealth, as well as income flows.

The second part of the book studies two themes: state redistributive policies and attitudinal measures of social inequality and familial responsibility. In chapter 4, I describe the role that asset-based policies in the United States have played in generating and transmitting socioeconomic advantage across generations. After a discussion of these policies, I summarize the key features of the liberal welfare regime, which relies on intensive use of means-tested (residual) forms of welfare, on the one hand, and private, market-based insurance on the other hand, leaving many Americans dependent on familial resources. Chapter 5 complements the assessment of asset-building and welfare policies, with a study of beliefs and practices that sustain control of material resources through private transfers of financial resources. The issue of *generational conflict* versus *generational contract* is examined in terms of older people's disposition of their accumulated wealth and the willingness of younger generations to support the elderly financially. This question concerns the nature of public and private transfers across generations and of attitudes and norms regarding such transfers. Chapter 5 also explores parental investment in child's economic well-being and analyzes the social and demographic factors that underlie this pattern. Cross-national comparisons with other industrial societies further illuminate the distinctive relationship in the United States between individualism and familism.

An analysis of racial and ethnic inequality is elaborated in the third part of the book. The socioeconomic divide between racial and ethnic groups is a central and persistent cleavage in American society. In contrast to education and labor market differentials, analysis of minority-white gaps in wealth is relatively scarce and research on wealth inequality beyond the black–white divide is almost nonexistent. Due to immigration and ethnic variation in birth rates, the proportion of nonwhite Americans is expected to grow drastically; by 2050, about one-half of the population will be nonwhite. In chapter 6, I present several competing explanations for the extreme racial and ethnic gap in the volume and composition of assets and study the sources and socioeconomic consequences of asset inequality between non-Hispanic whites, non-Hispanic blacks, and Hispanics. Special attention is given in this chapter to the impact of demographic processes—immigration, marriage, and divorce—on the unequal distribution of wealth. Empirical findings illuminate the extent to which racial and ethnic variation in immigration status, family structure, and intergenerational transfers are responsible for the white-minority gaps in asset holdings and wealth.

Chapter 7 focuses on intragroup wealth inequality among racial groups and proposes alternative explanations for the increasing socioeconomic polarization *within* the black and Hispanic populations. The discussion also expands the work on the race-class nexus by exploring the effects of family transfers on intragroup wealth inequality among the black, Hispanic, and white populations. The chapter builds on the growing evidence suggesting an increasing class differentiation within the black community and discusses the debate over the "declining significance of race." I argue that previous explanations of the race-class nexus largely overlooked the role that asset holdings and intergenerational transfers play in determining intragroup polarization in material resources. Empirical analysis of wealth distribution among white and minority households reveals that assets are distributed less equally within the minority communities. Because family transmission of material resources captures a long-term, cross-generational process of stratification, its inclusion in models of intragroup inequality is essential to an understanding of the race-class nexus. In the last section of the chapter, I explore the potential impact of racial and ethnic homogamy in marriage patterns, as a distinct form of social closure and exclusion, on the distribution of wealth across racial and ethnic lines.

The concluding chapter presents an elaborated model of production and reproduction of socioeconomic inequality. This theoretical framework provides a link between the labor market and the commodity market. Although at the macro level, the labor and commodity markets are two distinct arenas of socioeconomic inequality, governed by autonomous economic structures, the two markets are linked through intragenerational and intergenerational transactions at the household level. As the United States continues to weaken the social welfare safety net for young householders, the poor, and children, a family's stock of asset holdings has become increasingly important as a protection against economic crisis. Policy implications of this study, to current debates on asset-based policies, are discussed in the final section of the chapter.

PART ONE

FINANCIAL INSTITUTIONS, DEMOGRAPHIC TRANSITIONS, AND ECONOMIC POLARIZATION

CHAPTER ONE

The Institutional Foundation of the Commodity Market

In his property a person exists for the first time as reason.

—G. W. F. Hegel, *The Philosophy of Right*

Property is impossible, because it is the negation of equality.

—P. J. Proudhon, *What Is Property?*

Private Property

As a gauge of economic status, wealth differs from other economic measures in that it captures more than sheer monetary advantage. To understand the significant role of accumulated wealth in people's lives, we must first examine how private property is acquired and distributed. Private property is defined as tangible assets (that is, real estate, land, stocks, bonds, vehicles) and property rights that reflect the owner's ability to control the use of an asset and to consume an asset, either directly or through exchange (Barzel 1997 in Sorensen 2000).[1] This definition acknowledges the dual nature of property both as control over personal possessions—such as a home and car, stocks and bonds—and as a source of financial capital; the owner can use the asset and any revenues derived from the property through discretionary arrangements (renting, leasing, loaning, and so on), sell it for cash, transfer or give it as a gift, bequeath it through a will, and exclude others from using the asset.

As a stock of material resources, control over assets has unique consequences to economic, social, and psychological well-being (see Sherraden,
Page-Adams, and Yamada 1995: 248–51). The accumulation of wealth enables people to live in financial security and provides them with reasonable
comfort. Wealth can finance consumption during times of economic crisis—
illness in the family, losing one's job, divorce, or unexpected expenses—and
can be used to overcome liquidity constraints. Since wealth is held in a variety of forms, it tends to grow or decline over time, according to the value that
people assign to the property and the rate of appreciation and interest rates
associated with individual assets (Nembhard and Chiteji 2006).[2] In addition
to financial advantages, research has linked asset holdings to greater household stability and lower likelihood of domestic violence and family disruption. Recent evidence reveals that, net of other demographic and socioeconomic characteristics, property ownership is associated with better physical
health and lower mortality; the wealth-health association is particularly
strong for older adults in the postretirement age (Sherraden, Page-Adams,
and Yamada 1995; Sherraden et al. 2005). Asset ownership is also linked to
higher self-esteem and self-efficacy associated with control over property, an
attribute which is deeply rooted in American culture (Sherraden 1991). Assets create long-term planning of investment and consumption cycles and,
through intergenerational transfers of wealth, are associated with investment
in children's educational attainment and career development.

Property ownership not only leads to greater care and effort in maintaining assets, but also extends the owners' responsibility beyond the sphere of financial planning and into the domain of individual responsibility and civic
accountability. Private property creates economic and social distinctions between individuals, as well as increases social exchanges and interactions. On
the one hand, as the French sociologist Emile Durkheim observed, property
rights are critical to the manifestation of the individual as a distinct and separate entity from the "shadow of the group" (Parkin 1973). The notion of
"property as exit" (Penalver 2005), for example, captures the self-sufficiency
of property owners and their ability to avoid the demands of the collective,
to decrease dependency on members of the community, and to exclude others from using their property. On the other hand, the institution of property
is itself a product of cooperation; property ownership is key to the development of social contacts between people engaged in exchange.

> It makes sense to argue, as Hegel does, that it is partly in the process of com-
> ing to own things, and to be recognized as their owners, that human beings
> learn to behave rationally and responsibly, to lead an ordered life. It is partly

the process of learning to distinguish mine from thine that a child comes to recognize itself as a person, as a bearer of rights and duties, as a member of a community with a place of its own inside it. (Plamenatz 1975: 121 in Parkin 1979: 127)

The French observer Alexis de Tocqueville viewed widespread property ownership as the foundation of voluntary association in nineteenth-century America (see Sherraden, Page-Adams, and Yamada 1995) and contemporary studies on homeownership show that homeowners are more likely than renters to have a greater investment in the neighborhood, more involvement with their neighbors, and higher participation in local organizations—even after such factors as education, income, and other sociodemographic characteristics are accounted for (Penalver 2005).

Property and Power

As the two quotations at the outset of this chapter imply, tension exists between the individual's financial and social advantages, associated with property ownership, and the macro-level socioeconomic implications of property ownership and its distribution in the population. Property rights are strongly related to the distribution of power in society and the exclusion of others from access to desirable goods. Indeed, power and property are often viewed as two sides of the same coin: "Great fortunes brought their owners public prominence, gross and refined pleasures, and even the chance to do good. But the ultimate gift of colossal wealth, at least for the founders of the richest families, was power" (Jaher 1980: 215). While the exact definition and social context within which power takes place may vary, sociologists generally agree that *power* is "the ability to control events or determine the behavior of others in the face of resistance, and to resist attempts at control by others" (Rothman 2002: 4).

Asset holding is critical to the distribution of power on two complementary levels. First, in the political arena, ownership of large sums of wealth is associated with influence on decision making at the federal, state, and local levels (see Domhoff 1998). Historian Nedelsky (1990: 218), who studied the development of wealth in America, recognized the importance of wealth in shaping policies as well as the absence of a discourse on the relationship between economic and political power: "Even the countless attacks on the power of big business during the progressive era failed to make the political power of wealth or 'business' a basic issue in mainstream American politics." Drawing on recent data on the costs of political campaigns, Perrucci and

Wysong (2003) conclude that while wealth has always been an important factor in political campaigns, the growing use of sophisticated communication and marketing technologies has dramatically increased the costs of campaigning and shifted wealth to center stage.[3] The second feature of the property–power nexus, which directly affects millions of Americans, is the inverse of the first: lack of assets is equated with powerlessness. Indeed, property ownership, even the smallest possession, is a concrete means of having control over one's life and stands as a bulwark against powerlessness and reliance on individuals (employers, landlords) or institutions (welfare agencies, the state) for maintaining an adequate standard of living (Nedelsky 1990: 207).

> A man with much property has great bargaining strength and a great sense of security, independence, and freedom. . . . He can snap his fingers at those on whom he must rely for an income; for he can always live for a time on his capital. The propertyless man must continuously and without interruption acquire his income by working for an employer or by qualifying to receive it from a public authority. An unequal distribution of property means an unequal distribution of power and status even if it is prevented from causing too unequal a distribution of income. (Meade 1980: 105)

How do people acquire assets and accumulate wealth? The distribution and allocation of private property takes place in the market, the arena in which financial institutions operate as vital intermediaries linking individuals and families to various desirable assets. The next section introduces the concept of the commodity market and asserts that the backbone of the stratification system today lies in the link between labor and commodity market processes. I argue that in the present-day multi-asset and post-transitional society, a comprehensive understanding of the stratification system necessitates an analysis of commodity market inequalities (such as asset holdings, net worth, asset portfolio) and their relationships to disparities in human capital and labor market attainment.

The Commodity Market

> Whoever controls the property of a nation becomes thereby the virtual leader thereof.
>
> —W. I. King, *The Wealth and Income of the People of the United States*

In contrast to most contemporary research on social inequality, earlier works give private property and its distribution a critical role in the study of stratification processes. The seminal works of Karl Marx and Max Weber acknowledge that, in addition to inequalities that emerged from the division of labor, capitalism raises new—and not necessarily equal—opportunities for ownership of tangible property. The connection between production and capital accumulation processes, the relationship between income and wealth, and the role that achieved and ascribed factors play in the production and reproduction of asset-based inequality are strongly embedded in the classical works of social stratification (Weber 1958, 1964: 281; Marx 1962: 627–31, 754–75; Durkheim 1992: 123–26, 174–76, 215–16).

According to Marxian theory, the relevant economic divisions between owners of means of production and workers are formed within the division of labor in the production processes (Parkin 1978; Robinson and Kelley 1979). While the Marxist analysis emphasizes the possession of productive property and exploitation of the propertyless laborers, ownership of unproductive property is not entirely ignored. The distinction between the "industrial capitalist" and the "owner of property"—who "by virtue of title to a portion of the globe has become a proprietor of these natural objects" (Marx 1962: 754)—serves to demonstrate how ownership of natural forces (such as waterfalls, rich mines, and undeveloped land) can be monopolized. A "surplus profit"—the difference between the price received for the commodity and the capital invested in it—is guaranteed to property owners, regardless of their role in the production process. Under these conditions, the owner can gain profit from renting his property to the industrial capitalist, who uses it as a means of production, as in the case of a waterfall, or to the propertyless laborers, as in the case of rented housing units (Marx 1962: 754–55).

Undoubtedly, the work of the German sociologist Max Weber offers the most coherent analysis of asset-based inequality (see also Saunders 1978; Burrows and Marsh 1992; Rex and Moore 1967). The Weberian analysis views the economic structure as a complex, multidimensional phenomenon. In contrast to Marx, the Weberian framework explicitly recognizes that social cleavages that arise from consumption patterns do not overlap with, and may be more fundamental than, socioeconomic divisions arising from the social organization of production (that is, ownership of productive property) (Saunders 1984, footnote 1: 217). Specifically, the Weberian scheme acknowledges that control over material resources creates specific life chances—that is, the chances of gaining access to scarce and valued resources—and is critical to an understanding of the stratification system. According to this perspective, unequal distribution of material resources is determined by competition over economic interests in both the labor market and the commodity market:

> We speak of "class" when (1) a number of people have in common a specific causal component of their life chances, so far as (2) this component is represented exclusively by economic interest in the possessions of goods and opportunities for income and (3) is represented under the conditions of the commodity or labor market. (Weber 1958: 181)

This definition explicitly suggests that economic position is identified with market situation; the assets that one holds, and which determine his or her life chances, only have social and economic significance in the context of exchange in the market (Breen 2005: 41). Drawing on the Weberian notion that the market distributes life chances according to the resources that individuals bring to it, we can portray the commodity market as an arena in which individuals and social collectives—such as families, households, communities, and financial intermediaries—are engaged in exchange and determine the prices and quantities of productive and nonproductive tangible assets, as well as property rights that function in much the same way as physical property. Consequently, the unequal distribution of property and wealth reflects competition for opportunities of exchange and the exclusion of others from desirable assets such as housing, land, and businesses.

Social Stratification Dichotomies

One important feature of the stratification system that stems from the Weberian analysis is the inclusion of both labor and commodity market processes in the model. Contemporary works on social stratification often overlook the concept of the commodity market and its relations to labor market characteristics. This oversight resulted in the neglect of those processes of wealth accumulation that occur in the commodity market but bear little or no relation to labor market processes. Indeed, one of the noticeable characteristics of the literature on social stratification is that the independence of labor from commodity market processes is a key assumption underlying the study of economic inequality. This is unfortunate, because the relationships between the two markets hold clues to questions that intrigue social scientists on the distinctive nature of stratification systems and the types of social processes that serve to preserve or alter class, race, and gender inequalities. Specifically, I argue that six dichotomies dominate the stratifi-

Analytical Components	Empirical Attributes		
1. Market	Labor	-	Commodity
2. Unit of analysis	Individual	-	Family/Household
3. Principle for placement	Production	-	Accumulation
4. Exclusionary criteria	Individualist	-	Collectivist
5. Form of financial advantage	Flow (income)	-	Stock (wealth)
6. Intergenerational mobility	Human capital	-	Tangible capital

Figure 1. Social Stratification Dichotomies

cation processes (figure 1), and the analysis of the relationships between and within two sets of attributes is of critical importance to the understanding of the contemporary stratification system.

Most studies of inequality are confined to the left-hand side of the dichotomy. These works study individual attainment in the labor market, measured by flow of financial resources (wages and salaries), as the key principle of placement in the stratification system; workers' productivity—seen as a function of their skills, capabilities, formal education, and on-the-job-training—is rewarded by high wages and occupational prestige. Consequently, research on intergenerational mobility studies the economic advancement (or decline) across generations by focusing on labor market outcomes and on the transmission of occupational status among individual males in two generations (fathers and sons) (Hauser 1998; Haveman and Wolfe 1995).[4]

A relatively small number of works, whose theoretical framework is based on the Weberian class analysis, better represent the right-hand side of the dichotomy. These studies tend to emphasize differences based on consumption and wealth accumulation, measured by asset holdings and wealth, while using the household as the unit of analysis. In this literature, households are seen as units made up of members with different labor market capacities, marital history, and financial resources. Different types of households—in terms of size, structure, and age—have different needs and opportunities in regard to accumulation and composition of private property; these variations lead to diverse socioeconomic outcomes.

To provide a more complete picture of the structure and reproduction of social inequality, both labor and commodity market processes need to be addressed. To achieve this goal, one needs first to acknowledge the autonomy of these two markets and then study the distinct factors that link them and shape the distribution of material resources.

Wealth and Labor

In colonial America, the notion of private property as a natural right was embedded in religious and educational institutions and eventually manifested as the Fifth Amendment, which states that no person should be "deprived of life, liberty or property, without due process of law; nor shall private property be taken for public use, without just compensation" (see Schlatter 1951: 193–94).[5] The significance of private property as a natural right stemmed from the strong interrelationship between property and inequality. Concern about wide asset-based inequality and the concentration of land in the hands of the few led Thomas Jefferson to claim in 1785 that small landholders "are the most precious part of a state" and called on legislators to enhance the subdivision of landed property and restrict the concentration of wealth through inheritance (Brown et al. 2005).[6] The need to protect and expand private property derived from the notion that property ownership is strongly linked to liberty and economic independence.

> The problem of property arose for the Framers because their conception of property was inseparably tied to inequality. The link to inequality was liberty. Property was important for the exercise of liberty and liberty required the free exercise of property rights. (Nedelsky 1990: 205)

The assumed linkage between private property and liberty stems from the belief that the universal basis for both property rights and socioeconomic autonomy is embedded in the concept of *labor*. In pre-industrial America, the economy was largely based on agriculture, and tangible wealth derived from land ownership inherited from fathers to sons.[7] Independent labor—which by the mid-eighteenth century was typically farming—and the personal character and merit associated with such self-sufficiency was seen as the only means to free people from subordination to superiors (Katz 1976: 474). The availability of vast areas of agricultural land created the enticing possibility of private ownership, which enabled even the poorest families to achieve economic self-sufficiency (Warner 1968: 16 in Dreier 1982: 181). Private property was considered to be a sign of attachment to the new society and an indication of one's character and merit. In 1893, John Hay, later appointed secretary of state, expressed these views: "That you have property is a proof of industry and foresight on your or your father's part; that you have nothing is judgment of your laziness and vices, or of your improvidence" (in Dreier 1982: 181–82).

Major policies that aimed to boost land ownership and independent labor were first introduced in the mid-nineteenth century. Signed into law on May

20, 1862, the Homestead Act facilitated settlement in the Western territo-
ries by turning over vast amounts of the public domain to private citizens.
Between 1863 and 1939, nearly 3 million people applied for homesteads; almost 1.5 million households were given title to nearly 246 million acres; almost 10 percent of the area of the United States was claimed and settled under this act (Shanks 2005).[8] Under this program, citizens with few or no
assets could find unoccupied land, file a homestead application, and, after
living on and cultivating the land for five years, own the parcel, and achieve
financial independence (Shanks 2005: 23).[9] While the robust belief in the
connection between private property and individual merit has remained a
strong ethos in the United States, institutional, economic, and demographic
changes that took place during the twentieth century have dramatically
changed the visible link between work and property rights.

The Property-Labor Link and the
Rise in Homeownership

In the early twentieth century, the direct link between participation in the labor market and position in the commodity market was altered as government
policies and private financial intermediaries broke into the labor-property
nexus. Two institutional changes that underlie this historical process merit attention. The first involves the decommodification of the welfare state. The
concept of decommodification captures the idea that social policies of the
modern welfare state provide sufficient income, which allows individuals to
"opt out of work," thereby reducing the necessity to sell their labor as a commodity that can be bought by potential employers (Van Voorhis 2002: 6).
Critical theorists view this trend as a sign of the emergence of the exchange-
value orientation, which challenges the dominant meritocratic ideology; such
a system is demonstrated by the increasing number of people who do not support themselves through income from work, but rather rely on the state to
provide them with economic security (Habermas 1989: 280).

Even in the United States, a nation with limited social welfare provision,
the role of the government in assuring the welfare of its citizens had expanded in the early twentieth century. Until the 1930s, the United States did
not have economic and political imperatives toward a provision of welfare,
but the Depression changed the nation's view of the government's role in
protecting citizens from poverty and starvation. The social insurance reforms
of the New Deal represented a relatively rapid and sharp expansion of welfare through programs such as Social Security, Aid to Dependent Children

(ADC), and various housing programs (Shammas, Salmon, and Dahlin 1997). These programs, in particular the 1935 Social Security Act, reflected the recognition among policymakers that interruptions in earnings, which often lead families to impoverishment, could not be resolved through the market economy: "Perhaps it was a small step, but it was probably the largest step that could have been taken at that time, and it was a step in a new direction. With the Social Security Act, the United States had begun" (Levine 1988: 257).

The second, more significant, yet understudied, shift in the connection between labor market position and wealth accumulation involves the changing role the state and financial institutions play in the commodity market. This transition began with the shift in privately owned property from predominantly productive property (land) to domestic property (homeownership); with increasing industrialization, urbanization, and, later on, suburbanization, a growing number of middle-class families had access to homeownership—a functional, nonproductive asset that today symbolizes a core component of the American dream. From the late nineteenth century until 1930, less than half of all households in the United States owned their primary residence (figure 2). The Great Depression drove homeownership rates to their lowest level of the century—43.6 percent in 1940. But during the post–World War II period, a dramatic increase in homeownership occurred: Between 1940 and 1960, homeownership rates increased by almost

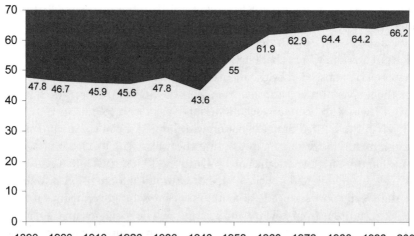

Figure 2. Owner-Occupied Units as a Percentage of Occupied Housing Units, 1890–2000

half, from 43.6 percent to 61.9 percent (Hobbs and Stoops 2002, figure 4–6: 125). This sharp increase was boosted by postwar economic prosperity; an invigorated home-building industry; favorable tax laws; increasing opportunities for home ownership through the GI Bill of Rights (Serviceman's Readjustment Act); and generous government financing through the Federal Housing Administration (FHA). Established in 1934, the FHA has provided government mortgage insurance on loans made by FHA-approved lenders (Brown et al. 2005; U.S. Department of Housing and Urban Development 1996). During the booming 1950s, one third of all private housing was financed by FHA or Veterans Administration (VA) programs (Dreier, Mollenkopf and Swanstrom 2001: 109).

The rapid spread of homeownership and the emergence of housing as the single most important means of wealth accumulation for most Americans signify an important stage in the detachment of labor from commodity market processes characterized by a shift from productive property to domestic property associated with family economics and consumption.[10] After two decades of rapid increase, homeownership rates continued to rise at a substantially slower pace (Hobbs and Stoops 2002, figure 4–6: 125) and the past four decades have witnessed a new stage in the commodity market, characterized by the emergence of various financial assets and increasing diversity in asset portfolios. At the risk of oversimplifying the economic changes that took place during the past four decades, and particularly since the early 1970s, data on labor and commodity market processes generally suggest a growing importance of household wealth accumulation in determining life chances and placement in the stratification system, as well as a growing autonomy of the labor and commodity markets. These trends occurred largely because of structural changes in the labor market and the institutional development of the commodity market.

The Changing Structure of the Market

In contrast to the steady rise in median income and relative stability in earnings disparity during the post–World War II years, the early 1970s marked a dramatic reversal in income trends. Over the past three decades the United States has experienced relative stagnation in earnings levels and growing polarization in earnings inequality; Morris and Western (1999) report that "by the early 1990s, nearly 80 percent of workers earned less than their counterparts in the 1960s." Deindustrialization and economic restructuring, along with the dynamics of globalization, have had a major impact on the changing distribution of labor income and have contributed to the growing disconnection between labor and commodity market outcomes.[11] In the early 1970s, global competition between the United States and the economies of Western Europe and Asia led to a rapid process of deindustrialization and economic restructuring (Bluestone and Harrison 1982) that included outsourcing, subcontracting, and the shifting of employment away from manufacturing and manual employment. The result was a dramatic shift toward nonmanual, precarious, and part-time employment in the service sector. In 1982, services surpassed manufacturing as the largest employer among major domestic industry groups, and the trend has continued since.[12] Many positions in the emerging private service sector are characterized by low wages, a high number of part-time jobs, and limited access to pension benefits.[13] Deindustrialization and economic restructuring contributed to overall stagnation in labor income (Levy 1995; Morris and Western 1999) and disproportionately affected men, who were more likely to be employed in manufacturing. Consequently, this group's earnings have become more bifurcated over the past three decades.

The past three decades have also witnessed dramatic institutional changes in the commodity market. From the mid-1970s, as deindustrialization accelerated—and corporate profits from the domestic economy declined—private investments became less tied to domestic manufacturing and continued to grow: "In 1970, direct investment by U.S. firms abroad was $75 billion, and it rose to $167 billion in 1978. In the 1980–1985 period, it remained below $400 billion, but thereafter increased gradually each year, reaching $4716 billion in 1994."[14] Moreover, during the 1980s, large segments of the economy were deregulated and experienced a wave of mergers (Stearns and Allen 1996). These trends, which were made possible by changes in the legal environment (Stearns and Allan 1996), involved the closing of plants and increase in layoffs, but worked in favor of investors and contributed to the increasing impact of financial investments on the distribution of household wealth and property income (Kesiter 2000). While in the past, opportunities for investment and access to financial assets were limited to a relatively small segment of the population, the second half of the twentieth century saw the proliferation of numerous financial institutions and private corporations that function as intermediaries between households and financial and income-producing assets.[15]

These institutional changes are part of a more general trend of financialization, that is, the increase in the importance of "financial markets, financial motives, financial institutions and financial elites in the operation of the economy and its governing institutions, both at the national and international level" (Epstein 2002: 3). At the international level, increased openness of economies in the second part of the twentieth century led to greater saving and investment opportunities as financial institutions were no longer limited to lending domestically and were not bound to accept funds from domestic investors. On the domestic level, financialization creates growing demand for financial services; on the one hand, the expansion of the financial sector leads to increases in output by making funds available to finance new and existing enterprises. On the other hand, the expansion of the aggregate output generates stronger demand for financial services and thus further expands the financial industry (Levine 1997; Levine and Zervos 1996; Berglof and Bolton 2002). Since the mid 1970s, financialization has transformed the functions of the American economic system, elevated the significance of the financial sector relative to the real sector, and contributed to the marked increase in household access to credit (and debt) (see Palley 2007). As will be seen in the next section, these institutional changes have slowly opened up the market to larger segments of the population, and the utility of property as a source of revenue, unrelated to one's position in the labor market, became more visible.

The Emergence of the Multi-Asset Society

As noted above, from the early 1960s, the homeownership rate has risen at a relatively slow pace. While the overall rate of homeownership grew between 1995 and 2005—reaching a record high of 69.1 percent in the first quarter of 2005—this increase did not match the dramatic rise of the post–World War II period, and was not evenly distributed across various demographic and economic categories. Recent evidence suggests that the homeownership rate for younger segments of the population, in particular working families with children, is lower today than it was in the late 1970s (Center for Housing Policy 2004).[16]

While the United States mortgage market has historically consisted of two segments—the conventional "prime" mortgage market and the government subsidized home loan market—the 1990s witnessed phenomenal growth in what came to be known as *subprime* mortgage lending. Subprime mortgage loans entail higher than average interest rates to accommodate borrowers with a wide variety of individual circumstances—such as low credit quality, few assets available for down payment, unstable income, or heavy debt loans—that prevent them from qualifying for prime loans at lower interest rates in the conventional mortgage market. In 2004, subprime loans accounted for 19 percent of all home mortgage loan originations in the United States (Hearing before the Subcommittee on Financial Institutions and Consumer Credit 2006: 130-131; FRBSF 2006).

The "democratization of credit" and the rise in ARM (adjustable-rate mortgage) loans, which made it possible to make smaller down payments and take out more substantial loans with higher interest rates when purchasing homes and vehicles—functional assets associated with household consumption—coincided with growth in household debt, particularly among young and low income families (Draut and Silva 2004).

> In the residential mortgage market, lenders have developed products that have broadened the base of household debt by enabling borrowers with impaired credit or limited funds for a down payment to purchase homes. . . . In the auto finance market, more drivers than in the past are leasing cars instead of purchasing them (Bucks, Kennickell, and Moore 2006: 147).

During the last fifty years, the ratio of total household debt to personal disposable (after tax) income grew fourfold; between the mid-1950s and the mid-1960s, the ratio grew from 35 percent to 65 percent, and after two decades of relative stability it has almost doubled, reaching 118 percent in 2005 (Teplin 2001; Bahchieva et al. 2005).[17] More than two-thirds (70 percent) of family debt in 2004 is attributable to the purchase of a primary residence, while the share of debt on residential real estate other than a main residence and on vehicles—the second- and third-largest reasons for borrowing—were 9.5 percent and 6.7 percent, respectively (Bucks, Kennickell, and Moore 2006). While the increase in household debt and, more recently, the rise in foreclosure among low-income families (Bahchieva et al. 2005) had a diminishing impact on the net equity held in functional assets (cars and homes) that are central to family consumption, access to financial and income-producing assets became more widespread through the operation of various financial intermediaries (corporations, banks, insurance companies) that manage savings and investment portfolios. These intermediaries provide fertile ground for the creation of new forms of financial assets, such as various securities, depository claims, and other contract rights that further enhance the diversity of an asset portfolio (Langbein 1991).

Data on historical trends in asset ownership show that, as a component of household wealth, financial assets (such as money-market funds, stocks, bonds, and other financial securities) have had the most dramatic increase, particularly in the second part of the twentieth century (Wolff 1994, 1996). Comparison of data from the early 1960s and the early 1990s reveals that the percentage of household assets held in real estate other than a primary residence had increased from 6 percent to 11 percent, the percentage held in pension wealth had increased from 2 percent to 9 percent, and the percentage held in business assets had grown from 15 percent to 18 percent (Keister and Moller 2000). During the 1980s and 1990s, diversity continued to dominate the market as people utilized more options to invest their wealth and shift money from one asset to another. The percentage of households that directly or indirectly own stocks in publicly traded companies increased from fewer than one-fourth in 1983 to almost half in 1998. The booming stock market has inflated the amount of wealth held in stocks; the percentage of households with stocks worth $10,000 or more has tripled from 10.8 percent in 1983 to 31.8 percent in 1998 (Wolff 1996; Engen, Lehnert, and Kehoe 2000).[18]

The appeal and availability of structured savings, in the form of retirement plans with automatic enrollment and restricted withdrawals, have contributed to the visible increase in the number of individuals and families that have access to financial and income-producing assets (Bernanke 2006). Indeed, the growth in household ownership of financial assets, particularly stocks, is explained in part by the proliferation of mutual funds available to families, as well as the growth in tax-deferred retirement saving accounts offered by employers, which often allow workers to invest in corporate equities (Kennickell, Starr-McCluer, and Sunden 1997; Engen et al. 2000). In 1984, fewer than 12 percent of all U.S. households owned shares in a mutual fund, and by 1992 the proportion had grown to 27 percent. As of June 2000, an estimated 50 million households, or about half of all households, owned shares in at least one mutual fund. Mutual funds have become an important intermediary between households and financial markets; between 1990 and 2000, total mutual fund assets increased nearly sevenfold, making them the largest type of financial institution (as measured by assets under management), even larger than commercial banks.[19]

Traditional and Roth IRAs, as well as employer-sponsored retirement accounts such as the 401(k), provide multiple tax-advantages and federal subsidies that enable workers to boost their retirement savings in order to enjoy greater economic security and independence in post-retirement years (Brown, Kuttner, and Shapiro 2005: 13). By 2000, 41 percent of all U.S. households owned at least one type of IRA, up from 35 percent in 1989, and across all but the highest income levels, households were more likely to own stock indirectly through retirement accounts rather than directly (Engen, Lehnert, and Kehoe 2000). And while government-subsidized savings accounts were primarily made available to augment the retirement nest egg of individuals and families, in recent years these mechanisms of wealth accumulation have expanded to include savings for other purposes, such as the college education of younger members of a household (education IRAs) (Brown, Kuttner, and Shapiro 2005: 12–13).[20]

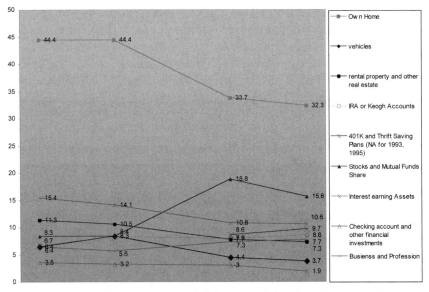

Figure 3. Percent of Aggregate Household Net Worth by Asset Type, 1993–2000
Source: Orzechowski and Sepielli (2003)

Figure 3 reports statistics from the 1993, 1995, 1998, and 2000 Survey of Income and Program Participation (SIPP) on the various forms in which household net worth is held. The data reveal noticeable changes in the composition of household wealth during the 1990s. While housing prices have gone up since the mid-1990s, the substantial amount of debt associated with functional assets and the growing appeal of financial investments and savings led to an overall decline in the *proportion* of household net worth held in functional assets (main residence and vehicles) from half (50.8 percent) in 1993 to about one-third (36 percent) in 2000. In 1993, 44 percent of the net worth of U.S. households was held in main residences, while in 2000, the figure was 32.3 percent.[21] As seen in figure 3, the proportion of net worth held in stocks and mutual funds nearly doubled, from 8.3 percent in 1993 to 15.6 percent in 2000, and the proportion of wealth held in IRA or Keogh accounts and in 401 and thrift saving plans totaled 18.2 percent in 2000. Using data from the 1983–2004 Survey of Consumer Finances (SCF), and analyzing temporal trends in household ownership of fungible assets (assets that can be readily converted to cash), Wolff (2007) reports two seemingly contradicting trends: While the share of gross housing wealth of total assets rose from 30.1 percent in 1983 to 33.5 percent in 2004, the share of net home equity (the gross value of the owned house minus any outstanding mortgages) fell from 23.8 percent in 1983 to 18.2 percent in 1998, and then rose to 18.8 percent in 2001 and 21.8 percent in 2004. The discrepancy between gross housing wealth and net home equity is attributable to the rise in median housing prices by 18 percent between 2001 and 2004, and the equally remarkable growth in mortgage debt from 20.9 percent in 1983 to 34.8 percent in 2004.[22] Shapiro (2006: 73) explains:

> Americans cashed out $333 billion worth of home equity between 2001 and 2003 when interest rates were low and refinancing was advantageous. . . . However, a majority of households used their newfound wealth . . . to cover living expanses and repay credit and debt. . . . Cashing out home equity is particularly troublesome given the decline in homeowner's equity between 1973 and 2004. In other words, Americans own less of their homes today than they did in the 1970s and early 1980s.

As mentioned above, the portfolio composition of household wealth varies significantly across wealth brackets. Because wealth is so unevenly distributed, and the wealthiest 5 percent of the population holds about two-thirds of all corporate stocks (Kennickell 2003; Wolff 1996), many of the changes in aggregate data on wealth composition reflect the booming stock market in the 1990s, which has mainly affected the wealthiest segments of the population (Kennickell 2003: 393). Accordingly, while the overall proportion of home equity declined during the 1990s, the primary residence remains the major source of wealth for the vast majority of Americans. Data from the SCF show that for those Americans in the 50–95 percentile category of the wealth distribution, the proportion of wealth held in principal residences declined from 53.8 percent in 1989 to 45.9 percent in 2001, whereas for those in the 0–50 percent of the distribution, the proportion had slightly increased over the same period, from 56.7 percent to 59.7 percent (Kennickel 2003, table 11: 23).

Commodity Market Segmentation

While the intrinsic utility of functional assets (main residence and vehicles) is their use value, financial assets such as stocks, bonds, and retirement accounts are held as a means of generating more wealth and accelerating consumption in the future. The temptation to consume or sell an asset, the level of control over an asset, the impact of asset holding on economic security and civic responsibility, and the ability to liquidate and pass on property to children and other family members, vary greatly across asset type (Sherraden

1991, chap. 6; Levin 1998; Rohe and Stegman 1994; Galster 1987; Massey and Basem 1992).[23] Ownership of financial and income-producing assets such as corporate stocks, rental property, and businesses, which generates "real" wealth and steady income, is qualitatively different from ownership of functional assets associated with consumption patterns and family economics (Oliver and Shapiro 1995: 105). Financial and functional assets do not require the same care and management and the size and function of the financial institutions that are involved in their transactions vary substantially by asset type. Whereas homeowners legally own their homes, in most cases the asset is mortgaged and under some circumstances it can be taken from the owner. In contrast, financial assets, such as stocks and bonds, are more easily liquid and are increasingly negotiated on national and global markets. There are also notable differences in the taxes levied on the various forms of capital; while homeownership is encouraged by generous tax benefits, capital gains are taxed (Clignet 1992: 82).

To argue that the commodity market is becoming more visibly diverse and segmented along the functional-financial line is not to deny the strong link between functional and income-producing assets. While financial and functional assets are located in distinct sectors, and their value is shaped by specific market circumstances and may move in opposite directions—for example, home prices may be inversely correlated with interests generated from savings accounts or the appreciation of stocks at the household level—possession of functional and financial assets are closely interconnected. A household's allocation of resources often follows the functional-to-financial sequence, starting with the purchase of a vehicle and a home to establish itself financially, and progressing into a more diverse portfolio. Furthermore, functional and financial assets have become increasingly interrelated through the role of financial intermediaries and the recent advancement in home equity lending, which has made it easier for homeowners to extract equity from their homes through a home equity line of credit or a cash-out refinancing. This way, homeowners are able to convert functional assets to financial ones or to consumer items, a flexibility that further enhances the diversification of wealth portfolio; rising home prices and falling interest rates have increased the desire of many homeowners to convert their home equity into liquid funds. These new borrowing opportunities have prompted many households to refinance their mortgages (Dynan, Johnson, and Pence 2003: 217; Brady, Canner, and Maki 2000) and created strong incentives for homeowners to engage in repeated market transactions (Penalver 2005: 1950). Not surprisingly, the proportion of homeowners who refinanced their mortgages rose sharply during the 1990s. Survey data show that the main reasons for refinancing included obtaining a lower interest rate, changing the term of the loan (such as conversion from an adjustable-rate to a fixed-rate mortgage), and liquefying equity (Brady, Canner, and Maki 2000). Consequently, whereas a household's decision to invest in one type of asset typically involves the decision not to invest in another, the development of financial institutions creates borrowing mechanisms that inflate the volume and diversify the portfolio of household wealth. While many households have benefited from these opportunities and improved their position in the commodity market, large segments of the population remain unaffected by these mechanisms of wealth buildup, and their relative position in the market has worsened; poor and minority households are often unable to take advantage of these favorable opportunities in the commodity market, due to lower levels of financial literacy, discrimination in credit availability, and limited access to financial institutions and government funds (Dymski 2006).

The expansion and diversity in wealth portfolios among the nonpoor, as well as the relaxation of credit standards, the ability to liquefy equity, and the appreciation of financial and income-producing assets over the past two decades (Kennickell, Starr-McCluer, and Sunden 1997), led to two important outcomes. First, these changes have contributed to the increasing polarization in asset holdings and wealth. The distribution of household net worth is especially unequal in the United States and it has become more so since the early 1980s, as the increase in wealth among the top heavy (Wolff 1995) coincided with an increase in the number of households with zero or negative net worth. [24] Not surprisingly, a cross-national comparison of wealth inequality ranks the United States as both the wealthiest and the most unequal (Wolff 1996). Between 1983 and 2001, the number of American households that owned property worth $1–5 million increased by 123 percent, those with property worth $5–10 million increased by 304 percent, and the number of households with more than $10 million increased by 409 percent, from 66,500 to 338,400 (New York Times 2005). These changes in the commodity market resulted in an increasing detachment of income (which represents the national productive capacity) from wealth (which represents investment opportunities and consumption potential), and has led policymakers to express concern that this "wealth effect" would result in an outbreak of inflation (Greenspan 2000). While between 1980 and 1994 the ratio of household net worth to household disposable income (inflation-adjusted after tax) ranged between 4.3 and 5.0, this figure surged beginning in 1994, reaching more than 6.0 in 2000—the highest recorded value in the 50 years for which wealth data are available—and fell back in 2003 to just under 5.0 (Bernanke 2003).

In addition to its impact on the distribution of wealth, the development of the commodity market and the proliferation of new forms of financial assets have important implications for the income that derives from the property system in the form of capital gains, dividends, interest, and rent.[25] Contrary to earnings and wages, the income generated from assets does not require a tradeoff with leisure, it does not decline with illness or unemployment, and it is often treated much more favorably under tax laws. In the past several decades, capital income has become an increasingly important component of the total income of many middle-class households, and the portion of income emanating from asset holdings has increased. Over the years, as life expectancy has risen and more people have retired, income from earnings has dropped steadily, while the share of assets and saving component in the income composition of the American family has increased. Since the early 1970s, inequality in the labor income of heads of household has increased drastically but the importance of this component as a source of household income has fallen.[26] Data from the Panel Study of Income Dynamics (PSID) reveal that the rising inequality in property income, particularly dividends, interest, and rent, has played the most important role in the increase of overall inequality in family income between 1975 and 2000 while rising inequality of labor income played only a secondary role (Pryor 2007). A recent study found that the contribution of wealth-adjusted income[27] to the overall increase in income inequality over the past two decades was substantial; this finding led the authors to conclude that the so-called working rich have not "fully replaced the 'coupon-clipping rentiers' at the top of the economic ladder" (Wolff and Zacharias 2006: 7). To illuminate the consequences of asset-based inequality and the extent to which commodity market processes are shaping the life chances and economic well-being of individuals and families today, it is critical to recognize the significant effect that the changing demographic structure has on the distribution and intergenerational transmission of economic advantage. The next chapter addresses these relationships and their socioeconomic consequences.

CHAPTER TWO

~

Demographic Changes and the Distribution of Wealth

The ownership of personal or material productive capacity is based upon a complex mixture of inheritance, luck and effort, probably in that order of relative importance.

—Frank Knight, *The Ethics of Competition*

Property, in fact, is not exclusively acquired by labor, but may be derived from other sources: (1) by exchange, (2) by donations inter vivos or legacy by will, (3) by inheritance.

—Emile Durkheim, *Professional Ethics and Civil Morals*

The Missing Link:
Demographic Trends and Economic Outcomes

The historical changes in the portfolio composition of household wealth—from a limited number of productive assets (including land, plants, and equipment) to a multi-asset portfolio—have developed with equally important changes in the role that the family plays in the production and capital accumulation processes. Throughout most of the pre-industrial period, the family functioned as the central productive unit of society. Children worked in their parental household, or in someone else's household, and received training to prepare them for future occupations (Vinovkis 1987). With the acceleration of industrialization and urbanization after the Civil War, the structure and function of the family altered in three notable ways. First, a fundamental trend underlying the changes in household and family formation during the nine-teenth century was the movement of production processes from the household into the workplace, a move that transformed the family-based economy and resulted in a new configuration of family systems—characterized by a gradual separation of market economic production (work) from household activities (Coontz 2006: 70; Ryan 1983; Cherlin 1983; see also Tilly and Scott 1978). As more goods and services were produced outside the home, and opportuni-ties in the urban labor market attracted a growing number of young men away from the farm or family business, the need to live and work in a multigenera-tional family setting became less prevalent (Coontz 2006; Cherlin 1983).

Second, the direction of intergenerational wealth flow changed. During the first demographic transition (FDT), which began in the early nineteenth century and continued into the first half of the twentieth century, fertility and mortality rates declined, while incentives to invest in child education and economic well-being grew (Coale and Watkins 1986; McLanahan 2004). The demographer Caldwell (1978) describes this change as a shift from pre-transitional to post-transitional society. In pre-transitional soci-eties, having children is profitable, as children's labor contributes to the eco-nomic status of the family; these societies are characterized by high fertility and mortality rates and by net wealth flows from younger to older genera-tions. In post-transitional societies, rearing children is costly and women limit their fertility; these societies typically have lower birth rates, higher life expectancy, and are characterized by downward net wealth flows, from older to younger generations (see Bergstrom 1996).

Third, during the second part of the twentieth century, with the institu-tionalization of the commodity market and the expansion of financial inter-mediaries, another stage in the changing functions of the family emerged: the movement of capital accumulation out of the household and into the mar-ketplace.

> The ever-larger capital requirements of technologically advanced enterprises require modes of financing that exceed the capabilities of the family. The cor-poration, as well as specialized financial institutions, arose to facilitate the pooling and allocation of capital. Corporations, banks, insurance companies, and other financial intermediaries displaced the family from its former role as the primary unit of capital accumulation. In turn, these intermediaries created new forms of wealth in financial assets—various securities, depository claims, and other contract rights. (Langbein 1991: 19)

The proliferation of new forms of private property necessitates a greater re-liance by the family on financial institutions to manage its increasingly diverse portfolio, a state that has further enhanced the proliferation of new forms of assets and dependence on financial intermediaries. Complete reliance on household and kin members as the primary source of credit allocation and valuable assets is currently a phenomenon that is documented almost exclusively among immigrant minorities with limited access to formal markets; research documents how immigrant families and ethnic groups displace labor market functions (such as screening, recruitment, and training) from the labor market and the firm to family, kin members, and ethnic communities who operate to provide jobs, housing, and access to credit (Sassen 1996; Waldinger 1996 in Tilly 1998: 159; Townsend 2005).[1] With the passage of time, however, immigrants gradually rely on formal markets and institutional agencies in their search for better opportunities in the labor, credit, and commodity markets.[2]

Temporal and Functional Dimensions of Market Disengagement

Figure 4 illustrates the historical changes in the relationships between labor and commodity market processes as they coincide with the changes in the functions of the family. The temporal axis shows the gradual movement of production and, later, capital accumulation out of the domestic and into the corporate realm. As the asset portfolio of the average family became more diverse during the second half of the twentieth century and included possession of numerous assets (stocks, bonds, savings accounts, real estate, primary residence, among others), unrelated to one's direct role in production processes, a structural shift toward a greater separation between labor and commodity market processes occurred. As seen in figure 4, in the contemporary multi-asset, post-transitional society, the labor and commodity markets are two distinct arenas of stratification; the two markets are independent in the sense that changes in one do not necessarily correspond to changes in the other. Although commodity and labor market processes are autonomous, one must not ignore the strong and reciprocal links between the two markets; how do jobs and asset holdings relate in a functional way? More specifically, how does one's position in the labor market translate into her/his position in respect to living standards and private property?

At the macro level, labor and commodity market processes are linked through market mechanisms of competition and exclusion. Because property rights are, by definition, a form of exclusion that limits access of nonowners to valuable and scarce resources, competition and exclusion are inherently embedded in property relations.[3] Lack of asset holdings reduces the bargaining power of the worker and leaves him/her more vulnerable to exploitation in the

TEMPORAL DIMENSION

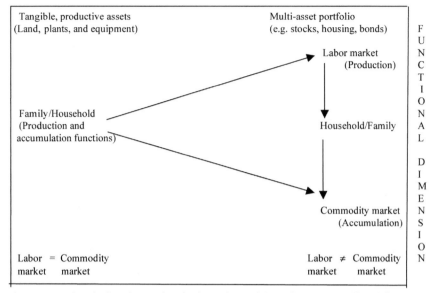

Figure 4. **Historical and Functional Dimensions of the Labor-Commodity Linkage**

production processes. This vulnerability depresses the worker's earnings and limits the ability of her/his family to save money and build a modest safety net. This property-labor nexus, which involves exclusion from both production and accumulation processes, has received some attention in Marxist interpretations. While, according to the Marxist scheme, the sources of both types of exploitation—and their remedy—are to be found in the capitalist mode of production, the cumulative effect of exclusion in production and accumulation processes intensifies the principal inequalities that are inherent within the capitalist mode of production. A case in point is housing. Limited access to housing leads to financial vulnerability and results in potential exploitation in the labor market; the combination of low wages in the labor market and high rent in the housing market can be used against workers as a means of "practically expelling them from the earth as a dwelling place" (Marx 1962: 754). Consequently, workers who own a home can no longer be seen purely as proletarians; as the economic interests of property-owner workers align with the interests of other property owners, the class consciousness of these workers becomes blurred (Engels 1975 in Gilderbloom and Markham 1995; for contemporary applications of the linkage between labor and housing market processes see Marcuse 1987: 121; Stone 1980; 1993; Katznelson 1992, chap. 6).

At the micro level, the answer to the question regarding the labor-commodity nexus is straightforward and is to be found in the distinct units of measurement—individual and household—that operate in labor and commodity market processes, respectively. Labor and commodity markets are linked primarily through the ability of households to save, invest, and acquire varying quantities and qualities of private property. Therefore, one's position in the labor market forms a functional link between the two markets—and any attempt to develop a model of commodity market inequality requires an understanding of labor market inequalities. This observation is in agreement with the neoclassical theory of socioeconomic inequality, which attributes wealth inequality to education, skill, and labor market differentials. Over time, however, this link has become increasingly indirect. As we have seen in figure 4, the movement of production and capital accumulation out of the family and into the corporate realm has altered the direct link between labor market success and commodity market attainment. This historical detachment of labor from commodity market processes coincided with the increasing importance of family-based transfers of wealth, as a means to enhance the social and economic well-being of property owners, and resulted in growing socioeconomic polarization.

To better understand the social origins of this polarization, two forms of social closure that function as pathways that intervene in the relationship between individual attributes and household position in the commodity market should be analyzed. The first form of closure is intergenerational transfers of tangible wealth, accumulated by previous generations and transferred to the current generation in the form of bequests and inter vivos gifts (transfers that people make during their lifetime). The second factor that affects wealth accumulation is family structure and its effect on division of labor and economies of scale within families. The next sections elaborate on these family-based mechanisms of wealth buildup. Specifically, I argue that during the second half of the twentieth century, changing demographic structures have altered the form and magnitude of these two family-based forms of economic transactions and further complicate the direct link between individual labor market attainment and household capital accumulation processes.

The Aging Society

In coming decades, many forces will shape our economy and our society, but in all likelihood no single factor will have as pervasive an effect as the aging of our population.

—Ben Bernanke, *The Coming Demographic Transition: Will We Treat Future Generations Fairly?*

The population of the United States, as in many other industrialized societies, is aging. Over the course of the twentieth century, the number of Americans aged 45–64 has increased by 50 percent and the number of those older than age 65 has tripled (see figure 5). This demographic change stems from the sustained decline in fertility that followed the post–World War II baby boom and the continuous lengthening of life expectancy. Historical trends in fertility rates of American women show a drastic increase from the mid-1940s through late 1950s; the average number of births per women rose from 2.2 in 1941 to more than 3 during the baby boom (1946–1964), reaching almost 3.8 in 1957, a level not seen in the United States since the earliest years of the twentieth century. In the mid 1960s, fertility rates began to fall, and have leveled off since the mid-1970s; in 2001, the rate was 2.1 children per woman, a number that reflects the sharp increase in the number of childless women aged 40–45, from 10.1 percent in 1980 to 19 percent in 2000 (U.S. Census Bureau 2004b; NCHS 2002; Bachu and O'Connell 2001). The rise in life expectancy, which is partly attributed to the overall improvement in health provision, progressed in a linear form; in 1900, life expectancy was 47.3. By 1950, it jumped to 68.2 years and in 2003, life expectancy at birth for the total population reached a record high of 77.6 years (NCHS 2002; Bernstein 1995; Hoyert, King, and Smith 2005). Consequently, the elderly (65 years and over), who comprised only 1 in every 25 Americans (3.1 million) in 1900, made up 1 in every 8 Americans (33.2 million) in 1994 (Bernstein 1995). While between 1990 and 2000, for the first time since 1900, the elderly population grew more slowly than the total pop-

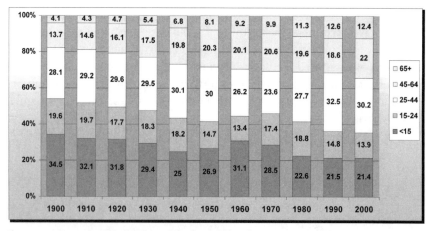

Figure 5. Percent Distribution of the Population by Age Categories: 1900–2000
Source: U.S. Hobbs and Stoops 2002. Census Bureau, Decennial Census of Population: Figure 2-4: 56.

ulation, this relative decline is linked to the low fertility of the late 1920s and 1930s and is expected to reverse as the baby boom generation (born from 1946 to 1964) reaches age 65, starting in 2011 (Hobbes and Stoops 2002). It is estimated that between the mid-1980s and 2040, the population aged 65 to 74 will grow by about 85 percent, the population aged 80 and older will grow by about 300 to 400 percent, and the population aged 90 and older will grow by about 500 to 700 percent (Lamm 1999). Most of the growth in the older population will occur between 2010 and 2030, when the majority of baby boomers enter their elderly years (Bernstein 1995). By 2050, 1 in 5 Americans could be elderly. The increase in life expectancy and overall improvement in health status enables many American households in the "third age"—a concept developed to reflect the increasing financial independence, accumulated wealth, and personal fulfillment of middle-aged persons in an aging society (Angel and Angel 1997: 169)[4]—to maintain active and productive post-retirement lives.

The Bell Curve and the Pivot Generation

A comparison of historical data on wealth distribution by age categories from three different studies at three points in time—1774, 1870, and 1962— reveals a surprisingly stable pattern:

> The age profiles yielded by these three major studies of the wealth distribution spanning two centuries are quite similar. In all instances except for gross wealth in 1870, the peak is in the 55–65 age interval. The mean gross wealth of the 35–44 age group is about half of the mean of the 55–64 age group in all three instances, while net worth is about a third. (Kearl and Pope 1983: 153)

The data presented in table 1 describe recent patterns of net worth distribution along age categories and reveals a similar relationship vis-à-vis the association between age and wealth; young households are the most economically vulnerable, whereas middle-aged households are the most financially secure. In 2001, for example, the median net worth rose from $11,600 for householders under 35 years of age to a peak of $181,500 for those 55 to 64 years of age. It then stabilized and slightly fell off, reaching a low of $151,400 for householders 75 years of age and older (U.S. Census Bureau 2006a). Data on the mean value show a similar curvilinear pattern. However, in comparison to the median, the mean value for each age category is substantially higher, a pattern reflecting the extreme inequality in household net worth.[5] In addition to the strong correlation between age and net worth, the portfolio composition tends

Table 1. Family Net Worth: Mean and Median Net Worth in Thousands of Constant (2001) Dollars, 1992–2001

	1992		1995		1998		2001	
	mean	median	mean	median	mean	median	mean	median
All families	230.5	61.3	244.8	66.4	307.4	78.0	395.5	86.1
Age of family head								
Under 35	56.2	11.4	49.9	13.9	69.5	9.9	90.7	11.6
35-44	164.8	55.1	165.9	60.3	213.6	69.0	259.5	77.6
45-54	331.7	96.8	342.4	107.5	394.1	114.8	485.8	133.0
55-64	418.0	141.1	442.3	133.2	579.3	139.2	727.0	181.5
65-74	354.6	121.7	402.9	128.0	507.9	159.5	673.8	176.3
75 and over	264.0	107.5	298.5	107.5	338.3	136.7	465.9	151.4

Source: U.S. Census Bureau, *Statistical Abstracts of the United States* (2006)

also to vary substantially across age groups. The peak-wealth age group tends to hold a higher share of their wealth in financial assets, and the proportion of wealth held in housing assets tends to decline at age 40; the amount of financial assets held by the 55–64 category, for example, is 17 times greater than the mean wealth held by the youngest (under 35) group (Tracy et al. 1999). These age differentials are translated into higher property income (interest, dividends, and rental income), an increase that compensates for some of the loss in earnings and other sources of income (Radner and Vaughan 1987; Torrey and Taeuber 1986).[6]

Why do the middle-aged have more wealth than members of other age groups? The curvilinear, bell-shaped pattern of the wealth distribution is consistent with the Life-Cycle Hypothesis (LCH), according to which household wealth follows the course of labor market participation; increasing income during work life is correlated with increasing wealth, while the spending down of financial resources is more common during the post-retirement years. Moreover, the growth in public investments in education over the past fifty years is clearly reflected in the educational attainment of today's older working-age population compared to that of earlier cohorts. The proportion of women aged 55 and older with a high school education increased from 25 percent in 1960 to more than 65 percent in the mid-1990s. The comparable figure for men shows a threefold increase during the same period. Not only did this age cohort have better job opportunities early in life, along with a more favorable pension coverage and better health status, but it also benefited from better investment opportunities and rates of return (Samuelson 2000). The pattern of gradual accumulation in later stages of the life cycle is also consistent with an age-cohort explanation, according to which there is no significant dissaving at old age, but rather a lower rate of accumulation by younger cohorts (see Spilerman 2000: 508). Recent data also show growing debt and a decrease in the wealth level of young cohorts, relative to the wealth base of older households, and a shift of wealth away from young households, particularly those under age 35, and toward those in the 55–64 age group (Wolff 2007). This pattern can be partially explained by the decline in homeownership rates among young couples, a pattern that deprives young families of several years' participation in the wealth buildup that frequently derives from homeownership (Spilerman 2000: 507–8). Finally, the distinct wealth level and portfolio composition of middle-aged households is also attributed to the unique financial decisions and saving behavior of this age category. These decisions are likely to be influenced by the cost of college education for their children and the need to save for their own retirement (Kennickell, Starr-McCluer, and Sunden 1997). As the number of middle-aged people increases, the overall proportion of financial assets held by the average American households rises.

The distribution of wealth by the rigid age categories seen in table 1 is somewhat misleading, as it masks some of the key features that characterize wealth buildup; wealth accumulation involves collective and durable effort of individuals, families, and generations. Rather than looking at age groups as distinct age cohorts—that is, those people born in the same time interval—or according to the life-cycle sequences of education, work, and retirement ("welfare generations"), wealth analysis requires the study of age categories as "family generations" that focuses on lineage between grandparent, parent, and child (Attias-Donfut and Arber 2000; Ryder 1965; Schuman and Scott 1989). In the post-transitional society in which wealth flows predominantly downward from older to younger generations, a life-cycle theory of wealth accumulation that excludes intergenerational transfers provides a partial picture of the process of capital accumulation in the U.S. economy (Kotlikoff and Summers 1989). Many middle-aged Americans experience a significant increase in wealth generated from their double advantage in both saving opportunities and intergenerational wealth transfers they receive from their parents. Their parents, who were born in the early twentieth century, were granted access to new sources of wealth and income, thanks to government support via the New Deal programs, the GI Bill, mortgage guarantees, and the Great Society–era expansion of benefits to the elderly (McNamee and Miller 1998: 207; Newman 1993; Reich 1964). Since 1935, when the Social Security Act was passed, the economic circumstances of the elderly have improved dramatically. In the mid-1960s, the poverty rate among the elderly (65 years and older) was about 30 percent, while about 10 percent of adults (18 to 64 years) were defined as poor; in 2005, the comparable figures were 10.1 percent and 11.1 percent. The elderly today are less dependent on their children's assistance (DeNavas-Walt, Proctor, and Lee 2006; Levy 1995: 39) and are likely to transfer large amounts of wealth to their adult middle-aged children:

> Reared in an age of frugality, earning incomes during a period of rapid expansion and prosperity, and having purchased homes that have greatly appreciated in value, this generation is expected to disperse accumulated assets in excess of $10 trillion between 1990 and 2040. (Shapiro 1994 in Miller and McNamee 1998: 207)

Family and Wealth: Intergenerational Transfers

> The man who dies thus rich dies disgraced.
>
> —Andrew Carnegie, *The Gospel of Wealth*

> The rich man dies like the poor man; of all his wealth he takes not a penny with him.
>
> —Arthur J. Eddy, *Property*

The most common approach to studying the intergenerational transmission of material resources focuses on production processes and involves an examination of the paths by which parental education and labor market status are replicated. The social mobility literature tends to emphasize parental human capital and labor market success as the main factors determining social and economic outcomes of children (Blau and Duncan 1967; Duncan 1968; Duncan, Featherman, & Duncan 1972; Hauser 1998; Haveman and Wolfe 1995) by focusing on the transmission of occupational status among individual males (fathers and sons).[7] Though parental education and occupational position have a considerable effect on children's attainment (Jencks 1979; Sewell and Hauser 1975; Hill and Duncan 1987), education and occupation are not directly transferred. Rather, direct transfers of material advantage are made from the stock of assets, in the form of inter vivos gifts and bequests (Spilerman 2000), and this process encompasses a wide social network that includes members of the extended family (aunts, uncles, grandparents, and parents-in-law). In other words, an understanding of the *mechanisms* that underlie intergenerational transfers of material advantage necessitates the study of wealth transfers across generations.

The classical works on stratification acknowledge the influential role of wealth transfers in the replication of social inequality. The Marxian view holds that intergenerational transmission of property rights enhances the concentration of relatively small and scattered private properties into a huge private property in the hands of the few (Marx and Engels 1962: 928). Since inherited property perpetuates the concentration of productive property and promotes the exploitation of the propertyless laborers, the abolition of inheritance rights is seen as a necessary step toward a society in which "the free development of each is the condition for the free development of all" (Marx and Engels 1962: 54). Emile Durkheim—widely regarded as the founder of the structuralism-functionalism theory—describes a similar picture of growing class polarization due to wealth transfers and warns of some imperative moral consequences of ascribed economic advantage. Defining exchange by contract and inheritance as the two critical sources of tangible property, Durkheim posits that in contrast to exchange, which creates new objects of ownership and enhances social bonds and solidarity among people, the institution of inheritance—viewed as a survivor of an earlier stage of communal property—is an immoral source of property, because inheritors are not the originators of the property (Durkheim 1992: 123, 173).[8]

> The inheritor is endowed with goods and chattels of which he is not the originator and which he does not even owe to any act of the one who did create them. In certain circumstances, it is kinship alone that confers the right to property. (Durkheim 1992, 123)

American sociologist Talcott Parsons (1970) has developed this idea by emphasizing the inherent contradiction between individual merit and ascriptive criteria and stresses the need to dismiss inheritance as a major institution in modern society. According to Parsons, in order to understand social stratification processes, one needs to focus on a universalistic definition of merit rather than on kinship inheritance: "Social stratification in its initial development may thus be regarded as one primary condition of releasing the process of social evolution from the obstacles posed by ascription" (Parsons 1970: 500). Indeed, in many scholarly works, the view holds that the transmission of wealth stands in sharp contrast to economic attainment through individual merit, and is often seen as a hindrance to the "natural" distribution of resources and the healthy functioning of supply and demand.[9] The neoclassical literature views the practice of inheritance as incompatible with basic values or ideas that underlie capitalism, because inheritance is not an act of exchange in the marketplace but rather is the transfer of material resources that takes place in the private sphere. As such, inherited advantage leads to concentration of wealth and power, hinders the free operation of the market and contradicts the three fundamentals of capitalism as put forward by Milton Friedman: the ideal of distribution according to productivity, the principle of equal opportunity for all to pursue the occupation of their choice, and the idea of liberty, which is defined as a free market that mutually benefits the parties that take part in the exchange (Friedman 1962: 161 in Haslett 1986).

While inheritance was predicted to vanish as an institution of social stratification, empirical evidence generally supports the strong association between inherited wealth and the growing concentration of wealth. In the early twentieth century, studies on wealth and power focused on the wealthiest entrepreneurs, as these individuals best symbolized the American dream of individual innovation and effort as a means of amassing wealth. This body of work investigated the processes responsible for the wealth buildup of the very rich and found a strong intergenerational link.[10] Although they build up enormous fortunes, many of the corporate rich in America today are inheritors who owe the bulk of their wealth to gifts and bequests they received from parents and relatives. This finding is not surprising. The number of children and family members who benefit from the passing on of businesses and tangible wealth is larger than the number of the so-called self-made men in the previous generation: "The fabled entrepreneurs of this century, like John D. Rockefeller and Henry Ford, are gone, but their families and much of their fortune endure" (Allen 1989: 4). A comparison of data on the origins of wealth among the very rich in 1892 and 1989 found that the proportion of inheritors among top wealth holders has doubled in less than a century (Inhaber and Carroll 1992: 138; see also Allen 1989).

The growing proliferation and diversity of wealth composition and the rise in median wealth levels over the past three decades have made more common the practice of cross-generational transfers as a means to promote the economic well-being of family members, not only among the super-rich but also among a growing number of middle-class households. Survey data reveal that one-fifth of respondents in the United States say they have received an inheritance (in an average amount of $64,906) and 28 percent say they are expecting to receive an inheritance (Joulfaian and Wilhelm 1994). And while most elderly people plan to bequeath a modest financial inheritance, about 25 percent expect to leave inheritances worth $100,000 or more, a pattern referred to as "bifurcated bequest motive" (Smith 1997). While the exact time of death is unknown to most people, and the passing on of bequests is not directed at a particular end, such as the purchase of a home or business (Kohli and Künemund 2003:125–31), research on transfer motives suggests that, notwithstanding the unpredictability of the exact time of death, many families deliberately accumulate and diversify their financial resources in order to pass on wealth to their offspring (Gale and Scholz 1994a; Bernheim 1991 in Spilerman 2000).

It is true, however, that because of demographic and institutional changes that took place during the twentieth century, intergenerational transfers of material advantage have become more complex, materializing in different forms and through different social mechanisms.[11] As a result, the socioeconomic impact of this specific mode of "opportunity hoarding" (Tilly 1998) has become more difficult to predict. Attempts to measure the impact of financial transfers on the economic status of heirs have resulted in controversial conclusions and different methods of analysis yield different results. Contemporary estimates suggest that intergenerational transfers account for at least half of total net worth accumulation (Gale and Scholz 1994a), though variant calculations range from 20 percent (Modigliani 1988) to 80 percent (Kotlikoff and Summers 1988; see Menchik and Jianakopolos 1998). The discrepancy between the two extreme estimates emerges from the varying definitions and measurement of wealth transfers; while Modigliani (1988) includes only bequests and major gifts between households and imputes to the contribution of bequests only the actual amount of these transfers, Kotlikoff's (1989) measure is broader—consisting of college education fees and other parental spending—and includes the accumulated interests on all transfers received by adult children (Arrondel and Masson 2006; Blinder 1988). While exact figures are unknown, estimates of the amount of wealth transferred at death in 1982 came to approximately $200 billion, with two-thirds of this amount passed from parents to children (Wilhelm 1996). Avery and Rendall (1994 in Wilhelm 1996) report that in 1990 children inherited $39.4 billion, but they add that this is likely to be an underestimate. Research on wealth flows across generations found that the gross flows of inter-household gifts and transfers are overwhelmingly downward, from older ages to younger ones, and estimated the average net payment in gifts and bequests from the parental generation to their children at roughly $25,000 per child (Lee and Miller 1994; see also Bergstrom 1996). Kotlikoff and Summers (1989: 43), who study aggregate saving rates in the United States, conclude that the life-cycle component of savings is very small, and that "American capital accumulation results primarily from intergenerational transfers."

The Inheritance Transition:
Bequests and Inter Vivos Gifts

The emergence of new types of assets with different levels of desirability and profitability, the availability of fluid capital, and the changing demographic structure of society have drastically altered the form and structure of intergenerational transfers. While wealth transmission from parents to children once tended to center upon major items of patrimony, such as the family farm or the family firm, wealth transfers today may skip a generation, pass from aunt to niece or sister to brother, and need not necessarily take place at death (Atkinson 1972: 184–5). Historians studying the American family in the nineteenth century have documented the transition from predominantly testamentary to inter vivos gifts and linked the shift in forms of family transfers to the growth of financial institutions in the late nineteenth century that made it easier for wealth holders to liquefy tangible assets:

> The passing of physical property, often the family farm, was of central importance in early America. Colonists, if they could, avoided liquidation of production capital . . . gradually, during the nineteenth century, there was a major change. . . . Instead they liquidated, and children more often received cash shares . . . with the growth of financial institutions and corporate forms in the nineteenth century, wealth holders found it easier to convert physical property into liquid assets. The transference of a viable business was no longer necessary. (Shammas 1987: 209)

In the second half of the twentieth century, however, and mainly since 1970, as the institutionalization of the market has accelerated and the proportion of wealth held in financial and income-producing assets has risen, the shift from predominantly testamentary to inter vivos gifts in which parents use their financial resources as a means to invest in their children's skills and human capital became prevalent, involving an increasingly large number of American households (Langbein 1991; also see discussion in Hall and Marcus 1998).

Inter vivos transfers differ from inheritance in some fundamental ways that shape the impact of intergenerational transfers on economic stratification. In contrast to bequests, the timing and goal of inter vivos gifts are planned, and are more likely to be targeted at specific ends, such as the purchase of a home or the acquisition of human capital. Empirical estimates conclude that a substantial amount of inter-household transfers occur between living people; Gale and Scholz (1994: 156) report that intended transfers account for "at least 20 percent of U.S. wealth and possibly more" while

Cox and Raines (1985) assess the fraction of inter vivos of total (inter vivos and bequests) transfers at about 60 percent. Explanations of voluntary (inter vivos) transfer motives range from pure altruism to strategic exchange. Some studies accept the possibility of altruism and see it as the primary motive in intergenerational family relations (Becker 1991; Spilerman 2000). This line of research concludes that the social and economic well-being of the child is the key incentive underlying transfers from parents to children. Under this assumption, parents give more resources to the child with the least resources. According to the exchange model, by contrast, parents transfer resources to children because they expect to get goods and services in return, such as visits, telephone calls, and financial resources to secure care in old age.[12]

The Inheritors

> If it had been my good fortune to come into the world a struldbrug, as soon as I could discover my own happiness, by understanding the difference between life and death, I would first resolve, by all arts and methods, whatsoever, to procure myself riches.
>
> —Jonathan Swift, *Gulliver's Travels*

As life expectancy increases, intergenerational transfers in the form of bequests pass on in a later stage in the life cycle, namely when the heirs are in their fifties and sixties. Data on intergenerational transfers by age categories reveal that inter vivos transfers are more frequently received by the young, and the incidence declines steadily with age. Consequently, the total accumulative amount of transferred wealth tends to increase until the age category of 40 to 44, and this age group receives the largest flow of inter vivos transfers (Wilhelm 2001:146; see also Hamnett 1991; Hamnett, Harmer, and Williams 1991). Thus, to capture the impact of intergenerational transfers on the distribution of wealth in aging societies, it is appropriate to focus on the older, rather than the youngest, households. Table 2 displays data from a nationally representative survey of middle-aged American households and describes the extent to which the demographic and socioeconomic characteristics of receivers of material resources differ from those households who did not benefit from these transactions.[13] The table includes detailed information on three forms of transfers—inheritance, gifts from relatives, and life insurance benefits—as reported by middle-aged American households.

Two key findings emerge from the information displayed in table 2. First, receivers of intergenerational transfers have socioeconomic and demographic characteristics that distinguish them from nonreceivers. Second, there is a

Table 2. Selected Characteristics of Households by Receipt (versus Nonreceipt) of Intergenerational Transfers (Weighted by Household)

	Received Inheritance/Trust		Received Inter Vivos Gifts		Received Life Insurance	
	Yes	No	Yes	No	Yes	No
Race:						
White	.94	.75	.94	.78	.85	.79
Black	.024	.128	.030	.113	.086	.10
Hispanic	.017	.088	.018	.078	.043	.075
Other	.013	.025	.010	.024	.015	.023
Total	100	100	100	100	100	100
Marital Status:						
Married	.72	.64	.74	.65	.32	.67
Partner	.020	.020	.017	.023	.019	.029
Separated	.023	.038	.013	.037	.021	.035
Widow	.068	.086	.054	.085	.55	.055
Never Married	.044	.048	.057	.047	.009	.050
Divorced	.12	.16	.11	.15	.068	.15
Total	100	100	100	100	100	100
Age	56.5 (4.9)	55.9 (4.8)	56.0 (5.0)	56.1 (4.8)	56.1 (4.4)	56.1 (4.9)

Gender (male)	.55	.52	.56	.52	.24	.54
Parental education	11.3	9.9	11.6	10.0	10.6	10.1
	(3.4)	(3.6)	(3.4)	(3.6)	(3.3)	(3.6)
Professional/managerial occupation	.40	.27	.42	.29	.30	.30
Employed	.69	.66	.74	.66	.66	.67
Education (years)	13.5	12.1	13.8	12.3	12.7	12.4
	(2.6)	(3.2)	(2.6)	(3.1)	(2.5)	(3.1)
Household income ($1000)	57.2	58.1	67.1	48.5	43.5	50.4
	(51.0)	(53.3)	(69.1)	(51.0)	(35.9)	(53.7)
Size of household	2.4	2.6	2.6	2.5	2.2	2.5
	(1.1)	(1.3)	(1.2)	(1.3)	(1.3)	(1.3)
Number of children	2.9	3.1	2.9	3.1	3.2	3.1
	(1.9)	(2.1)	(1.9)	(2.1)	(1.9)	(2.1)
Native-born	.95	.89	.95	.90	.94	.90
Mean Net worth (in $1000)	362	211	480	222	219	244
	(641)	(488)	(812)	(489)	(304)	(537)
N	1423	6184	549	7058	373	7234
	18.7%		7.2%		4.9%	

*Source: HRS-92.
Note: Family Transfers include three categories: (1) inheritance (2) transfers from relatives in the amount of $10,000 or more (3) life insurance payments. The transfer categories are not exclusive: respondents who received more than one type of transfer are included in more than one column.

noticeable variation in the sociodemographic characteristics among receivers, based on the type of transfers being made. Compared with nonreceivers, receivers of inheritance or inter vivos gifts are more likely to be white, and are more likely to be married than divorced, separated, or widowed. They tend to have higher levels of education, to be employed, and to hold prestigious professional occupations. Receivers of inter vivos gifts, in particular, tend to have the highest level of both household income and wealth. One possible explanation for this pattern is that, in contrast to bequests and life insurance benefits, voluntary transfers are likely to be targeted at specific ends. Recipients of life insurance benefits differ from recipients of inheritance and gifts in some fundamental ways: the racial composition of life insurance beneficiaries is similar to that of nonbeneficiaries, as are their labor market and education characteristics.

What are the sources of these private transfers of wealth? As noted earlier, studies on intergenerational mobility tend to focus on the economic status of parents and their children. Less attention has been given in the past to direct transfers of private resources from relatives other than parents. However, given the gradual increase in life expectancy and the longer years of "shared lives" across generations (Bengston 1996; Riley and Riley 1993 in Bengston et al. 2003), the expansion of intergenerational support networks available to individuals and families is notable. The data displayed in table 3 suggest that wealth transfers are not limited to parents and children, but involve wide networks of exchanges that link individuals, extended families, and generations. While parents remain the main source of transfers in the form of inheritance and gifts—approximately 65 percent of transfers reported were from parents—other members of the extended family play an important role in shaping the economic status of younger generations. The fact that 12 percent of the inheritance reported and 14 percent of the gifts reported were received from parents-in-law, and that 4 percent of the gifts were received from a spouse or ex-spouse, highlights an important material advantage associated with marriage. Transfers from aunts and uncles intensify the role that the extended family plays in promoting the economic well-being of its members; almost 12 percent of bequests and 9 percent of inter vivos gifts come from aunts and/or uncles. Siblings and children are less likely to be the source of either inheritance or gifts. As expected, the main source of life insurance benefits is the spouse, and life insurance beneficiaries are more likely to be widowed and females. Finally, an interesting finding concerning the relationship between inheritance and inter vivos gifts is the relative independence of these two forms of transfers (table 3): Whereas 8.5 percent of inheritors report receiving

Table 3. Selected Characteristics of the Recipients of Family Transfers, by Transfer Type

	Inheritance/Trust		Inter Vivos Gift		Life Insurance	
	Yes	No	Yes	No	Yes	No
Source of transfer (among receivers)						
Grandparents	5.4		1.6		—	
Parents	63.5		66.1		6.0	
Parent-in-law	11.7		14.3		3.2	
Child		—		.2		9.8
Aunt/Uncle	11.6		8.9		.7	
Respondent's sibling	1.3		1.8		4.0	
Spouse/Partner sibling	.5		.7		.9	
Spouse/Ex-spouse	2.7		4.3		72.5	
Other	3.4		2.2		2.9	
Total	100		100		100	
Other types of transfers received:						
Inheritance	—	—	.22	.20	.23	.20
Inter-vivos	.085	.078	—	—	.093	.079
Life insurance benefits	.060	.052	.062	.053	—	—
N	1423	6184	549	7058	373	7234
	18.7%		7.2%		4.9%	

*Source: HRS wave 1.

Note: Family Transfers include three categories: (1) inheritance (2) transfers from relatives in the amount of $10,000 or more (3) life insurance payments. The transfer categories are not exclusive: respondents who received more than one type of transfer are included in more than one column.

gifts, 7.8 percent of noninheritors were also recipients of inter vivos gifts. Whereas 22 percent of the households that received gifts also received inheritance, 20 percent of those who did not receive gifts reported that inheritance was transferred to them in the past. Note, however, that many receivers benefit from multiple transfers; the average number of inheritance and gift received is 1.3 and 1.6, respectively.

Family and Wealth: Marriage

> There is certainly no country in the world where the tie of marriage is more respected than in America or where conjugal happiness is more highly or worthily appreciated.
>
> —A. de Tocqueville, *Democracy in America*

In addition to aging and its impact on intergenerational transfers, a key demographic transition that has a substantial effect on the distribution of wealth is the changing structure of the American family. In comparison to other industrialized Western nations, marriage is more prevalent in the United States and the vast majority of American adults—about 95 percent of whites and 88 percent of blacks—eventually marry (Cherlin 2005).[14] Marriage and wealth are closely related; the amount of net worth among households maintained by married couples is about five times greater than the amount of net worth held by households maintained by either single women or single men (U.S. Department of Commerce 1995a). Moreover, the longer couples stay married, the greater their wealth accumulation becomes and the greater the parental wealth is that they leave to children and other relatives. The economic function of legal marriage has clear advantages in terms of possession and accumulation of financial resources and clear disadvantages when marriages dissolve and the assets are divided (Wilmoth and Koso 2002). A compilation of empirical works provides evidence and explanations for this association between marriage and wealth buildup (Waite and Gallagher 2000: 113).

First, division of labor between married couples enables them to be more productive and efficient. The possibility of social exchanges between husband and wife results in a total product that is larger than the sum of the outputs that each produces separately: "It is often forgotten that the modern domestic household is very much an economic unit even if it is no longer a farming unit" (Goode 2005). Furthermore, research on the "marriage premium" indicates that married men have higher wages than nonmarried (separated, divorced, and never-married) men, even after controlling for demographic and labor market characteristics, and taking into account the selection of men with higher education and greater earning power into marriage (see review in Thomas and Sawhill 2005). Married couples also benefit from economies of scale—the sharing of house, car, and domestic commodities—that allow them to maintain higher standards of living than do single people with similar socioeconomic characteristics.

Second, with the drastic increase in two-earner families, married people are more likely to have higher incomes and greater savings. Although labor force participation has increased for all women during the second half of the twentieth century, the subgroup whose participation rate has increased more rapidly over the past three decades is married women with children. In more than 60 percent of marriages, both spouses work, and in about one-quarter of dual-earner couples, the wife's earnings are higher than the husband's (Thomas and Sawhill 2005: 59).[15] While the above-noted economic rewards in labor market remuneration may also be advantageous in cohabitation, that is, the sharing of a household by unmarried persons, cohabitation remains more transitory than marriage (Bumpass and Sweet 1989; Bumpass and Lu 2000) and it lacks the legal and institutional bonds of marriage that are critical for the long-term processes of wealth accumulation. A multivariate analysis of the effect of marital status on wealth accumulation among pre-retirement adults in the United States found that cohabitors who never married have 78 percent less wealth than couples in intact marriages (Wilmoth and Koso 2002).[16]

Third, research reveals that married couples have the forethought to save for unforeseen events, such as death, disability, or unemployment, which would potentially leave their spouses and children without sufficient material resources (Waite and Gallagher 2000). Finally, the likelihood of receiving financial assistance from family members increases because of the expansion of the family and social networks. As seen above, intergenerational transfers today involve not only parents and children but a wide kin network that includes parents-in-law, aunts, uncles, and nonrelatives.

Divorce and Single Parenthood

While marriage is associated with wealth, divorce has a strong negative impact on living standards and socioeconomic well-being. The amount of assets each party receives at the time of divorce affects their post-marriage economic well-being (Holden and Kuo 1996). One of the major demographic trends in the second half of the twentieth century, affecting the accumulation and transmission of wealth, is the increase in divorce rates. While marriage is more prevalent in the United States than in other developed countries, the United States also has one of the highest rates of divorce in the industrialized world, and the likelihood of divorce has increased during the past fifty years (Monnier and de Guilbert-Lantoine 1996).

Historical records show that in the late nineteenth century, about 5 percent of all marriages ended in divorce. During the following decades, divorce rates fluctuated until the mid-1960s, when the United States experienced a significant increase in divorce rates, fueled by the growing labor force participation of women, the women's rights movement, and the adoption of no-fault divorce laws in most states. But divorce rates have stabilized since the 1980s; recent estimates predict that almost 50 percent of marriages will end in divorce within twenty years (Cherlin 1992, figure 1-6: 22; Cherlin 2005: 36). Some argue that the high expectations Americans have for the institution of marriage is a main cause of divorce, as such unrealistic hopes lead to great disappointments and hence separation. Yet survey data show a decrease in the proportion of adult Americans who seem to believe that marriage is associated with happiness. In 1988, about 53.4 percent of American respondents either agreed or strongly agreed with the statement that "married people are happier than unmarried" and only 15.7 percent disagreed or strongly disagreed with the statement, whereas fourteen years later, in 2002, the comparable figures were 41 percent and 26.5 percent, respectively (sda.berkeley .edu/cgi-bin/hsda3). The marked increase in divorce rates had a crucial impact on the distribution of financial resources across gender lines. Because the unit of observation in wealth analysis is the household, family members living in the same household share the same economic status. Accordingly, if all adult men and women in a given society were married, we would expect to find no gender differences in poverty, net worth, and other family/ household-based measures of economic attainment. As seen in figure 6, the proportion of married couples' households has decreased drastically over the past sixty years (1947–2006). In 2006, married-couple households constituted about three-fourths of all households and about 50 percent of all family households.[17]

The trends seen in figure 6 reflect the sharp increase in single parent households. During the past fifty years, the United States has experienced a drastic rise in single parenthood, as a result of divorce and of births to unmarried women. While in 1955 about 4.5 percent of all births reported were to nonmarried women, by 2003 the figure was 35 percent (Cherlin 2005: 35). The sharp increase in nonmarital births and the breakup of the two-spouse family have been cited as key factors that have shaped the feminization and

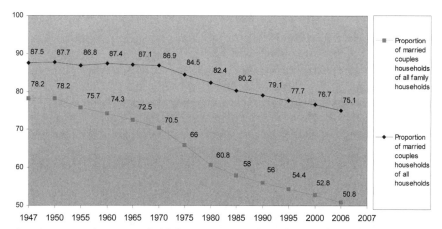

Figure 6. American Households by Type: Proportion of Married Couples Households of Total Family Households and Total Households, 1947–2006
Source: Author calculation based on US Census Bureau 2006b. Table HH-1: Households by Type: 1940 to Present. (www.census.gov/population/socdemo/hh-fam/hh1.xls)

juvenilization of poverty (Pearce 1978; Bianchi 1999). Copious evidence shows that women are more likely to be poor than men, and single mother households are at greater risk of falling below the poverty line than two-parent households or single-father households.[18] Whereas researchers have acknowledged that the association between economic resources and family structure may not be causal, a growing number of studies report that marital status has a direct effect on the family's economic resources, and that child poverty rates would likely decrease if single mothers were to marry (see review in Thomas and Sawhill 2005).

While scarce, research on wealth inequality across gender lines reveals similar patterns in financial resources according to family structure. Among the nonmarried (widowed, divorced, and never married) heads of households, women have lower levels of net worth and are more financially vulnerable than men of the same marital status (Conley and Ryvicker 2005; Chang 2003), while never-married women are the most economically vulnerable, with the lowest median net worth of all household types (Chang 2003). Recent evidence on middle-aged families shows that single parents are financially disadvantaged in comparison to adults without children, and single mothers suffer the most severe economic penalties in household wealth accumulation (Yamokoski and Keister 2006). A multivariate analysis of the distinct effect of marital history on the wealth levels of women and men on the verge of retirement found that being never married, divorced from a first or second marriage, or separated from a second marriage is significantly more detrimental to women than it is to men (Wilmoth and Koso 2002: 265). In addition to marital status and family structure, the gender gap in household net worth has been attributed to gender differences in human capital and labor market attainment (earnings, employment status, and access to employer-sponsored retirement plans), gender-differentiated family roles (for example, caregiving for children and elderly parents), and the higher dependency ratio in single-mother families, as well as gender differences in financial risk tolerance, financial literacy, and savings rate associated with greater expenses such as payments for child care (Chang 2003; Conley and Ryvicker 2004).

The Family Transactions Model

Drawing on the institutional changes that have shaped wealth accumulation processes, and the demographic and social changes that have altered intergenerational transfers and family structure during the past fifty years, figure 7 presents a tentative model of wealth stratification and provides a visual description of the functional link between two stratified subsystems, the labor market and commodity market. The Family Transactions Model (FTM) is particularly useful in studying wealth accumulation among the pivot generation. Since life expectancy has increased and bequests are transferred to people when they are in their mid-fifties, and because more people today face one or more family breakups, studying the effect of accumulated and transmitted resources among households on the verge of retirement can better illuminate the economic consequences of both attainment and ascription processes over the life cycle. As a result of distinct opportunity structure early in life, and intergenerational transmission of wealth later on, this age group is at the peak of its economic success and holds high levels of wealth and privileged positions in the labor market. In addition, the middle-aged are an important age cohort to the study of the distribution and replication of economic inequality because this age group serves as a mediating link between generations, as providers of financial assistance to both elderly parents and young adults—a function that places them at an important intersection in the stratification system. Whereas elderly Americans are better off today than they were in the past—the poverty rate of the elderly has declined drastically since the 1960s—the group is not economically homogeneous and, with the increase in life expectancy and high eldercare costs, poor elderly parents are becoming more socially and financially dependent on their middle-aged children.[19]

The model starts with individual attainment in the labor market, which is formed by various mechanisms that are exogenous to this model, and in which parental wealth and investment in children's human capital play an

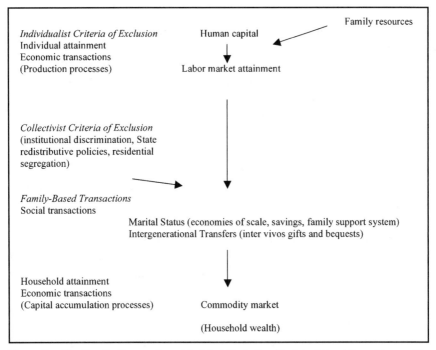

Figure 7.   The Family Transactions Model: A Tentative Model of Asset-Based Inequality

important role (Axinn, Duncan, and Thorton 1997; Alwin and Thornton 1984; Conley 2001; Zhan 2006). Positions in the labor and the commodity markets are linked through the ability of the household to earn money and acquire varying quantities and qualities of private property. Thus, at the basic level, educational attainment and earnings form a critical functional link between labor market remuneration and position in the commodity market, measured by the possession, composition, and value of various types of assets. Moreover, those employed in rewarding occupations have easier access to financial institutions through structured savings, in the form of retirement plans with automatic enrollment and restricted withdrawals. Employment in part-time, temporary jobs is often characterized by low wages and limited access to employer-based health insurance and retirement accounts. Consequently, any real understanding of how wealth is accumulated requires an analysis of the ways in which the labor market influences levels of income, and hence levels of household net worth. Over time, however, the link between labor market remuneration and wealth has become increasingly indirect making it impossible to simply "read off" the commodity market position of an individual from his/her labor market position (Randolph 1991).[20]

Increasing access to financial intermediaries enhances both the accumulation and the unequal distribution of private wealth; the increasing diversity in asset composition boosts household capital that is generated within the commodity market in the form of capital gains, dividends, and rents, affecting the household wealth portfolio and volume and contributing to the growing disconnection between one's success in the labor market and his/her position in the commodity market. The fact that wealthier families have better financial literacy and access to financial institutions such as banks, savings and loan institutions, and insurance companies, and the fact that low-income and minority households historically have a more limited access to such institutions, have contributed to the wealth gaps that stem from the commodity market. Evidence indicates that exclusionary practices in formal credit markets restrict access to credit and tend to exclude poor and minority borrowers, even when they are creditworthy (see Bolton and Rosenthal 2005; Dymski 2006). Additional collectivist exclusionary practices (Parkin 2001), such as institutional discrimination in the housing market, discriminatory practices by financial institutions, and limited access to government funds and contracts, affect the commodity market status of financially vulnerable families. Moreover, in mediating the outcome of the commodity market by redistributive intervention, estate taxes, and tax subsidies that encourage retirement pensions and homeownership, the state's actions have broken into the operation of a pure market relationship. The combined effects of economic gaps in both labor and commodity market outcomes result in a much greater inequality in wealth and asset holdings than in labor market remuneration.

Demographic changes, such as aging and changes in the structure and the function of the family during the second part of the twentieth century, also play a crucial role in shaping the unequal distribution of private property. Households represent aggregations of individual labor market participants, thus breaking the direct link between individual labor market position and his/her household accumulation potential (see Randolph 1991). The increase in the number of women in the labor force in the World War II era, and changes in marriage, divorce, and fertility rates, since the mid 1960s, have further complicated the direct link between individual labor market attainment and household status in the commodity market. As seen in figure 7, in the contemporary post-transitional and multi-asset society, two social mechanisms—*family structure* and *inheritance*—intervene in the connection between labor market and commodity market processes. These mechanisms of accumulation, distribution, and transmission of economic advantage that take place in the private sphere of the family, are governed by conversation-type (Tilly 2000) processes of inequality,[21] and forge a functional link between position in the labor market and position in the commodity market. Accordingly, asset-based inequality and its socioeconomic consequences can be analyzed through the understanding of the key role that the family plays in providing its members the economic wherewithal to own property. Because family structure and intergenerational transfers play an important role in linking the labor and the commodity markets, it is useful to highlight the extent to which the functions and objectives of familial exchanges of goods and services in the private sphere differ from economic exchanges that occur in the marketplace.

Economic and Social Exchanges

Kinship relations and familial exchanges of goods and services are often viewed as buffers against self-interested individualism and a contrast to the formal and divisive nature of financial exchanges in the marketplace (Bellah et al. 1985)—be it the labor or the commodity market. Yet the changing demographic structure and functions of the American family over the past few decades have accentuated the association between family social ties and the economic well-being of its members and brought it to the forefront of stratification processes.

The motives that underlie exchanges of goods and services among family members differ considerably from those that characterize economic exchanges in the market. Economic exchange involves competition and opposition of interests between two parties: "The exchange of money for a commodity is an economic exchange. When I buy a house, the money paid is a loss, whereas receiving the deed is a gain. For the seller the money is a gain and the house is a loss" (Willer 1999: 28). Social exchange, in contrast, is defined as transactions that occur between people who are socially close; these exchanges rely on primary, intimate, informal family connections that are associated with strong emotional content, and often, no conflict of interest or competition exists between the actors: both parties gain from the exchange, as one party wants to provide a positively valued resource and the second wants to receive it (Michalski 2003). These attributes are particularly visible in exchanges between family and kin members: "Parents who send their children to college know that sustained one-way flows can and do occur in social exchange relations" (Willer 1999: 28). This does not mean that all voluntary (inter vivos) family transfers are altruistic, but rather that all family exchanges are based on informal social bonds, based on normative obligations to the well-being of family members (see chapter 3). However, because wealth transfers among family members are informal, and the strength of

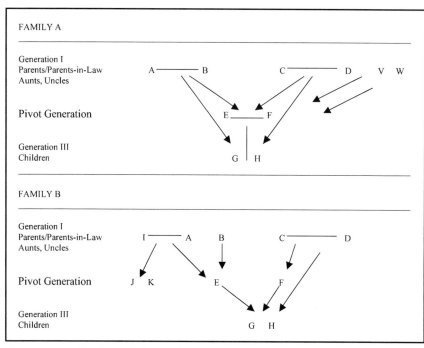

Figure 8. Family Ties and Financial Transfers

family ties and filial responsibility is not fixed, the type and volume of family transfers tend to vary from one family to another.

The importance of family ties as a means of economic mobility can be demonstrated in figure 8, which represents two ideal types of family and kin networks: Family A has closed social ties and Family B has an open network (see Coleman and Hoffer 1987). In Family A, the social bonds between kin members are strong and financial resources are shared among family and kin members. Parents AB and parents-in-law CD maintain strong social ties with their married children and grandchildren. Other relatives (aunts, uncles, and others) in Generation I (V and W) are also involved in exchanges of wealth and services. Because receipt of family transfers is associated with willingness to pass on resources to the younger generation (children G and H), this norm of familial responsibility and the socialization of family members to assist members in need (Attias-Donfut and Wolff 2000; Spilerman and Elmelech 2003; Kohli and Künemund 2003) maintain closure and exclusive access to resources by family members.

When the social bonds within families and between generations are weak, the transfers are often more limited and less dependable (see Family B).

Coleman and Hoffer (1987) coined the terms *structural deficiency* to describe absence of family members (single-parent families, for example) and *functional deficiency* to describe absence of strong relations between children and parents, despite the physical presence of parents. Recent evidence suggests strong association between family structure and intergenerational contacts and transfers of goods and services. First, parental marital disruption tends to have a negative effect on intergenerational transfers between elderly parents and their adult children (Pezzin and Schone 1999). Research on middle-aged Americans on the verge of retirement found that couples where at least one spouse experienced divorce or widowhood had substantially lower levels of income and accumulated assets than couples in first-time marriages (Holden and Kuo 1996). A critical factor determining the subdivision and magnitude of financial transfers to children is a child's age at the time of their parents' divorce (Furstenberg, Hoffman, and Shrestha 1995). Second, the increase in divorce rates and the number of children living apart from their fathers (Elwood and Jencks 2004) enhances the feminization and juvenilization of poverty and increases the dependency of many mothers on parental resources (Chiteji and Hamilton 2005; Bengston 2001). Because single parenthood has a negative effect on wealth level and its transmission to children, all things being equal, those parents (Generation I) who experience divorce earlier in life (A and B) are likely to transfer fewer resources to adult children. In addition, parents who remarry (A with I) and establish new families are likely to share their wealth with more children (J, K, and E). Divorce among couples in the pivot generation (E, and particularly F, who has custody over the children G and H) may also increase demand on parents and other family members to provide financial assistance. As recent data suggest, since the early 1960s, single motherhood has become more visible in all demographic groups, but the increase in single motherhood has been greatest among women with low educational level (Elwood and Jencks 2004), a pattern that accentuates economic disparities along family structure.

~

CHAPTER THREE

Social Class and Private Property

"[P]roperty" and "lack of property" are, therefore, the basic categories of all class situations.

—Max Weber, *Class, Status, Party*

Class, Status, Property:
Social Closure and Economic Advantage

So far, we have primarily discussed the significant role marriage and family transfers play in determining wealth accumulation processes at the household level, by largely overlooking the wider societal context that underlies these family patterns. For students of social stratification and mobility, however, the family operates as a main social institution that forms social closure and exclusion along kinship, race, ethnicity, and class lines. Sociologists define *social closure* as a process of monopolization, which is directed against competitors and maximizes rewards by restricting access to social and economic resources and opportunities to a "limited circle of eligibles" (Weber 1978: 339–48). In this context, the distinction between classes and status groups has significant relevance for the distribution of private property. In his seminal essay "Class, Status, Party," Weber (1958) writes: "With some oversimplification, one might say that classes are stratified according to their relations to the production and acquisition of goods; whereas status groups are stratified according to the principles of their consumption of goods as represented by special life style" (see also Saunders 1984). The distinction between life chances and lifestyle maintains that classes and status communities represent two possible modes of group formation in relation to the distribution of power in society (Giddens 1971). While membership in a particular class does not necessarily correspond with membership in a particular status group, the two may overlap. Indeed, in the realm of property relations, class and status groups are particularly interrelated.

> Status affiliation may cut across the relationships generated in the market, since membership of a status group usually carries with it various sorts of monopolistic privileges. Nonetheless, class and status groups tend in many cases to be closely linked, through property: possession of property is both a major determinant of class situation and also provides the basis for following a definite "style of life." (Giddens 1981: 44)

Social scientists have long acknowledged the social and economic consequences that stem from this dual nature of property. Property ownership not only determines life chances and common economic interests through exchanges in the marketplace (class), it also creates social affiliation and networks based on lifestyle differentiation (status groups) that arises from its "consumptive and conspicuous nature (ownership of summer residences or luxury cars)" (Conley 1999; see also Rex and Moore 1967; Saunders 1978, 1984). A distinct lifestyle can be expected from members of the same status group, and this social distinction is associated with specific restrictions on, and distinct opportunities for, social interactions (which are not subservient to economic interests)—in particular those related to marriage patterns and wealth transfers. The social networks that define the boundaries of status groups and link individuals, households, and generations, as well as religious, racial, and ethnic groups, through marriage patterns and intergenerational transmission of wealth, also delineate the boundaries of wealth and its distribution. In extreme cases, restrictions on access to social circles "may confine normal marriages to within the status circle and may lead to complete endogamous closure" (Weber 1978: 932). In the context of property relations, exclusion and monopoly of certain types of assets are placed in homogeneous marriage patterns and kinship inheritance.

> Property considerations, then, cannot be divorced from class as an economic construct. Yet, the "holding" of property is necessarily outside of the market: the biography of property is a particularistic one, bound by social relationships that channel its inheritance within particular sets of personal biographies, such as those linked by kinship and marriage. (Brudner and White 1997: 162)

Assortative Mating

But how prevalent are class-based homogenous marriage patterns in contemporary U.S. society? The propensity of wealthy families to intermarry has been extensively documented. Research on the corporate rich reports strong centripetal kinship norms that emphasize the importance of ties with kin and secondary relatives (such as aunts, uncles, nieces, nephews, and first cousins) and depend on the existence of some common economic interests that both unifies the family and distinguishes it from other families (Allen 1989: 102; Coontz 2006: 72). The prevalence of class homogamy and the normative practice of transmitting wealth to family and kin members lead to limited redistribution of private property. In his "stylized pattern of wealth transmission," economist Atkinson (1975: Figure 8.1: 147) describes a model of wealth transfers among the rich that includes three trajectories, corresponding to three generations. The scheme begins with a self-made man (Generation I), who passes on wealth to his heirs (Generation II) who may also inherit from other members of Generation I (such as aunts and uncles), and may marry into wealth. The total wealth received through inheritance and marriage provides a start in life and may be augmented through further savings and active entrepreneurship; alternatively, it may be dissipated. The resulting wealth then passes on to heirs in Generation III and the process continues.[1]

Anecdotal evidence on educational and economic assortative mating in the marriage market is abundant. A glance at the *New York Times*' Weddings and Celebrations section reveals clear patterns of homogamy among the financially better-off segments of society. While the sample is not representative and clearly overrepresents couples from middle- and upper-class backgrounds, the information posted in these announcements provides ample information on education, occupation, and place of residence of the newly married couple, as well as information on the clergy who officiated at the ceremony and socioeconomic information on the couple's parents. Endogamy by class, race, age, faith, and occupation is common in these announcements.[2]

Rebecca Ariel Pearlman . . . is to be married today to Benjamin Saul Stieglitz . . . Rabbi H. Jacob Simckes is to perform the ceremony at Beth Yeshurun synagogue in New Rochelle. The bride, 26, and the bridegroom, 28, graduated from Columbia University, where they met. . . . The bride's father was a senior manager in Albany, N.Y., for Rottman & Mclean, the accounting firm . . . the bridegroom is a production assistant at Fox News Edge . . . his parents own the Oriental Carpet Company, a store in Kingston, N.Y.

Sarah Margaret MacKay, a daughter of Emma H. MacKay and Dr. Robert C. MacKay of Tenafly, N.J., . . . was married yesterday to Peter Matthew Mitchell. . . . The Rev. Robert Donnelly, a Roman Catholic priest, performed the ceremony. . . . The bride and bridegroom, both 35, are stock analysts in New York. . . . The bride graduated from Yale and received an M.B.A. from Columbia. . . . Her father is a partner at Zelnick, MacKay and Morris, a law firm in Manhattan. The bridegroom graduated from the College of the Holy Cross and received an M.B.A. from Princeton.

Although numerous variables play a role in the choice of a spouse, empirical research based on nationally representative samples shows persistent homogamy with respect to such attributes as parental background, income, and education (Kalmijn 1998). Testing both cultural and economic endogamy, Kalmijn (1994) found that economic-status homogamy has increased between 1970 and 1980 at the expense of cultural-status homogamy. Recent studies report that the increasing similarity of spouses' educational levels continued through the 1980s and 1990s and conclude that the odds of homogamy for prevailing marriages increased substantially from 1960 to 2003 (Schwartz and Mare 2005). Analysis of data on white women entering first marriages found an increasingly strong and positive association between women's premarriage wages and occupational status and the expected earnings of the men they married (Sweeney and Cancian 2004), according to which, "the highest-earning men are increasingly married to the highest-earning women, and the lowest-earning men to the lowest-earning women" (England 2004). This homogamous economic pattern in the marriage market is particularly relevant to the perpetuation of inequality. Cross-generational transfers of wealth are likely to decrease socioeconomic inequalities between families when these resources are distributed equally in the population. When these transfers benefit some sectors of the population but are denied others, asset-based divisions are likely to increase. As mentioned above, asset holdings have critical implications for social, psychological, and economic well-being. However, the process that creates distinct boundaries between the haves and have-nots is embedded in social relations based on marriage and kinship. Through social closure and restriction of social and economic opportunities to outsiders, kinship and marriage patterns function as the main social mechanisms that form and reproduce socioeconomic inequality between distinct social groups, such as classes, ethnic groups, and racial categories. These cumulative processes are embedded in practices that sustain network-based control of resources; homogamous marriage patterns along education, race, and class lines, and the monopoly of intergenerational transfers of material resources within households, social classes, and kin groups.[3] Since asset-based inequalities are a product of *both* individual performance in labor market processes and collectivist criteria of social exclusion by families, households, and other social collectives (figure 2), they result in substantial economic disparities:

> Under capitalism, inequality in regard to inherited wealth generally exceeds inequality in regard to monetary income, since the wealthy customarily draw important returns from their wealth in nonmonetary forms and hoard some portion for transmission to heirs . . . in this case, beliefs in wealth as property, in the inviolability of property rights, and in the priority of interpersonal ties based on birth and marriage, all reinforce the centrality of inheritance as a mode of opportunity hoarding. (Tilly 1998: 155–56)

Classes: Past and Present

Since the seminal works of Marx and Weber in the nineteenth century, the concept of class has received much attention in social research, and analysis of class formation and structure is often seen as one of sociology's "crowning achievements as a discipline" (Braun 1997: 7). While this field of research encompasses a range of distinct lines of theoretical perspectives and empirical approaches, the central premise in class analysis is that the stratification system consists of small, identifiable, and distinct groups of people defined by their *economic position* (Rothman 2002). Most models of class structure operationalized the term "economic position" as position in the production processes, measured by occupation, authority, or the ownership or control of productive assets (such as factories, offices, malls, airlines, rental properties, and small businesses) (Wright 1997: 25 in Rothman 2002: 27).

During the past two decades, however, the concept of class as an analytical tool has been questioned and numerous studies have revolved around the definition and measurement of the concept (see review in Braun 1997: 367; Grusky and Sorensen 1998). Indeed, one of the major challenges in contemporary class analysis is how to study the increasing complexity of the socioeconomic structure, while maintaining the concept of class as defined exclusively through economic status. Some scholars view the complexity of the social stratification system as evidence of the absence of a definable class structure; this literature concludes that the United States is a classless society and calls for the adoption of a multidimensional perspective system of social stratification involving multiple hierarchical positions (Kingston 2000). Other studies, however, see the growing complexity of the social stratification system as a new stage in class relations, and expand the concept of class to include not only the economic dimension, but also measures of human and social capital (Perrucci and Wysong 2003). Whereas the two perspectives differ over whether a multidimensional approach represents a new stage in a more polarized society or signifies a classless, yet unequal society, both are in agreement that the emphasis on production-based economic disparities portrays a partial and insufficient picture of class structure. Indeed, the notion that class is determined primarily, and occasionally exclusively, by individual position in the production processes (how much a person earns), rather than wealth accumulation processes (whether a person owns or does not own property), is key to an understanding of the withering of the concept and the current debate on class formation and structure.

> Having gutted the concept of any serious social meaning, these sociologists then turn around and discover . . . that "class" has no social meaning. Thus the concept of "class" is prevented from performing its central function in social analysis, namely, to serve as an intervening variable, a bridge, between strictly individual behavior and truly social behavior, hence the gateway into the role of consciousness and volition in history, culture, politics and so forth. (Mc-Dermott 1991, 6–7)

Adding to the skepticism that surrounds the validity of the concept is the growing evidence suggesting not only that wealth accumulation processes have become more visible as a stratifying mechanism in recent years, but the functions of production processes in the context of class formation and identity have weakened. Recent data show growing divisions within the labor movement; the percentage of U.S. workers who were union members has decreased from 31.8 percent in 1948 to 12.5 percent in 2004 (Greenhouse 2005). The sharp and steady decrease in the number of unionized workers, which began in the mid-1970s, is partly attributed to globalization, economic restructuring, and the movement of manufacturing jobs abroad. This decline coincided with a general trend toward part-time employment in trade and service industries that tended to decrease workers' attachment to the labor market.[4] Since the early 1970s, involuntary part-time and temporary employment has expanded, and the number of people unable to find full-time jobs, and thus work as part-time and temporary employees, was estimated at about 6 million Americans, or 5.5 percent of the labor force (Tilly 1996: 6).[5]

Class and Property

The power and privileges emanating from the possession of wealth and capital are analytically separate from those which stem directly from the division of labor. A model of class, which addresses itself only to the latter, is a lopsided one indeed.

—Frank Parkin, Social Stratification

Early attempts to develop an asset-based typology of social classes were developed in response to the rapid increase in homeownership rates in the post–World War II period. Some Marxist analyses of class acknowledge that conflicts over housing issues may be significant in bringing together classes "such as the proletariat and the petty bourgeoisie, in a broad anti-monopoly-capital alliance" (Castells 1975 in Saunders 1978: 239), but reject the idea that these conflicts themselves constitute a basis for class formation.[6] A different Marxist interpretation views the conflict between tenants and landlords as a struggle between capital and labor and claims that the spreading of homeownership by the state can be interpreted as an attempt by the ruling class to undermine the solidarity of the working class (Clark and Ginsberg 1975: 25).

Drawing on the Weberian perspective, which posits that class struggles are likely to arise wherever people in a market situation enjoy differential access to property—not merely around the use of the means of industrial production but also around the control of domestic property—British scholars developed the concept of "housing classes." This literature flourished during a period of a substantial increase in home equity, which led scholars and policymakers to the realization that homeowners can accumulate sizeable wealth through house-price inflation, favorable interest rates on housing loans, government subsidies on house purchases, and the option for owners to use their own labor to increase the value of their dwellings (Saunders 1986: 323). Consequently, "a family may gain more from the housing market in a few years than would be possible in savings from a lifetime of earnings" (Pahl 1975: 291 in Hamnett 1999). The main idea that underlies these property-based class typologies is that struggle over scarce and desirable housing is parallel to class struggles that occur in the labor market with respect to the distribution of labor-based remuneration. As such, housing classes have to be understood as a distinct phenomenon of the distribution of social and economic power (Rex and Moore 1967; Saunders 1978; Savage, Watt, and Arber 1992).[7]

The scholarly emphasis on one type of asset (housing), however, seems insufficient to build a sustainable theory of class structure and the literature on housing classes waned during the latter part of the twentieth century.[8] The proliferation of new types of assets, and in particular the expansion of wealth held in financial and income-producing assets, necessitates a new framework of asset-based class analysis that captures the changing structure of the commodity market. Sorensen (2000) has recently proposed two approaches to study class formation and structure. The first approach—Class as Life Condition—is based on the quantitative dimension of asset holdings; classes are defined based on the volume of total net worth they hold, which determine their standard of living: "By shaping welfare and well-being, as well as economic opportunities and the investments that maximize these opportunities, the total wealth and its composition create the behavioral dispositions that are accountable for the inoculation and socialization mechanisms associated with class as life conditions" (Sorensen 2000: 145). Although scarce, several studies attempted to conceptualize the structure of wealth-based inequality. Keister (2000), for example, defines wealth classes by the relative value of the wealth they hold; in this scheme, the middle class is defined as those in the second and third quintiles of the wealth distribution.

The second concept coined by Sorensen (2000: 1490)—Class as Exploitation—views classes as socioeconomic distinctions based on the forms in which wealth is held. Because wealth is held in different, tangible assets and its volume and composition are influenced by different, relatively autonomous, forces, such as housing policies, taxation on capital gains, or estate taxes, ownership of financial and income-producing assets (business, real estate, and stocks) is qualitatively different from ownership of functional assets (homes and vehicles) and cannot be fully grasped by an analysis of the total amount of wealth that is held by a household. Moreover, as noted by the Weberian analysis of class stratification, classes and markets are closely related concepts; class struggle over valuable resources determines one's life chances and "only have value in the context of a market" (Breen 2005: 41). The institutionalization and segmentation of the commodity market have changed the contemporary class structure; as growing and unequal access to financial assets is associated with increasing disparities in wealth and income, variations in asset portfolio are becoming increasingly relevant to class analysis. Specifically, control over financial and income-producing assets may involve, directly or indirectly, the exploitation of others—be it the workers in the company in which one holds stocks, or the tenants of the rental property that one owns. Thus, in contrast to functional assets, ownership of financial assets "may generate benefits obtained at the expense of someone else, who would be better off with a different distribution of control or property rights to the various attributes of the assets" (Sorensen 2000).

Ownership of financial assets differs from functional assets, not only in terms of the consequences and effects on the owner's life chances but also in its origins. Elaborating on the literature of asset-based classes, we can use the

Family Transactions Model (FTM) to explore these determinants among the pivot generation. A multivariate analysis that aimed to measure the socio-economic and demographic determinants of the proportion of household wealth held in financial assets (see table A.2 in Appendix A),[9] reveals three noteworthy findings. First, education and employment are positively associated with investment in financial assets and, as expected, the amount of net worth the family has is positively associated with the percentage of wealth held in financial assets: the higher the total wealth held by the household, the more likely it is to be invested in financial assets.[10] Second, holding other characteristics constant and after household net worth is controlled for, married couples, and those who are living with partners or are separated, are more likely to hold a high proportion of their wealth in financial assets than householders who have experienced divorce. The magnitude of the effect is especially strong for cohabiting couples. In addition, analyses also show that marriage, particularly intact marriage, is strongly associated with ownership of a primary residence, while the effect of marriage on ownership of financial assets is relatively inconsequential (see table A.3 in Appendix A). Indeed, research on homeownership and home equity has reported that marriage has a consistent and robust effect on these outcomes (Lewin-Epstein, Elmelech, and Semyonov 1997). Finally, family transfers in the form of gifts and inheritance are strongly and positively associated with investment in financial assets. Especially strong are the effects of bequests and gifts on both the likelihood of ownership of, and the proportion invested in, financial assets (tables A.3 and A.2 in Appendix A, respectively). These findings indicate that, all things being equal, receipt of inheritance and gifts enhances financial assets—thus directly contributing, not only to wealth buildup in general but, particularly, to possession of income-producing assets.

Asset Poverty

Because the allocation of household wealth among various types of assets is a privilege of property owners, the findings reported above are limited to this population. Millions of Americans, however, have either an insignificant amount of wealth or negative net worth. While there is an abundance of information on the income poor, relatively little is known about those individuals and families at the bottom of the wealth ladder (but see Caner and Wolff 2004).[11] Lack of assets is particularly consequential for the well-being of members of the pivot generations and their dependents. While the amount of wealth held by those mid-life adults is significantly higher compared to other age categories, future upward mobility in the commodity market—as a result of either labor market attainment or through receipt of significant private transfers—is unlikely. In fact, these households will more likely experience a gradual decrease in the value of the material resources they hold in the following decades as they enter the "fourth age" (Laslett 1991). Evidently, being asset poor on the verge of retirement reflects an extreme case of socioeconomic disadvantage and slim chances for advancement. Moreover, these economic circumstances have important consequences for the well-being of frail elderly parents and adult children who rely on the financial resources of the pivot generation. Findings from logistic regression analysis of data from the HRS-92 sample of middle-aged households (table A.4 in Appendix A) reveal that the likelihood of households to belong in the lower quintile of net worth distribution is strongly determined by family and labor market characteristics. Consistent with the Family Transactions Model (FTM), the effect of intergenerational transfers is striking; even after taking into account the head of household's education, race, employment, age, and marital status, as well as other demographic and socioeconomic attributes, the probability that inheritors will be asset-poor is about half that of non-inheritors and the effect of inter-vivos gifts on asset-poverty is even larger.[12] Moreover, when compared to divorced householders, intact marriage is strongly and inversely associated with asset poverty. This finding suggests that, net of human capital and labor market attainment, married couples who did not experience marital disruption early in life are less likely to be asset poor than divorced householders are. As expected, employment, age, and education are negatively associated with asset poverty and native-born householders are less likely to be asset poor than those who are foreign born. All things considered, white householders are less likely to be asset poor than nonwhite householders.[13]

Property Classes Redefined

Although class membership may, under specific circumstances, become a meaningful determinant of social action and identity, the key feature of classes is that of a group of people who share roughly common life chances as a result of their economic position in the market. In this context, classes can be characterized as collectives of individuals and families with comparable command over material resources. One important implication of earlier schemes of property-based classes is that the individual position within the commodity market is determined by distinct and unequal access to desirable resources and is defined by ownership status, as well as the value and the composition of private property; even though ownership versus nonownership of valuable assets is an important basis of class division in a competitive market, "those who own property can be differentiated according to what they own and how they use it for economic ends" (Giddens 1981: 164). Building on these assumptions, the proposed asset-based classification incorporates the two dimensions of asset classes—class as life condition and class as exploitation (Sorensen 2000)—and takes into account both the value of the assets (wealth) and their composition (portfolio).

Finally, if one accepts the assertion that "mobility into the classes of the wealthy is the key attribute to look for, not what anyone earned in a given year" (Cowell 1977: 2), both marriage and intergenerational transfers of wealth need to be studied as an integral part of class formation. In contrast to production-based classes, the unit of analysis in wealth-based typology includes households and individuals as members of households. In that respect, asset-classes can be viewed as a product of consistent and durable opportunities for wealth accumulation over the life span that take place in the market and the private sphere. Persistent economically homogeneous marriage patterns and the exclusion of outsiders from access to family material resources reinforce social (status groups) and economic (class) boundaries and shape the standard of living and future life chances of individuals, families, and kin members.

Any attempt to develop an empirical scheme of mutually exclusive and relatively explicit classes requires arbitrary decisions on where the boundaries between the classes are drawn and what they represent.[14] The current proposed taxonomy is no exception to this limitation. Drawing on the work of Turner and Starnes (1976), four property classes are identified: estate capitalist; pseudo-capitalist, which comprises two categories—home owners and investors—and the propertyless underclass investors.

The *propertyless* underclass includes those households that are practically excluded from significant property-based power and lack control over their socioeconomic status.[15] They typically have negative net worth due to debt; indeed, while some propertyless households own assets (business, main residence, cars), they also have high debts, an attribute that determines their disadvantaged position in the commodity market. Thus, as Turner and Starnes (1976) observe, the ladder of wealth begins with debt, liquid assets, vehicles, and some business equity at the upper interval. Because they have little accumulated resources, the standards of living and economic well-being of the asset-poor are completely dependent on the flow of financial resources, and they must rely on their labor or on welfare as a source of income.

As seen in table 4, which describes class divisions among the pivot generation, not all middle-aged households benefit from the economic independence and self-fulfillment that characterizes members of this age group. Those who are at the bottom of the asset ladder experience a "triple disadvantage."

Table 4. Percent Distribution and Mean Values (Standard Deviation) by Asset Classes (Weighted by Household Weight): Selected Variables

	Propertyless	Homeowner	Investor	Estate-Capitalist
Household Characteristics				
Total net worth ($)	−3,555	96,997	127,329	780,287
	(39,583)	(63,147)	(72,443)	(905,069)
Total Household income ($)	21,855	43,258	47,588	85,712
	(21,853)	(29,309)	(34,732)	(85,992)
Capital gains ($)	623	1,489	3,743	19,032
	(8,601)	(6,538)	(9,884)	(44,026)
Family transfers:				
Inheritance	7.9	17.0	24.7	33.6
Gifts	2.5	6.1	8.4	15.1
Life insurance	3.1	5.1	7.3	5.8
Individual Characteristics (Head of Household)				
Age (years)	55.4	55.9	56.0	56.9
	(4.4)	(3.2)	(4.8)	(5.0)
Education (formal education)	10.5	12.1	13.0	14.0
	(3.5)	(2.8)	(2.7)	(2.6)
Employed	49.7	69.9	72.9	70.2
Occupation:				
Managerial/Professional	11.7	25.0	35.2	49.8
Race:				
White	56.1	79.6	85.0	92.7
Black	24.6	10.8	7.2	2.4
Hispanic	16.0	7.5	4.9	2.4
Other	3.1	1.7	2.7	2.3
Marital Status:				
Married	32.1	71.4	67.4	82.2
Married (intact)	18.0	52.5	43.9	61.7
Married (remarried)	13.3	18.9	23.3	20.5
Cohabit	4.1	1.7	2.0	1.9
Separated	10.1	2.3	2.7	1.1
Widow	13.5	7.5	9.3	4.7
Never	9.4	3.2	7.1	1.9
Divorced	30.4	12.5	15.3	7.9
Assets (reported in $):				
Housing equity	-4,298	31,576	26,822	151,923
Business equity	2,792	1,047	9,323	161,523
Liquid	1,129	8,218	22,254	62,156
IRA and Keogh	316	6,007	17,278	60,476
Stocks and mutual funds	188	2,700	10,745	74,618
Bonds	7.6	192	859	12,705
Real estate	652	3,210	26,077	195,778
Debts	6,720	2,467	2,002	2,934
N	1,537	3,170	1,366	1,521

Source: HRS-92

First, they have a clear disadvantage in human capital and labor market attainment; low levels of education, high levels of unemployment, and concentration in low-skilled occupations are prevalent among the propertyless underclass. Second, they are less likely to be married and more likely to experience family disruption early in life than other classes. Propertyless households are more likely to be female headed and, relative to other classes, the number of nonwhite householders is quite high. Third, they are less likely to benefit from financial assistance in the form of family transfers (e.g. inter vivos gifts, bequests, life insurance benefits), and thus have no financial resources to support adult children, elderly parents, or other family members in need.

At the other extreme on the wealth ladder, we find the *estate capitalists* or asset affluent, whose wealth is invested in various forms, primarily financial and income-producing assets. These households occupy the upper quintile of the net worth distribution that includes the segments of the population whose wealth is held in forms that are "central to the definition and operation of the capitalist economy" (Turner and Starnes 1976: 33). One distinctive characteristic of the asset portfolio of this category is found in the high rate of ownership and the substantial volume of wealth held in business and real estate. These households dominate not only the distribution of financial assets in the aggregate, but also have more wealth held in specific functional and financial assets (for example, homes, business equity, stocks) (see also Turner and Starnes 1976: 33–4).[16] Compared with other classes, these households benefit from advantages in education and labor market remuneration, tend to higher rates of marriage, particularly intact marriages, and are more likely to receive intergenerational transfers. In addition, the number of racial/ethnic minority members among this class is small.

The broad middle ranks of the *pseudo-capitalists* are further separated into two classes. The *homeowner* category includes households that hold the bulk (more than 50 percent) of their wealth in functional assets (homes and vehicles) associated with family economics. As mentioned above, earlier schemes of asset-based classes view homeownership as the defining characteristic of the middle class. Today, the segmentation of the commodity market and diversity in asset portfolio coincide with the emergence of the *investor* class, which includes those households in the middle of the wealth distribution that hold the bulk (more than 50 percent) of their wealth in a variety of nonfunctional assets (such as liquid assets, stocks and mutual funds, other real estate, and retirement accounts). Compared with *home owners, investors* are wealthier and more likely to receive intergenerational transfers, but are less likely to be married and are more likely to experience family disruption earlier in life.

Households belonging to the *investor* category are more likely than those in the *homeowner* class to report receipt of intergenerational transfers, to own businesses, and to hold professional and managerial positions.

Among asset holders, inequality in "flow" of financial resources (property income) is attributable to the higher share of wealth that the affluent and *investor* classes hold in financial and income-producing assets. Indeed, each form of financial and income-producing assets has a linear pattern across asset classes; the higher the position of the household in the asset ladder, the more likely the household is to own financial assets and the higher the value of the asset. This pattern is especially important to the understanding of inequality among the pivot generation. Reviewing contemporary studies on the socioeconomic well-being of middle-aged and elderly households, Angel and Angel (1997: 169) conclude that this literature "makes it clear that income from assets and accumulated wealth are major factors separating those who are well off in retirement from those who are not." Clearly, the idea of "people's capitalism" (Kolko 1962), according to which stock ownership will become widely diffused, does not seem to be factual: stock ownership and stock equity tend to be highly concentrated in the hands of the better off households. Whereas business ownership is the main type of asset that distinguishes the asset affluent from other classes, these great fortunes need not be seen simply as an individual enterprise. Instead, ownership of a business, and other remunerative assets, are products of multigenerational efforts; receipt of intergenerational transfers shows a linear pattern, according to which the propertyless are the least likely and the asset affluent are the most likely to receive transfers in the form of inheritance and inter vivos gifts.

In sum, the analysis of asset-based classes reveals that in contrast to the assumptions that underlie functionalist and neoclassical schemes (Parsons 1970; Haslett 1986), embedded in asset-based class typology is the notion that ascription and achievement are strongly related processes. Specifically, households that receive family transfers have a much better chance of achieving a higher position in the commodity market and are more likely to invest their material resources in diverse assets that are crucial to the operation of the capitalist market and can more easily be passed on to offspring. On the other hand, the two processes are autonomous in the sense that they exert independent effects on accumulated wealth. Assuming that receipt of family transfers indirectly measures parental resources and investment in educational attainment at earlier stages of the life cycle, we can presume that the findings presented in the analysis underestimate the effect of transfers on economic status. Given the continuous decrease in birth rates, the subdivision of assets among heirs is likely to have a stronger effect on socioeconomic inequality in the coming decades. The next chapter discusses some of the distinctive institutional and cultural features of American society that underlie the extreme inequality in private property and brings the family to the forefront of the stratification system as a key provider of a financial safety net to its members.

PART TWO

WEALTH AND WELFARE

CHAPTER FOUR

~

Social Policy and Economic Inequality

In the United States, where we have more land than people, it is not at all difficult for persons in good health to make money.

—P. T. Barnum, *Art of Money*

Self-made men, indeed! Why don't you tell me of the self-laid egg?

—Francis Leiber

The State and the Self-Laid Egg

Conventional market theory and the popular view of wealth creation tend to focus on personal characteristics, such as innate talent, character, and self-discipline, and have a propensity to overlook the significance of exogenous variables, such as political and economic conditions, and the normative structure that underlies wealth buildup and inequality (Bollier 2002). Andrew Carnegie (1885: 91-101), the nineteenth-century steel tycoon who epitomized the self-made-man narrative, had this advice to young people who want to be financially secure:

Let me indicate two or three conditions essential to success: . . . the first and most seductive, and the destroyer of most young men, is the drinking of liquor. The next greatest danger to a young business man in this community I believe to be that of speculation . . . the man of business knows that only by years of patient, unremitting attention to affairs can he earn his reward, which is the

result, not of chance, but of well-advised means for the attainment of ends.
. . . The third and last danger against which I shall warn you . . . is the perilous
habit of endorsing. . . . Before you endorse at all, consider endorsements as
gifts, and ask yourselves whether you wish to make the gift to your friend and
whether the money is really yours and not a trust for your creditors.

The emphasis on character and self-discipline, and the absence of any mention of formal education, is not uncommon in the rags-to-riches narrative. In fact, entrepreneurship is often seen as an alternative route to economic mobility for those sectors in the population facing limited educational and employment opportunities.[1]

Another prevalent version of the rags-to-riches narrative places the emphasis on luck. As a wealthy entrepreneur stated recently: "There are millions of people who have the qualities that make you successful in business, but who weren't lucky enough to be in the right place at the right time or to get the right help. So having the capabilities is necessary, but nowhere near sufficient" (in Collins et al. 2004: 21). Economist Lester Thurow argues that, in contrast to the principal assumptions of the classical model of wealth buildup, the accumulation of large fortunes is largely accidental; since insufficient information is available to secure the expected rate of return on an investment within each risk range, choosing an investment simulates a lottery: investors "bet" on some nonquantifiable factors of an investment, with some "winning big" and others "losing big" in a random way (Chester 1982: 6). Paradoxically, both the individualistic, merit-based account of economic success and the "luck" narrative resonate well with Americans, as both explanations are based on the assumption of the level playing field.

> Luck is random; anyone can be a potential recipient. A lottery winner, for instance, can instantly go from rags to riches and fulfill the American dream without discriminating against anyone else or personally taking advantage of anyone else in the process. (McNamee and Miller 1998: 194–95).

Both narratives, however, tend to overlook the larger economic, political, and sociodemographic structures that espouse the accumulation and unequal distribution of wealth. The chances of being born into great wealth, investing in a booming stock market, or winning a significant sum of money in a lottery are possible only in a wealthy but stratified society in which vertical mobility is feasible, the commodity market is developed, and property rights are valued and protected.

Over the years, the rags-to-riches narrative has been criticized on the grounds that it has failed to take into account extra-individual factors that promote wealth buildup. Books with unequivocal titles like *The Self-Made Men in America: The Myth of Rags to Riches* (Wyllie 1954) reiterate the importance of societal attributes to one's economic success. Whereas individual effort, self-discipline, and luck are critical to wealth accumulation, these factors are practically irrelevant without a strong social, economic, and political structure that enhances and protects private property. In one of the classic studies on American millionaires and multimillionaires in the late nineteenth and early twentieth centuries, Sorokin (1925) reports that many so-called self-made men had benefited from distinct opportunity structures in their native states and cities and concludes that the desire to succeed was especially strong in regions that had been transformed by the Industrial Revolution. About three-fourths of nineteenth-century millionaires were natives of New England, New York, or Pennsylvania, and more than two-thirds gained their wealth in manufacturing, banking, trade, or transportation— activities that were concentrated in old commercial centers like New York, Philadelphia, and Boston, or in new industrial towns such as Rochester or Pittsburgh (see Wyllie 1954: 16). To better understand processes of wealth accumulation today, in an era of a developed and more sophisticated market economy, one should not only study the determinants of economic inequality, but also analyze the social and political conditions that favor the causes of inequality.

Protecting Property Rights

The most common and durable source of factions has been the various and unequal distribution of property. Those who hold and those who are without property have ever formed distinct interests in society.

—James Madison, *The Federalist*

The role that private property plays in shaping the distribution of wealth and power increases as the market is more developed and regulated for sale of assets, and as the government facilitates property ownership and protects property owners against loss through theft or fraud (McDermott 1991). Although they need not be supported by the state to be effective, property rights are stronger if they are aligned with cultural norms and enforceable by the legal system (Barzel 1997). In the United States, the cultural value assigned to the protection of property rights dates back to the nineteenth century. James Madison, one of the primary authors of the U.S. Constitution, wrote: "Government is instituted to protect property of every sort. . . . This being the end of government, that alone is a just government, which impartially secures to every man, whatever is his own" (Madison 1792). Property rights are one of the most valued provisions of the U.S. Constitution and a strong system of property rights is considered by many to be one of the most fundamental requirements of a capitalist economic system; Bollier (2002) describes how—thanks to government protection of private ownership and lack of adequate protection for public ownership—"Americans are losing the right to control the commons," including such tangible assets as public forests and minerals, as well as critical infrastructure such as the Internet.[2] The government, however, cannot simply be viewed as the main line of defense behind private property; it is also one of its main generators. The United States has remarkably fertile soil for the creation of wealth: "This is probably the most important element of America's success narrative, and yet it is the most ignored or misunderstood" (Collins, Lapham, and Klinger 2004).

Asset-Building Policies and Wealth Creation

Since the mid-1940s, the American government has played a key role in wealth creation, developing a number of asset-based programs and initiating various practices, such as occupational licenses, government contracts, and subsidies to businesses, which have benefited the nonpoor almost exclusively (Reich 1964). Convincing evidence exists that these programs are effective and benefit corporations and wealthy families (Zepezauer and Naiman 1996). Almost one half of the *Forbes* 2000 largest companies, including the top three on the list—Citigroup, General Electric, and American Intl Group—are American owned. And of the *Forbes* list of the world's wealthiest people in 2005, more than half (11 out of 20) claim the United States as their country of citizenship. The top two names on that list—William Gates III, with a net worth of $46.5 billion, and Warren Buffett, with $44 billion—are Americans. Buffett (in Collins, Lapham, and Klinger 2004) has acknowledged the important role that social policies and legal regulation play in the creation of great wealth:

> I personally think that society is responsible for a very significant percentage of what I've earned. If you stick me down in the middle of Bangladesh or Peru or someplace, you'll find out how much this talent is going to produce in the wrong kind of soil. I will be struggling 30 years later. I work in a market system that happens to reward what I do very well—disproportionately well.

Americans benefit from public support in wealth buildup that includes investment in education, public infrastructure (ports, roads, communication), and research and innovation (mainly as grants to universities), as well as property rights law and investment in individual opportunity, such as tuition assistance (Collins et al. 2004). As one entrepreneur acknowledges recently: "The opportunities to create that wealth are all taking advantage of public goods—like roads, transportation, markets—and public investments. None of us can claim it was all personal initiative. A piece of it was built upon this infrastructure that we all have this inherent obligation to keep intact" (Collins, Lapham, and Klinger 2004: 28). The United States has no coherent and comprehensive asset-building policy but it does have numerous programs that collectively provide substantial financial benefits to asset owners (Woo and Buchholz 2007). Tax expenditures to individuals—for retirement accounts, homeownership, and financial or business investments—benefit millions of nonpoor families and total more than $300 billion per year. In fact, most benefits given to the nonpoor are asset-based programs that are structured into the tax system. The largest of these benefits are tax subsidies for corporate and individual retirement accounts and homeownership (Sherraden 1991).

Private saving for retirement is highly favored by the federal tax system and most retirement plans offer significant tax advantages. While federally sponsored incentives to saving for retirement are not new, these forms of subsidy have increased as more employers shifted from traditional defined benefits, which guarantee a specific pension income in the future, to defined-contribution plans, to which both employer and employee contribute (Woo and Buchholz 2007; Munnell, Cahill, and Jivan 2003). During the past two decades, the percent of wage and salary workers with defined-benefit plans has decreased from almost 60 percent in 1981 to less than 15 percent in 2002 while the percent of workers with defined-contribution plans has increased threefold from 20 percent to roughly 60 percent (Munnell, Cahill, and Jivan 2003: figure 2: 2). While nearly 40 percent of workers in the United States currently participate in employer-sponsored retirement, participation in these programs is positively correlated with income. Higher-income workers are more likely to benefit from these tax subsidies than their lower-income counterparts; Woo and Buchholz (2007: 7) report that almost three-quarters (73.2 percent) of workers who earn $50,000 or more enroll in their employer-sponsored plan, while only one-tenth of those (9.6 percent) who earn less than $5,000 participate in these plans.

Federal policies boost homeownership in numerous ways. Established in 1934, a key objective of the Federal Housing Administration (FHA) was to promote homeownership through the provision of government insurance to banks lending money to home mortgages (Dreier et al. 2001). The FHA today is the largest insurer of mortgages in the world, insuring nearly 33 million properties since its inception. The loans usually require much lower down payments than those approved by private lenders such as banks and mortgage companies (Brown, Kuttner, and Shapiro 2005; U.S. Department of Housing and Urban Development 1996). Homeownership is also boosted by generous mortgage policies and tax breaks that enable taxpayers to deduct mortgage interest and property tax, deductions that are not available to nonowners; totaling $72.6 billion in 2005, mortgage interest deduction is one of the largest single tax expenditures in the tax code, the biggest federal subsidy for homeowners (Dreler et al. 2001). The cost of owning a home is further subsidized through a sizable exclusion of capital gains on the sale of a primary residence (Munell et al. 2003: 4). Because the magnitude of tax benefits on homeownership is correlated with the value of the asset, a disproportionate share of these tax breaks flows to the wealthier households; recent data on total mortgage and property tax deductions show that in 2005, the bottom half of all earners received 2.9 percent of these tax benefits, while the top 10 percent of earners received 59.4 percent (Munell et al. 2003: 5; Dreier et al. 2001: 110–12). Moreover, in a pattern distinct from the one seen in other industrial societies, the publicly subsidized sector in the U.S. housing market is marginal and the law tends to protect the landlord while leaving the tenant more vulnerable to such acts as evictions (Dreier 1982). In view of these legal and economic circumstances, it is not surprising that the homeownership rate is higher in the United States than in most Western European countries.

The role of the government is crucial, not only to the creation and safeguarding of personal wealth but also to the ability of the owner to capitalize, liquidate, or transfer it to future generations. Contrary to its egalitarian values, the United States has a limited transfer-tax system, which play an important part in the replication of wealth inequality (McNamee and Miller 1998). In addition, there are numerous methods for tax avoidance, such as trusts, generous marital deductions, and the establishment of charitable foundations. The loopholes in the transfer-tax system have led some scholars to term the estate tax a "voluntary" tax and to conclude that the American public tends to believe in the existence of robust inheritance taxes that do not actually exist (Thurow 1976: 33 in McNamee and Miller 1998: 209): "This is how the rich stay rich—by passing on from generation to generation assets that have appreciated greatly in value, but on which they never pay capital gains taxes" (Barrlett and Steele 1992, in Oliver and Shapiro 1995: 184). At the end of May 2001, the U.S. Congress passed a tax bill that included the elimination of the federal estate tax, thereby enabling the wealthy to transmit their wealth without tax penalty (Perrucci and Wysong 2003).[3] In 2002, the estate tax was assessed only on estates worth $1 million or more and many of those were exempted. Under the current administration's tax cuts, the estate tax threshold will gradually increase to $3.5 million in 2009, while the tax rate gradually declines: "The estate tax will be totally repealed in 2010, but then reinstated in its pre-2002 form in 2011, absent further action by Congress" (Bartels 2004b).

The Welfare State

While asset-building policies boost private ownership and provide tax breaks to property owners, the main beneficiaries of these programs are the nonpoor. Those who are less likely to own assets and have little or no tax obligations, such as low-income families, racial and ethnic minorities, and many young families with children, are largely excluded from these programs (Sherraden 2005). Whereas asset-building policies are robust and durable, provision of welfare to families in need is based on income. In the United States, these income-based programs, like Medicaid and Supplemental Security Income, are offered on a means-tested basis; their beneficiaries are families undergoing extreme economic hardship who are incapable of supporting themselves through ordinary market mechanisms (Titmuss 1974; Goodin 1999).

> The underlying assumption is that poverty and hardship result from an inadequate distribution of flows of resources, and the solution is to make the flows more adequate. However, the income-based welfare state has not fundamentally reduced poverty (although it has alleviated hardship); it has not reduced class or racial divisions; it has not stimulated economic growth; and it has not developed a broad base of public support. Yet most welfare reform proposals, conservative and liberal alike, assume that income-based policies are the only answer. (Sherraden 1991: 3–4)

Quadagno (1987) attributes the late development of the American welfare state and the marginal provision of welfare to the continuing political weakness of organized labor; the legacy of American politics and formation of distributional policies in early democratization; and the dualism of the American economy between the more industrialized North and the South, which had few of the characteristics necessary for welfare state development (for example, industrialization, democracy, political parties, and a working class capable of pressing for social benefits). From a cross-national perspective, the unique features of the American welfare state are particularly visible. The literature on the welfare state typically identifies four models of welfare regimes: conservative, social democratic, liberal, and Southern European (rudimentary). The relevance of these models to the discussion on wealth and asset-based inequality lies in the distinct relationships these models form between the three cornerstones of the welfare structure: the state, the market, and the family (Esping-Andersen 1990; Titmus 1974; Castles 1998; Goodin et al. 1999, all in Rice et al. 2006; Van Voorhis et al. 2002; Gauthier 1996). The relationship between the three components holds key clues to the distribution of private and public resources and the extent to which the American family functions as a provider of financial support to its members.

The *conservative* regime, which characterizes Austria, Belgium, France, Germany, Ireland, Luxemburg, and the Netherlands, is identified with policies that sustain differentiation based on labor market attainment. Whereas the state is active in the provision of welfare services, different groups are entitled to different welfare services and the traditional family and gender division of labor is often explicitly favored, with marriage and childbearing strongly encouraged. Consequently, the state is not the sole provider of welfare services; the family as well as private, nonprofit organizations (churches, trade unions, and so forth) play an important part in the provision of welfare to their members (Rice et al. 2006; Goodin et al. 1999). The *social democratic* regime (including Denmark, Finland, Norway, and Sweden) is linked to middle-class universalism and social equality; in contrast to the conservative regime the provision of welfare services in these countries is dominated by the state and, as a result of the redistributive function of the state, income differentials are relatively low. This welfare system is characterized by universal state support for families and strong commitment to gender equality: "family policy is strongly oriented toward the interests of the 'next generation' and provides myriad forms of support to children and their careers out of a combination of egalitarian and pronatalist concerns" (Goodin, Rice, and Parpo 2005). The term "rudimentary welfare regime" is often used to describe the southern European welfare regime (specifically, Greece, Italy, Portugal, and Spain) whose welfare provision is characterized by a high degree of fragmentation along occupational lines (Ferrera 1997), absence of a national statutory income scheme, and limited child benefits. Accordingly, welfare provision is dominated by the market and the family; in comparison to other European countries, these countries are characterized by high rates of multigenerational living arrangements (co-residence), low rates of divorce and single parenthood, and more substantial financial dependence of young adults on their parents' economic resources (Barlow and Duncan 1994).

The United States belongs to the fourth category, the *liberal* regime (along with Australia, Canada, Japan, New Zealand, Switzerland, and the United Kingdom), which is characterized by limited state interference, residualist social policies, and strong market orientation (Van Voorhis 2002; Goodin 1999: 57–60). Instead of redistributing the country's financial resources, the liberal regime characteristically promotes the trickle-down effect, according to which financial benefits given to the upper classes and the wealth buildup of the rich will trickle down to the poorer segments of society through the operation of the free market. This framework aims to provide a mechanism whereby "the individual could prevent dependency through his own efforts" (see Brown 1956 in Goodin 1988: 353). Because public assistance is only provided to families with extremely low incomes and severe needs, this system is characterized by persistent economic differentiation that maintains class and status distinctions (Van Voorhis 2002). Not surprisingly, compared to other developed countries, the United States is spending very little of its gross domestic product (GDP) on social programs to support families in poverty (Smeeding et al. 2001; Gauthier 1996), and poverty rates in the United States are higher than in other industrialized societies.

Public Views on Economic Inequality and Mobility

Given this visible economic inequality, the high poverty rates (particularly among families with children), and the limited provision of welfare (especially family and child allowances), it is perplexing as to why Americans are consistently less supportive than people in other industrialized nations of redistributive policies as a means to reduce economic gaps between the rich and the poor (Kluegel et al. 1986). When adult Americans are asked whether

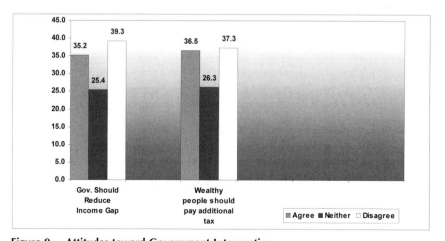

Figure 9.   Attitudes toward Government Intervention
Source: International Social Survey Programme, Social Inequality III, 1999.

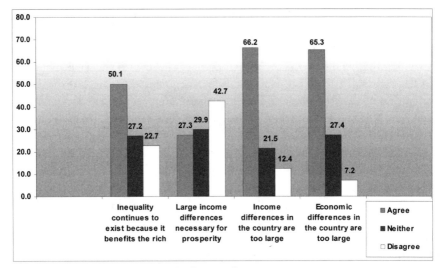

Figure 10. Attitudes toward Societal Inequality
Source: International Social Survey Programme, Social Inequality III, 1999.

the government should intervene to reduce economic disparities (see figure 9), about one-third agree with the statement, more than one-third disagree, and about a quarter neither agree nor disagree.[4]

One possible explanation for this attitudinal structure is that Americans are not aware of the widening economic disparities in wealth and income. The data seem not to support this hypothesis. Many Americans are aware of, and express dissatisfaction with, the growing economic gulf between the rich and the poor (figure 10). Almost two-thirds of Americans either agree or strongly agree with the statement, "Economic differences are too large," and a similar proportion (66.2 percent) expresses agreement with the statement, "Income differences are too large." When asked about the origins of these societywide economic disparities, about one half of the sample either agree or strongly agree that "inequality continues to exist because it benefits the rich," whereas less than a quarter disagrees with the statement. Moreover, more people are likely to reject than accept the notion that income differences are necessary for prosperity (42.7 percent versus 27.3 percent, respectively).

Another explanation for public indifference to government intervention is that Americans are generally less interested in the unequal distribution of economic resources—that is, the precise gap between the wealthy and the poor—and its remedy, than about their own opportunities for upward mobility (Samuelson 2001).[5] In the same vein, McCall (2003) suggests that the normative ambiguity pertaining to the concept of inequality stems from the

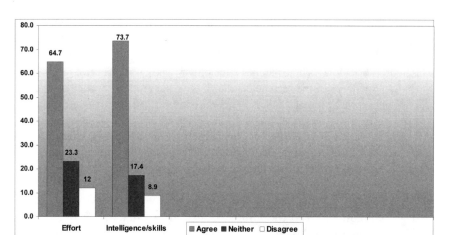

Figure 11.   Attitudes toward Individual Mobility: Effort and Intelligence/Skills
Source: International Social Survey Programme, Social Inequality III, 1999.

differences between trends in overall societal inequality and upward mobility and the possibility that an increase in inequality can coincide with an improvement in the overall population's standard of living.[6] This interpretation is closely aligned with the view that in the United States, economic upward mobility is viewed as a process based on merit and talent in a free market, and these opportunities for advancement are not only plausible but also prevalent. When asked whether individual effort is an important factor to success (figure 11), a majority of the respondents (64.7 percent) either agrees or strongly agrees with the statement. The proportion of the public who believes that "intelligence/skill is important for getting ahead" is also high; about three-fourths (73.7 percent) of the respondents express support for the statement. For both items, only about one-tenth of the population disagrees or strongly disagrees with the statement (12.0 and 8.9 percent, respectively).[7]

This strong belief in market economy, equal opportunity, and opportunities for mobility encompasses the notion that rewards for a given position in the stratification system are set by the functional contribution of the position to the society (Davis and Moore 1945). This portrayal of the stratification process has strong roots in stratification literature in the United States, which views social inequality as both functional and inevitable.[8] The robust belief in economic success as an individual endeavor has a clear downside: those individuals and families at the bottom end of the wealth distribution are often blamed for their own economic impoverishment.[9] Moreover, in contrast to the views expressed in figure 11, recent data on economic mobility reveal limited mobility and strong intergenerational inheritance of economic status (Hertz 2006: i):

> Children from low income families have only a 1 percent chance of reaching the top 5 percent of the income distribution, versus children of the rich who have about a 22 percent chance . . . children born to the middle quintile of parental family income ($42,000 to $54,300) had about the same chance of ending up in a lower quintile than their parents (39.5 percent) as they did of moving to a higher quintile (36.5 percent). Their chances of attaining the top five percentiles of the income distribution were just 1.8 percent.

While equal opportunity and the ethos of meritocracy unquestionably represent a dominant ethos in the United States, these views are often aggrandized in the literature. The findings shown in figure 12 suggest that alongside the strong beliefs in individual merit and innate attributes, a different ethos of economic success exists, according to which extra-individual factors, such as social networks and parental wealth, are widely seen as key determinants of socioeconomic mobility. More than four-fifths (85.5 percent) of respondents say they believe that "knowing the right people" is important for getting ahead in society, while 10.8 percent decide that is "not very important." The scholarly literature provides support for this observation, showing that social networks, including contacts through acquaintances rather than close

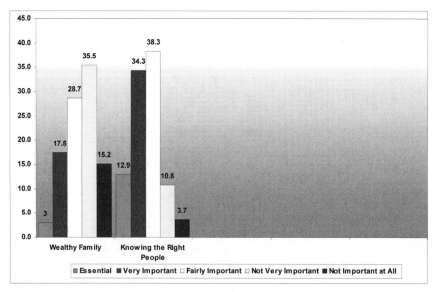

Figure 12.   Extra-Individual Determinants of Economic Mobility
Source: International Social Survey Programme, Social Inequality III, 1999.

friends, are important means of getting ahead and finding rewarding and desirable jobs (Granovetter 1983). In addition, about one-half of this nationally representative sample indicates that having a wealthy family is essential, very important, or fairly important for economic success, while only 15.2 percent hold the view that family wealth is not important at all.

The correlation matrix presented in table 5 enables us to elucidate the relationships between the above-mentioned attitudinal measures and to explore the extent to which specific sets of attitudes are associated with one another. Several findings merit attention. First, as expected, respondents that place a high value on individual effort as a key to social mobility are also likely to view intelligence/skills as important—the correlation between the two measures is positive and strong (r=.615). Positive association is also seen between the two extra-individual measures, social capital and parental resources (r=.522). Second, beliefs in intelligence and effort as a means of getting ahead do not seem to negate the value placed on social capital and parental wealth. Instead, the correlation between these two sets of measures is positive, although weak and/or not statistically significant. For example, the correlation between "wealthy family" and "intelligence/skill" is (r=.081). This finding implies that respondents who believe in individual merit do not necessarily reject the significance of ascribed attributes in determining economic success.

Third, beliefs in individual traits as an important means to economic mobility are inversely correlated with unfavorable views of inequality—that is, viewing economic gaps as too extreme—and with support in government redistributive policies. For example, support for the view that "people get rewarded for effort" has no clear association with the view that economic differences are too large (r=0.038, not statistically significant) and is negatively (but weakly) correlated with the view that the government should intervene to reduce economic gaps (r=–0.193). While no definite conclusion on the causal relationship can be derived based on these cross-sectional data, this finding provides support for the "equal opportunity" explanation, according to which those who place strong emphasis on individual effort as a means of mobility are less likely to support government intervention in the operation of a free market. Fourth, beliefs in extra-individual attributes are positively correlated with support in government intervention. Specifically, people who acknowledge the importance of parental wealth and social networks in determining economic mobility are also likely to view the economic gaps as extreme and to support government intervention as a means to reduce economic inequality. This correlation, however, is weak. For example, the correlation between "wealthy family" and the view that economic differences

Table 5. Correlation Matrix

| | Getting Ahead | | | | Society-Wide Inequality | | | | Government Intervention | |
	A	B	C	D	E	F	G	H	I	J
A	—									
B	.522**	—								
C	.044	.028	—							
D	.081**	.062*	.615**	—						
E	.155**	.162**	−.161**	−.115**	—					
F	.084**	.105**	.080**	.098**	−.028	—				
G	.069*	.107**	−.146**	−.084**	.396**	−.142**	—			
H	.061*	.110**	.038	.061*	.273*	−.069*	.382**	—		
I	.163**	.167**	−.193**	−.123**	.382**	−.035	.425**	.238**	—	
J	.130**	.100**	−.133**	−.074*	.245**	.037	.263**	.327**	.439**	—

**Correlation is statistically significant at the 0.001 level (2-tailed)
*Correlation is statistically significant at the 0.05 level (2-tailed)
Note: Missing cases are excluded.
Source: International Social Survey Programme, Social Inequality III, 1999.

Getting Ahead
A. Wealthy family
B. Knowing the right people
C. Get rewarded for effort
D. Get rewarded for intelligence/skills

Societywide Inequality
E. Inequality benefits the rich
F. Large income differences necessary for prosperity
G. Income differences are too large
H. Economic differences are too large

Government Intervention
I. Government should reduce income differences
J. Wealthy people should pay additional tax to help

are too large is (r=0.061). Finally, those respondents who view inequality as too extreme are also more likely to support government intervention; the correlation between "Economic differences are too large" and "Government should reduce income differences" is relatively strong and positive (r=0.425).

Because many people are aware of the extreme economic gaps, and the proportion of people who think that inequality is extreme tends to increase during periods of rising economic disparities (McCall 2003), the link between economic bifurcation, rising public resentment, and political polarization is of growing concern to policymakers (Greenspan 2005). However, in the United States, in contrast to other industrialized nations, inequality is typically conceptualized as a private matter rather than as a product of government policy (see also McCall 2003). Moreover, beliefs in the significance of extra-individual factors (such as parental wealth and social capital) as determinants of economic success do not seem to negate the equal opportunity ethos and are not strongly associated with either critical views on societal inequality or strong support in redistributive policies. The above-mentioned attitudinal patterns are in accordance with the liberal welfare regime model—which is dominated by a stark emphasis on private material resources—in which the family is "falling decisively on the 'private' side of the public-private dichotomy, unfit as the subject for any substantial public intervention" (Rice et al. 2006). It is in this intersection of the *public* and the *private* spheres that the American family takes its place at the forefront of the stratification system, not only in actual provision of a financial safety net to its members, but also in terms of the normative obligations and filial responsibility that Americans express toward family and kin members. To understand the role of the American family in the economic sphere and, in particular, the role that normative structure and expectations play in determining intergenerational transfers of social and economic advantage, we need first to elucidate the tension between two concepts—individualism and familism—and then to understand how the two strands are intertwined.

∽

CHAPTER FIVE

Families, Generations, and Familial Responsibility

It is often forgotten that the modern domestic household is very much an *economic* unit even if it is no longer a farming unit.

—William J. Goode, *The Theoretical Importance of the Family*

Familism and the Changing Nuclear Family

The classical sociology of the family, particularly those works that drew on the structuralism-functionalism and modernization paradigms, maintained that industrialization and the historical shift to market economy would lead to the rise of individualism and loss of the traditional centrality of the family. Specifically, the literature posits that industrialization and urbanization reduced the multigenerational living arrangements of the extended family and contributed to the emergence of the isolated nuclear family of parents and their young children living in the same household. The literature also predicted that with modernization and increasing individualization of social relations, intergenerational bonds would lose their salience (Kohli 1999; Kohli and Künemund 2003; Parsons 1970: 24 in Parkin 1978).

Family scholars continue to voice concern over the weakening of the traditional utility of the American family in three related areas: structural, functional, and normative. The literature on the structural decline of the family maintains that during the past fifty years, due to an increase in divorce (from about 30 percent in the 1950s to 50 percent today) and decline in fertility (from about 3.8 in 1950s to about 2.1 today), the nuclear family has become smaller and more isolated and vulnerable. The second, related dimension of the weakening family literature highlights the decline in the functions of the family. With industrialization and modernization, some argue, other social institutions, such as education and the labor market, replaced some of the key functions that the family had in the past. This transition has left the family weaker and today the family has only two functions: childbearing and the provision of affection and companionship to its members (Popenoe 1993).

Both the structural and the functional decline theses have some apparent limitations. A comparison of the family today with the average family in the 1950s is misleading. First, the demographic characteristics of the family in the 1950s represent a historical deviation, characterized by an exceptionally young age of marriage and parenthood, relatively high fertility rates, stable marriages, and low rates of divorce (Coontz 1995). While fertility rates are lower today than they were in the 1950s, the average number of births per woman in 1941 was about 2.2, and infant mortality rates were much higher than they are today. Note also that fertility rates in the United States today are substantially higher than those reported in other developed countries. In 2002, the fertility rate in the United States was 2.1 children per woman while the figures for western European countries averaged 1.5 children: in Germany the rate was 1.4, France, 1.9; Italy, 1.2; Austria, 1.3; United Kingdom, 1.7; Denmark, 1.6; Spain, 1.2; Canada, 1.6; and Australia, 1.8 (U.S. Census Bureau 2002: table A-9: 1).

The twentieth century also witnessed variation in marriage rates which range between a low of 7.9 per 1,000 total population in the Depression year of 1932 and a high of 16.4 in 1946 (NCHS 1989; 2004). In 2004, the marriage rate was 7.8. Consequently, the divorce rate has followed a similar trend: It increased from 1930 to the mid-1940s, decreased during the 1950s, and rose fairly steadily throughout the 1960s and 1970s, reaching a peak of 5.3 per 1000 in 1979 and 1981. In 2004, the divorce rate was 3.7 per 1,000 population (NCHS 1989; 2004). Moreover, most of those who divorce today tend to remarry, a pattern often cited to suggest that rather than showing a decline, the changing structure of the American family mirrors the increasing cultural, demographic, and economic diversity the United States has experienced during the past fifty years.[1] And while, in contrast to contemporary living arrangements, multigenerational residence was a norm among the aged population in the mid-nineteenth century, the overall number of multigenerational families was relatively low; shorter life expectancy, higher fertility rates, and the fact that an old parent could only live with one adult child at a time limited the actual number of years that individuals spent in multigenerational coresidence (Ruggles 2006).

Second, in contrast to the pessimistic view on its weakening functions, the family continues to play an important, albeit indirect, economic role. While other social institutions have replaced the family in directly providing human capital and occupational training, the indirect impact the family has on placement of its members in the stratification system remains significant. As mentioned above, parental wealth plays an important role in determining educational attainment and economic mobility. Empirical studies have found that, net of parental human capital and labor market success, inter vivos transfers of wealth remain a strong predictor on children's educational achievement and economic well-being (Axinn, Duncan, and Thornton 1997; Alwin and Thornton 1984; Conley 2001; Zhan 2006; Orr 2003) and the post–World War II decline in fertility rates has been linked to increasing parental investment in children (Becker 1991).

Third, despite the rapid increase in women's participation in the labor force, mothers' time with children has been relatively constant over the past few decades (Bianchi 2000). Studying changes in children's time with parents between 1981 and 1997, Sandberg and Hofferth (2001) found that overall, children's time with their parents did not decrease during the period. However, while children's time with mothers, fathers, and both parents has increased substantially in two-parent families, these changes were not paralleled in single-parent families.[2] Recent studies also report that low levels of education also are becoming more closely associated with divorce, single parenthood, and the transmission of fewer resources to children (McLanahan 2004, figure 2: 611; see also Ellwood and Jencks 2004, figures 1.4 and 1.5: 13–14).

Families and Generations: The Generational Conflict Hypothesis

At the core of the third dimension of the academic discourse on the changing American family lies the debate on family values and the seeming contradiction between individualism and familism (Zinn and Pok 2002). Heller (1976: 423) identifies three analytical levels of the concept of familism:

> Familism consists of a set of rights and obligations pertaining to members of a given kin network. Three interrelated conceptual levels of familism can be distinguished. Familism as social organization refers to role rights and obligations linking kin members to one another. Familism can also be viewed as behavior: i.e., kin members directly engaged in the fulfillment of role obligations. Finally, familism can refer to a kin member's attitudes concerning his obligations toward

other members. Individual family members possessing strong familistic attitudes perceive kinship rights and obligations as mandatory.

Citing the decrease in fertility rates and the increase in divorce during the past fifty years, the literature on the weakening family sees individualism and familism as two contrasting values in a zero-sum game; growing individualism and autonomy among today's adult women is coupled with deteriorating family values and the unraveling of social bonds (Popenoe 1993).[3] The normative discourse on the weakening of the family refers not only to the nuclear family, but the strength of ties that bind members of the extended family. Specifically, the generational conflict theory mirrors a growing concern about what is often viewed as an increasing tension between the generations. This literature portrays the economic well-being of the young and the old in terms of conflict and competition over limited public and private resources (Preston 1984).

> The hypotheses advanced regarding growing conflict between generations have focused both on the relationship between middle-aged parents and their children in the establishment phase, and on the relationship between elderly parents and their descendents (adult children and grandchildren) in terms of older people's disposition of their accumulated wealth. . . . [The] question of conflict or absence thereof between generations is . . . a question of the type and nature of transfers between the generations—both in the public and the private sphere—and of attitudes and norms regarding such transfers and inequality. (Gulbrandsen and Langsether 2000: 69–70)

The issue of limited public resources has received much attention from policymakers and family scholars. The generational equity (GE) perspective, for example, holds the view that each generation should provide for itself (Williamson, McNamara, and Howling 2003). Proponents of the GE perspective draw on evidence indicating that, because of excessively generous public spending on programs for the elderly, the improved conditions for the older population have been achieved, at least partially, at the expense of children whose economic status has deteriorated (Preston 1984). Indeed, one consistent finding from research on poverty is that children (under eighteen) are more likely than adults to live in poverty, while the elderly (over sixty-five) have the lowest level of poverty. Consequently, this literature contends, because old-age policies are unsustainable, the expectation that the pivot generation will support the older cohorts may lead to increasing conflicts between the generations. This approach often leads to proposals to cut back on entitlement programs for the elderly and to place more emphasis on privatized programs. Applying these policies, however, seems more difficult than ever. Economists and policymakers have expressed concern that, as their populations age, Western societies will have a large group of economically inactive, but affluent, voters. These elderly "who require expensive social services such as health care and who depend upon government for much of their income . . . are bringing down the social welfare state, destroying government finances, and threatening the investments that all societies need to make to have a successful future" (Thurow 1999: 93). Studies also cite changes in demographic and economic structures as factors that have negative effects on the type and amount of intergenerational exchanges of goods and services. The growth of external demands on young parents, particularly women who become increasingly involved in economic activities outside the home; the high level of marital instability, which depletes the financial resources of younger adults; and declining and postponed fertility are often cited as causes of the weakening of intergenerational ties and support networks (see Dwyer and Coward 1992; Logan and Spitze 1996).

Data from the ISSP social inequality survey of 1999 (figure 13) reveal that many Americans view the conflicts between generations as strong. Whereas the question is too general and does not clearly identify the nature of the conflict, more than 40 percent of the respondents view the conflicts between the old and the young as either strong or very strong and one half (49.8 percent) characterize the conflict as "not very strong." Only 7.1 percent answered "no conflict."

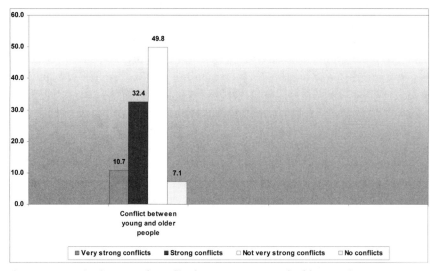

Figure 13.   Attitudes toward Conflict between Young and Older People
Source: International Social Survey Programme, Social Inequality III, 1999.

The Generational Contract

In contrast to the bleak view portrayed by the generational conflict thesis, various measures of depth and strength of intergenerational ties reveal strong associational and normative solidarity that bind individuals, families, and generations. Instead of exhibiting a competition between distinct age cohorts over limited economic resources, evidence indicates that private and public transfers coexist and that social and financial bonds between generations seem to be boosted, not weakened, by public transfers to the elderly; through intergenerational transfers in the form of inter vivos gifts, a substantial fraction of the public resources transferred to the aged is redistributed downward, from older to younger generations (Attias-Donfut and Wolff 2000). The elderly today are less likely to be poor than adults and children, many are engaged in paid work, and the activities of this group are not limited to work and often include involvement in civic organizations and familial exchanges (Zedlewski and Schaner 2006). Indeed, data on American retirees reveal that among people aged sixty-five to seventy-four, over three-fourths report engagement in a variety of productive activities such as paid work, volunteering, and family caregiving.

The strength of bonds among members of an extended family is often measured by analyzing family networks in the physical-spatial sense (such as co-residence and frequency of visits), and in terms of familial obligation and exchanges of goods and services (Taylor 2005a). Research reveals a significant increase in the acceptability of co-residence, especially among young adults (Alwin 1996) and actual co-residence of adult children with parents is on the rise (Goldscheider et al. 1999).[4] While the percentage of persons aged sixty-five and older who co-reside with their adult children has declined sharply since 1850, this trend has generally stabilized since 1980, and the percent of elderly blacks living with their adult children has actually increased since 1960 (Ruggles 2007). A recent report by the Urban Institute (Johnson and Schaner 2005) found that nearly 40 percent of older Americans (fifty-five years and older)—and about half of those aged fifty-five to sixty-four—provide care for family members such as spouses, parents-in-law, and grandchildren.[5] Grandchild care was the most common caregiving activity, pursued by nearly one-quarter of older adults, followed by parent care, spousal care, and child care. And about 7 percent of adults aged fifty-five and older cared for multiple generations of relatives. Provision of services to grandchildren ranges from looking after grandchildren on afternoons, evenings, and weekends to serving as legal guardians and primary caregivers when parents are unable to care for their children themselves; during the past thirty years, the number of children living with grandparents has increased by 73 percent (U.S. Census Bureau 2004b; Kreider and Fields 2005: 8).

The existence of familial ties across three generations is partly attributable to the changing age structure and the overall aging of the population (see chapter 2); the demographer Uhlenberg (1996; see Bengston and Lowenstien 2003) contrasted the age structures in 1900 with those in 2000 to examine some of the social outcomes of these changing demographic realities. The analysis shows that for those born in 1900, by age thirty, less than one-quarter (21 percent) had any grandparent still living. For those born in 2000, more than three-quarters (76 percent) will still have at least one grandparent alive. Whereas 83 percent of twenty-year-olds living in 1900 had their mother living, about 91 percent of twenty-year-olds living today have a grandmother still living.

The strength of associational solidarity (Bengston 2001), that is, the type and frequency of intergenerational contact between family members, is clearly seen in table 6, which shows data from the ISSP 2001 Survey on Social Networks on the frequency with which adult Americans visit their parents and siblings. To help us assess the extent to which social contacts between family members in the United States are prevalent, the table also displays data from other developed countries that represent the four above-mentioned welfare regimes—conservative, liberal, social democratic, and rudimentary (household sector). The data show that many Americans maintain both horizontal social contacts with siblings and vertical contacts with relatives from other generations such as parents, aunts, and uncles. More than half of the population reports visiting their kin (mother, father, and siblings) at least once a month and about one-third visit their relatives at least once a week. In other countries, with the exception of Spain, patterns of family co-residence and kin contacts are similar to those reported by Americans. Given the population size, geographical mobility, and strong emphasis on independent living and high homeownership rates in the United States, these findings are particularly striking.

So far we have emphasized the distinct structural conditions and processes that make the American family the core of social and economic support between generations. However, institutional arrangements and demographic structures that reinforce reliance on private resources do not necessarily side with, and may in fact contradict, cultural expectations vis-à-vis familial responsibility; the intergenerational transfer behavior of households may be driven by necessity, enforced by law, and accompanied by economic burden and distress on the part of those providing assistance, rather than guided by normative principles.[6] The subsequent pages report findings on normative

Table 6. Frequency of Family Visits: Parents, Siblings, Aunts, and Uncles

Welfare Regime	Liberal			Conservative		Social Democratic	Rudimentary Sector
	U.S.	Canada	Australia	France	Germany-West	Denmark	Spain
How often visit brother or sister							
Lives in same household	2.6	3.2	4.2	2.3	2.5	1.4	16.4
Daily	7.0	3.4	1.7	2.3	3.7	1.5	19.2
Several times per week	11.5	8.7	5.1	9.5	11.4	5.6	18.6
At least once per week	16.8	17.1	17.0	21.1	18.0	15.4	16.7
At least once per month	18.1	19.6	22.9	22.8	24.1	36.0	12.3
Several times per year	23.8	26.0	27.7	32.8	30.3	34.6	12.2
Less often	20.2	22.1	21.5	9.2	10.0	5.6	4.7
N	951	943	1088	1107	673	1081	986
How often visit father (adults with living father)							
Lives in same household	6.1	10.7	12.0	7.9	12.4	6.3	45.3
Daily	10.6	14.0	3.6	4.9	9.7	1.6	14.0
Several times per week	10.4	8.0	7.7	13.4	12.4	10.1	11.6
At least once per week	16.0	16.3	24.2	21.4	17.8	18.7	13.3
At least once per month	16.3	18.5	17.6	22.7	19.3	39.5	5.9
Several times per year	19.8	19.3	16.6	19.6	18.1	17.4	5.9
Less often	14.8	18.7	9.4	6.0	7.2	2.9	3.4
Never	9.6	4.3	8.9	4.2	3.2	3.4	.7
N	575	460	392	649	404	552	580

How often visit mother (adults with living mother)

Lives in same household	8.9	8.1	9.8	7.2	13.2	6.5	42.9
Daily	9.5	6.5	4.4	6.9	12.4	2.7	16.2
Several times per week	17.2	13.1	10.5	13.7	13.7	14.2	13.6
At least once per week	18.7	18.4	25.2	22.0	16.4	22.6	12.4
At least once per month	14.9	19.0	18.6	22.7	20.7	38.8	5.8
Several times per year	16.8	21.2	15.7	19.2	17.3	13.6	6.0
Less often	11.4	12.3	12.3	6.4	5.3	.8	2.7
Never	2.6	1.4	3.5	1.8	.9	.8	.4
	744	657	592	844	531	738	728

Frequency of contact with uncles or aunts for those with living aunts/uncles

More than twice in last four weeks	20.1	15.9	4.7	12.6	12.3	8.2	22.0
Once or twice in last four weeks	28.2	26.4	23.4	32.7	36.2	28.8	30.4
Not at all in last four weeks	51.7	57.7	71.9	54.8	51.5	63.0	47.6
Never	956	881	1024	946	667	879	935

Source: International Social Survey Programme, Social Relations and Support Systems, 2001.

perceptions and expectations toward familial obligations to the well-being of the old and the young.

Normative Solidarity and Familial Responsibility

Analysis of attitudes regarding familial obligation and their formation has three distinct, not necessarily exclusive, merits. First, people's attitudes are one of the key factors that shape their actual behavior (Ajzen and Fishbein 1980; Fishbein and Ajzen 1975; Manstead 1996). Studies on familial obligation report that positive attitudes regarding the primacy of intergenerational transfers have an independent effect on actual transmission of financial resources to children and older family members (see, for example, Lee, Netzer, and Coward 1994; Spilerman and Elmelech 2003; Ganong et al. 1998: 595; see also Barber 2001). Second, while attitudes have important implications for cultural expectations from family and kin members, they are also likely to influence policymakers. Research in the United States reports that public policy is strongly influenced by public opinion—particularly when issues are important to the public and the public's desires are clear—and concludes that the neglect of public opinion research in sociological analysis is becoming harder to justify (Burstein 1998). Finally, people's expectations and attitudes are formed during the socialization process, and reflect their attachment to societal normative structure (Goldscheider and Lawton 1998; Rossi and Rossi 1990 in Burr and Mutchler 1999). In this context, the study of attitudes concerning obligations toward family members constitutes an important aspect of familism (Heller 1976: 423) that is often discussed in lay and academic discourse on the normative weakening of the American family.

Attitudinal research on the family is particularly important in a cross-national framework, in which cultural distinctiveness is more likely to be reflected by attitudes than by specific behavioral contingencies, which are often reinforced by the state's political and economic organization. Analysis of family and intergenerational obligations are fundamental, insofar as the allocation of responsibilities among the state, the market, and the family constitutes one of the critical features for characterizing various welfare regimes (Martin 1997). The attitudinal measures presented in tables 7 and 8 focus on six developed countries that represent the four aforementioned welfare models: liberal, conservative, social democratic, and rudimentary. The aim of this comparative format is to illuminate the uniqueness of the U.S. attitudinal structure, rather than to contrast the typical features of each nation participating in the study.[7]

Table 7 reports findings from a general question measuring normative solidarity. As seen in the data, the views of respondents in the United States

Table 7. Attitudes toward Familial Responsibility

	Liberal			Conservative			Social Democratic	Rudimentary Sector
	US	Canada	Australia	France	Germany-West		Denmark	Spain
Agree strongly	43.4	12.0	15.1	33.3	12.1		23.9	27.9
Agree	39.9	51.3	53.8	31.1	38.6		33.7	51.8
Neither agree nor disagree	12.8	24.1	21.9	21.6	17.4		17.7	13.8
Disagree	3.6	11.7	8.7	9.1	24.4		15.0	5.6
Strongly disagree	.3	.9	.5	4.9	7.4		9.7	1.0
	1139	1509	1278	1281	889		1236	1207
	100	100	100	100	100		100	100

Source: International Social Survey Programme, Social Relations and Support Systems, 2001.

Table 8. Attitudes toward Provision of Care for Old Parents

	Liberal			Conservative		Social Democratic	Rudimentary Sector
	U.S.	Canada	Australia	France	Germany-West	Denmark	Spain
Agree strongly	36.1	18.9	6.9	48.1	20.2	16.7	27.6
Agree	37.1	36.7	35.5	27.8	48.7	33.2	51.8
Neither agree nor disagree	17.6	22.2	35.2	18.4	14.6	21.7	12.7
Disagree	7.0	16.7	18.9	3.8	12.5	11.5	6.5
Strongly disagree	2.2	5.5	3.4	1.9	4.0	16.9	1.4
	1125	1068	1278	1318	872	1197	1203
	100	100	100	100	100	100	100

Source: International Social Survey Programme, Social Relations and Support Systems, 2001.

seem surprisingly distinct from those expressed by citizens of other industrialized nations; four in five Americans accept the general notion that "people should take care of family before they help others," and about half of those supporting the statement strongly agree with it (43.4 percent). A small fraction (3.9 percent) of the sample disagree with the statement. With the exception of one country, which represents the rudimentary or southern European welfare regime (Spain), this level of agreement is substantially higher in comparison to other developed nations.

Strong familial obligation is also manifested in the second item, which measures the caregiving responsibility of adult children toward elderly parents. Almost three-fourths of the respondents either agree or strongly agree that adult children should care for old parents. Less than one-tenth of the U.S. sample disagrees with the statement.[8] These findings align with recent data on the changing size and functions of social networks in the United States. Analysis of temporal changes in core social networks between 1985 and 2004 reveals that over the past two decades, both kin and non-kin confidants were lost, but decrease in non-kin ties was more substantial, a pattern that led to a visible increase in intimate networks that center on close family members (McPherson, Smith-Lovin, and Brashears 2006).

Attitudes toward Financial Assistance to Elderly Parents: Age Differentials

Familial commitment to the well-being of older parents is also evident in the economic sphere, as seen when Americans are asked a more specific question pertaining to a child's duty to look after the financial well-being of their parents. Utilizing data from the U.S. Generations Survey,[9] Elmelech (2005) reports that when asking the question, "Do you think children should look after their parents economically when the parents have financial problems?" the answers were split almost evenly between those who chose the answer, "Children should look after their parents even if they have to make sacrifices," and those who expressed willingness to assist as long as the burden "does not become too great" (45.1 percent). Only 3.4 percent thought there was no reason for children to support elderly parents in need (see table 9).

The data presented in figure 15 reveal that, in contrast to common wisdom, expression in support of assistance to elderly parents (measured on the scale of 1 to 3) is strong for all age categories but is slightly stronger among the young (2.56 points) and weaker among the elderly segments of the population (2.26 points). A word of caution is warranted: Because different age cohorts might have distinct political and social experiences and value structures

Table 9. Assistance to Parents: Financial Support

"Do you think children should look after their parents economically when the parents have financial problems?"

	U.S.
1. As children have their own responsibilities, there is no need for them to look after their parents.	3.4
2. Children should look after their parents as long as the burden does not become too great.	45.1
3. Children should look after their parents even if they have to make sacrifices.	51.5
N	1473

Source: The Generations Survey, 1995

(Ryder 1965; Schuman and Scott 1989), the age differentials seen in figure 14 could reflect, in part, cohort effects. Because the data are cross-sectional, it is impossible to distinguish the life-cycle effect from the cohort effect.

Multivariate analysis (Elmelech 2005) that uses this measure of familial responsibility as a dependent variable reveals that this age pattern remains relatively stable even after socioeconomic and demographic characteristics are controlled for (see appendix B, table 2).[10] Specifically, the analysis shows that even when such variables as education, income, religiosity, and race are introduced into the model, the linear pattern of age remains salient; compared with the youngest age group, elderly people express less support in the notion that children are responsible for providing financial assistance to elderly parents.

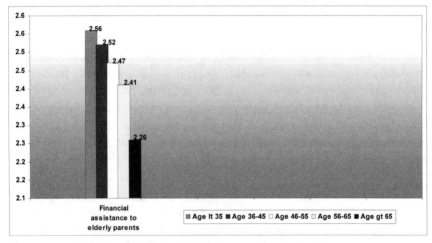

Figure 14. Attitudes toward Private Assistance to Parents, by Age
Source: The Generations Survey 1995

Overall, the findings reflect the high level of normative solidarity between generations, whereas the younger generation is inclined to express strong financial responsibility toward the elderly. The social norms held by older people may reflect their desire for autonomy and self-reliance—their sense that the role of parents is to provide, rather than receive, assistance, and their aversion to becoming burdensome to the younger generations (Bengston and Lowenstein 2003: 12–13).[11] The findings reported in appendix B also show two interesting findings on the impact of intergenerational exchanges on attitudes toward familial obligations. First, those respondents who expect to receive inheritance in the future express more positive views on assistance to the aged. Second, respondents who reported close relationships with their parents during childhood are also more inclined to support aiding elderly parents in need. These findings reiterate the link between social and financial exchanges in the family and the extent to which social and economic ties between generations increases financial responsibility between the old and the young.

Downward Transfers of Financial Resources

As illustrated by the shift from a pre-transitional to post-transitional society, the gross flow of interhousehold transfers today is overwhelmingly downward, from older to younger generations (McGarry and Schoeni 1995; Bergstrom 1996), and both the magnitude and the objectives of assistance to offspring differ from those characterizing assistance to elderly parents. Whereas gerontology research that studies support systems for the elderly focuses on the growing need for the family to provide services and care to elderly and ailing parents, "downward" flow of material resources emphasizes parental investment in the life chances and standards of living of young adults. As young people spend more time in school, and as the level of financial debt among the young rises and the cost of setting up and maintaining a household increases, many young adults are not financially well equipped to maintain an independent residence (U.S. Bureau of the Census 1997) and are more dependent on their parents' resources.

Direct and Indirect Transfers: Age Differentials

While often seen as two contradictory mechanisms of social mobility (Durkheim 1992)—one enhancing achievement and the other associated with ascribed advantage—investment in educational attainment and passing on of material resources are two complementary processes that families utilize to promote the life chances of the young. The historical shift in asset portfolio composition, from mostly tangible assets (such as land, plants, and equipment) to diverse portfolios—which affected intergenerational transfer behavior, leading to a transition from primarily testamentary to inter vivos gifts (Langbein 1991; also see discussion in Hall and Marcus 1998)—has brought parental wealth into the forefront of the debate on equal opportunity and the role of ascribed versus achieved mechanisms of mobility. Whereas the principle of equal opportunity is supposed to be provided by the system of public education, research has documented that the quality of education at the primary and secondary levels is linked to parental wealth, and the likelihood of attending college is based on parental ability to pay the increasing costs of tuition. A growing number of studies now report findings that underscore the importance of wealth transfers for children's education (Axinn, Duncan, and Thornton 1997; Alwin and Thornton 1984; Conley 1999) leading scholars to conclude that the "'rules of the game' that are the foundation for the class structure are designed primarily to transmit advantage and disadvantage across generations" (Perrucci and Wysong 2003: 34–36).

Table 10 displays findings from two attitudinal measures of parental responsibilities for the well-being of children that have been collected in the Generations Survey. The first question measures attitudes toward investment in children's educational attainment. The data show strong normative support for assistance to and investment in children's education. Not only did the vast majority (97 percent) of respondents agree with the statement, "It is a parent's duty to see that his/her child receives a good education even if it entails sacrifices," but more than three-quarters (75.5 percent) expressed "strong" agreement with it. The second item reported in table 10 measures attitudes toward

Table 10.   Attitudes toward Family Transfers to Children

1. Investment in Children's Education
"It is a parent's duty to see that his/her child receives a good education even if it entails sacrifices."

2. Transfers to Children: Inherited Property
"It is best to leave as much property as possible to one's children."

	Education	Property
1. Disagree strongly	0.1	11.6
2. Disagree somewhat	2.2	28.0
3. Not sure	0.8	4.9
4. Agree somewhat	21.3	35.1
5. Agree strongly	75.5	20.4
N	1500	1500

Source: The Generations Survey 1995

the passing on of tangible property. Responding to the statement, "It is best to leave as much property as possible to one's children," the majority (55.5 percent) of respondents either "somewhat" or "strongly" agreed with this statement and 11.6 percent disagreed strongly with the statement.

To assess age differences between old and young adults, figure 15 reports the distribution of expressions of family responsibilities by age categories. The data on parental obligations to the educational attainment of children reveal that Americans of all ages express a relatively strong and consistent support for this obligation. The age distribution of attitudes toward leaving an inheritance to children has a curvilinear (U-shaped) pattern; the elderly and the young are more likely, whereas the middle-aged are less disposed, to express support in passing of property in the form of inheritance.

Multivariate analysis (Elmelech 2005)[12] reveals that after controlling for socioeconomic and demographic attributes, including education, marital status, race, and income, the U-shaped age curve remains visible (see table B.3 in Appendix B). The distinct pattern seen among the pivot generation seems to reflect the relative economic security and independence of middle-aged households, who are more likely to benefit from these transfers in the near future. As for the old and the young, no evidence is found to support conflict between the elderly—those most likely to leave property in the next decade or two—and the young; elderly respondents tend to favor assistance to children in rates similar to, or even larger than, those that characterize the young. Another important factor that shapes attitudes toward family transfers is receipt

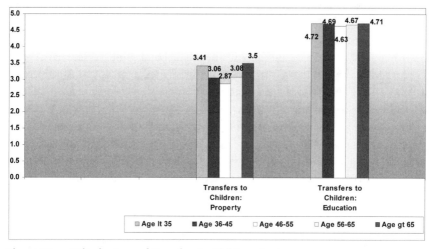

Figure 15. Attitudes toward Transfers to Children, by Age
Source: The Generations Survey, 1995

of intergenerational transfers; both receipt of inheritance and the expectation for future inheritance are associated with attitudes favoring parental responsibility to the well-being of younger generations. This pattern reflects the contribution of past transfers to the total wealth level of the receivers, as well as the social and multigenerational dimension of wealth transfers, according to which those who receive material resources from older generations are more likely to support such transfers to younger generations.

For sociologists who study the family, this may not be surprising; assistance to the old and the young is linked through the norm of reciprocity between generations (Antonucci and Jackson 1990; Pyke 1999) and ample evidence suggests that, through socialization, the norms associated with giving assistance to family members are transmitted from parents to children. As a recent study on family transfers in France reports, "The members of the pivot generation who receive financial transfers from their elderly parents are more likely to give financial help in turn to their own children" (Attias-Donfut and Wolff 2000: 42). Spilerman and Elmelech (2003) use the term *modeling effect* to describe similar findings from a sample of Israeli adults that show how receipt of family transfers in the early stages of marriage has a long-term effect on the respondents' disposition to provide financial support to family members. And evidence also shows that children are socialized to accept a general normative template of familial obligation, not only as part of direct exchange of goods and services but also from indirect reciprocity, "namely, that you give to a person other than the one from whom you expect the benefit of exchange" (Stark 1995 in Kohli and Künemund 2003: 129). In the absence of data on actual transfers to family members, the strength of the link between attitudes and behavior in the sample is impossible to examine. However, the literature on family transfers of financial resources (Spilerman and Elmelech 2003), as well as the high level of compatibility (see Manstead 1996: 10–13) between the attitudes measured in the survey and the actual behavior they refer to, suggest that these attitudinal measures are likely to correlate with actual transfer behavior.

Finally, the results reported in table B.3 in appendix B also reveal racial variation in attitudes toward private transfers; whites are less likely than nonwhites to favor intergenerational transfers to children in the form of inherited property. Previous studies report that black and Hispanic parents are more concerned than white parents with the long-term effects of cross-generational transfers of financial resources and are more likely than white parents to place the financial burden on themselves. Given the disadvantaged position of many racial and ethnic minority members, the need for parental assistance as a means of social mobility is favored more positively by racial and ethnic minorities

Table 11. Seeking Financial Assistance: First Choice (excluding "No One")

Welfare Regime	Liberal			Conservative		Social Democratic	Rudimentary Sector
	US	Canada	Australia	France	Germany-West	Denmark	Spain
Husband, wife, partner	**14.5**	**18.5**	**41.1**	**15.2**	**19.3**	**17.6**	**15.9**
Mother	18.7	9.2	7.1	15.1	11.5	8.0	17.8
Father	16.5	7.4	5.6	13.3	12.2	9.6	14.4
Parents (mother+father)	**35.2**	**27.7**	**12.7**	**28.4**	**23.7**	**17.6**	**32.2**
Daughter	3.2	1.1	4.3	1.1	1.5	1.3	8.6
Daughter-in-law	3.3	2.7	4.8	1.7	3.7	1.9	5.8
Son	5.6	2.5	1.9	2.4	2.3	.90	5.0
Son-in-law	6.4	1.9	2.9	3.2	3.5	.60	4.1
Children	**18.5**	**8.2**	**13.9**	**8.4**	**11.0**	**4.7**	**23.5**
Sister	3.6	.90	.70	1.8	.80	1.0	1.9
Brother	3.6	2.9	1.0	2.4	.80	1.8	.90
Siblings	**7.2**	**3.8**	**1.7**	**4.2**	**1.6**	**2.8**	**2.8**
Social Services agency	.60	.50	1.0	.30	.20	.30	.2
Someone you pay to help	8.8	49.5	26.1	38.7	39.3	54.6	21.2

Source: International Social Survey Programme (ISSP), Social Relations and Support Systems Survey, 2001.

Table 12. Marital Status of the Population Aged 15 and Over: 2000

| | Married | | | | | |
	Spouse Present	Spouse Absent	Widowed	Divorced	Separated	Never Married
Men						
Total	52.9	3.9	2.5	8.6	1.8	30.3
15 to 19 years	.07	3.1	0.1	0.1	0.2	95.8
20 to 24	12.9	6.0	0.2	1.2	0.9	78.8
25 to 29	38.6	5.5	0.2	4.6	1.9	49.2
30 to 34	55.0	4.9	0.3	8.0	2.3	29.6
35 to 44	63.3	3.8	0.5	12.0	2.6	17.9
45 to 54	69.4	2.8	1.0	14.7	2.4	9.7
55 to 64	74.6	2.4	2.8	12.6	1.9	5.6
65 to 74	74.9	2.5	8.3	8.3	1.4	4.6
75 to 84	67.3	4.6	18.2	4.9	0.9	4.1
85 years/over	45.4	10.9	35.3	3.3	0.8	4.3
Women						
Total	49.5	2.7	10.5	10.8	2.5	24.1
15 to 19 years	2.4	2.9	0.2	0.2	0.3	94.1
20 to 24	22.5	4.2	0.2	2.2	1.8	69.1
25 to 29	49.1	3.0	0.3	6.6	3.0	38.1
30 to 34	61.4	2.4	0.6	10.3	3.6	21.9
35 to 44	65.1	2.0	1.3	14.5	3.8	13.4
45 to 54	65.4	1.7	3.7	18.0	3.1	8.0
55 to 64	62.7	1.8	11.9	16.3	2.3	5.0
65 to 74	51.7	2.0	30.8	10.1	1.3	4.1
75 to 84	30.5	4.3	54.6	5.8	0.7	4.3
85 years/over	8.5	10.9	71.6	3.3	0.5	5.2

Source: U.S. Census Bureau 2001

(Steelman and Powell 1993; Lee and Aytac 1998). The racial and ethnic divide in wealth accumulation and asset holdings is discussed in chapter 7.

Reliance on Family and Kin Members

To study attitudes pertaining to familial responsibility, particularly in the context of reciprocity and exchange of goods and services, one needs to assess not only the normative structure of giving but also the extent to which people in need accept, and rely on, interpersonal transfers. From a cross-national perspective, Americans' reliance on private resources is salient. A recent ISSP survey (2001) that focused on social networks asked representative samples of the adult populations from twenty-nine countries to whom they would turn first for help if they needed to borrow a large sum of money.[13] For the sake of

Table 13. Seeking Financial Assistance: First Choice by Marital Status

	Married	Widowed	Divorced	Separated	Not Married
No one	11.3	25.0	17.1	11.1	6.2
Husband, wife, partner	21.4	—	4.7	11.1	7.7
Mother	12.3	4.2	17.6	15.6	26.0
Father	12.7	2.1	9.4	13.3	23.8
Parents: mother+father	**25.0**	**6.3**	**27.0**	**28.9**	**49.8**
Daughter	1.6	16.7	3.5	4.4	—
Son	2.4	15.6	2.4	2.2	.3
Children	**4.0**	**32.3**	**5.9**	**6.6**	**.3**
Sister	4.0	7.3	8.2	4.4	4.0
Brother	5.2	5.2	5.3	2.2	7.1
Siblings	**9.2**	**12.5**	**13.5**	**6.6**	**11.1**
Other blood relative	2.2	3.1	2.4	6.7	4.6
Other in-law relative	6.3	—	1.2	2.2	.6
Close friend	2.6	3.1	8.2	8.9	8.4
N=1130	496.0	96.0	170.0	45.0	323.0

Source: International Social Survey Programme (ISSP), Social Relations and Support Systems Survey, 2001.

parsimony, the data displayed in table 11 report findings from six countries that represent the four types of welfare state regimes. The data from the United States sample show strong reliance on parents and other kin as a source of financial assistance. More than one-third of Americans chose the categories "mother" or "father" (18.7 percent and 16.5 percent, respectively, totaling 35.2 percent), and a relatively large number of respondents selected children and children-in-law (18.5 percent) and siblings (7.2 percent) as their first choice. By contrast, a relatively small proportion chose social services agencies (0.6 percent) and "someone you pay to help" (8.8 percent).

Reliance on family support tends to vary by marital status. As mentioned earlier, increasing rates of divorce and the postponement of marriage during the past fifty years have increased the number of nonmarried adults in a given year. In 2000, almost half of all men (43.2 percent) and women (47.8 percent) aged 15 and older were not married (table 12). While women's marriage rate is highest for the forty-five to fifty-four age group, one-third of all women in this age bracket are not married (table 12). Note also that even among older men aged sixty-five to seventy-four—the age/gender category with the highest rates of marriage—about one in every four is not married. When studying the changing family structure, some scholars of the American family interpret the increase in divorce rates as a sign of the fragility of the contemporary family, and its diminishing ability to carry out its traditional social and economic functions such as socialization and education (Popenoe 1993).

Interestingly, however, the changing circumstances of nuclear families seem to enhance intergenerational dependence between older parents and adult children. In fact, as seen in table 13, people who experience divorce or separation and those who never married are more likely than married couples to rely on their parents, siblings, children, or other blood relatives, as a key source of financial assistance. Whereas age is obviously a mediating variable in the association between marital status and family transfers,[14] the increase in the number of single Americans—because of the postponement of marriage, divorce, and the higher rates of cohabitation (a pattern more common among people with low education and income levels)—is lengthening the financial reliance on parents and other family and kin members.

Discussion and Conclusions

The global aging of the population and the changes in fertility patterns and family formation have profound economic and social implications. Families and states worldwide have chosen different coping strategies in response to the problems and pressures that stem from the changing demographic structure and the impact that these changes have on cross-generational transfers of goods and services. Moreover, because individuals live longer and are likely to spend more years with relatives from other generations, intergenerational transfers among adult family members may be more important today than throughout most of the twentieth century (Lowenstein and Bengston 2003: 372). In the United States, the combination of generous asset-based policies for the middle class, residual income-based provision of welfare to the poor, and lack of strong support for government intervention coincide not only with visible financial reliance on family transfers, but also with strong normative support of these practices. The evidence of intergenerational solidarity—associational, normative, and financial—suggests that, contrary to previous predictions, the changing demographic structure since 1972 has led to increasing contact and consolidated economic and social bonds between members of the extended family (see also Walker 1996; Arber and Attias-Donfut 2000; Attias-Donfut and Arber 2000). American elderly express high levels of self-reliance and independence and are less likely than are younger respondents to favor sacrifices on the part of children as a way to provide financial support to elderly parents. And young Americans seem willing to financially assist elderly parents in need.

It is common to portray individualism and familism as two contrasting values; the decreasing importance of the traditional nuclear family is often linked to the increasing significance of individualism and the economic autonomy of women. However, when we adopt a more elaborated, multigenerational definition of family ties and familism, the picture that emerges is of strong family and intergenerational bonds often used as a means to improve the economic well-being and life chances of individual family members. Although the rise in divorce is associated with increasing economic hardship of single mothers and their children, in the absence of strong welfare support for families in need, kin members across several generations are called upon to fill the vacuum, draw on their accumulated wealth, and provide financial and social support. A continuing increase in the number of individuals who remain single, or experience divorce later in life—especially among young adults with low levels of income and wealth—leads to growing reliance on private resources. These private resources, however, are unevenly distributed in the population and this unequal allocation of private resources plays a key role in replicating one of the most persistent and salient economic cleavages in the United States: the racial and ethnic divide. The next chapter elaborates on the racial and ethnic wealth gap and the distinct patterns of marriage and family transfers that shape economic disparities between and within racial and ethnic groups.

PART THREE

INEQUALITY IN A
MULTI-ETHNIC SOCIETY

CHAPTER SIX

~

The Racial/Ethnic Divide

"A man without land is nobody. Remember that, Duddel."

—Mordecai Richler, *The Apprenticeship of Duddy Kravitz*

We are beginning to follow the American pattern of accumulating individual wealth and of considering that this will eventually settle the race problem.

—W.E.B. Du Bois, *The Problem of the Twentieth Century Is the Problem of the Color Line*

Race, Ethnicity, and Inequality

During the past five decades, immigration and racial variation in fertility rates have substantially changed the racial and ethnic makeup of the American population. The passage of the 1965 amendments to the Immigration and Nationality Act—which eliminated the restrictive provisions of the national origin quota system and instituted a series of preferences aimed largely at relieving occupational shortages and achieving family reunification—resulted in a shift in the ethnic composition of immigrants, away from a prevalence of Europeans to a majority of Asians and Latin Americans (Bean and Tienda 1987: 115–16). Between 1990 and 2000, the foreign-born population increased by 57 percent; according to the U.S. Census Bureau estimates, by 2050 about one in two Americans will be non-Hispanic white, 15 percent of the population will be black, almost 25 percent Hispanic, 8 percent Asian, and slightly more than 1 percent Native American, Eskimo, and Aleut (U.S.

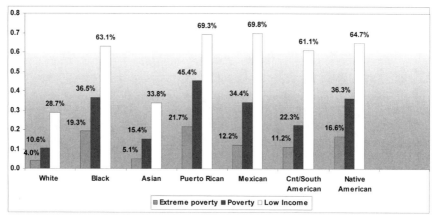

Figure 16a. Poverty Rates of Children by Racial/Ethnic Origin
Source: Author's calculations from the 1993, 1995, 1997, 1999, and 2001 surveys of the CPS.

Census Bureau 2006b).[1] The influx of immigrants in the late twentieth century coincided with persistent racial and ethnic disparities in human capital and socioeconomic characteristics, such as education, employment, and poverty. National figures show that among men and women alike, immigrants are more heavily concentrated in service jobs and have the lowest representation in managerial and sales jobs (Chiswick and Sullivan 1995) and, compared with earlier waves, immigration at the end of the twentieth century was characterized by greater social and economic diversity (Waldinger and Bozorgmehr 1996).[2] Even with the economic prosperity of the 1990s, the poverty rate among minority families with children remained substantial. As of 2000, almost 12 million children lived in poverty and the child poverty rate was 16.2 percent—considerably higher than both the elderly and the nonelderly adult poverty rates (10.2 percent and 9.4 percent, respectively) (Dalaker 2001, figure 2: 4). However, the rate and depth of poverty among minority children, particularly Hispanics and blacks, differ from those that characterize white children (Aponte 1991; Elmelech et al. 2002; Hernandez and Myers 1995; Lu et al. 2004).

Not only are minority children more likely than whites to live in poverty, but the white-minority gaps in extreme poverty—defined as those who live in families with income below half of the poverty threshold (in 2000, for example, the extreme poverty line was $6,940 for a family of three)—are particularly striking (figure 16a). The data reveal that a black child is almost five times more likely to live in extreme poverty than a white child, and 3.5 times

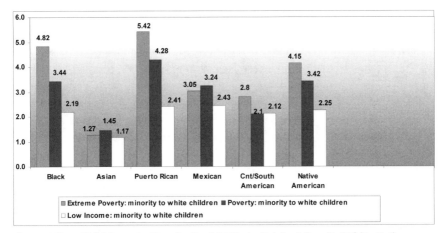

Figure 16b. Child Poverty Gaps by Racial/Ethnic Origin: Minority/White Ratios
Source: Author's calculations from the 1993, 1995, 1997, 1999, and 2001 surveys of the CPS.

more likely to live in poverty, while the comparable figures for Puerto Rican children are 5.4 and 4.3, respectively (figure 16b).

The racial/ethnic gaps in extreme poverty are alarming because they suggest that the financial resources required to lift poor children out of poverty are greater for minority, primarily black and Hispanic children, than white children. The persistent white-minority economic differentials, particularly among families with children; the prospects for future trends in racial/ethnic makeup of the population; and the extreme white-minority variation in family structure and parental resources continue to puzzle policymakers and social scientists. It is in this context that household net worth has become a focal point in the contemporary discussion on racial and ethnic stratification and racial/ethnic origin has become critical to an understanding of the extreme wealth inequality in contemporary U.S. society (Oliver and Shapiro 1989; Conley 1999; Nembhard and Chiteji 2006).

The Wealth Gap

Racial and ethnic gaps in household net worth are salient and exceed those disparities seen in labor market remuneration. Most previous studies on household net worth adopted a near-exclusive focus on black and white households (Blau and Graham 1990; Shapiro 2004; Henretta 1979; Conley 1999; Keister 2000; Oliver and Shapiro 1995; Parcel 1982). Whereas research beyond the black-white divide is still in its infancy (but see Hao 2004;

Krivo and Kaufman 2004), recent evidence on the fast-growing Hispanic population reveals a substantial white-minority wealth gap and shows that Hispanics hold about 12 percent of the net worth held by white households. In 2000, household median net worth was $79,400 for households with a non-Hispanic white householder, $7,500 for households with a black householder, and $9,750 for households with a Hispanic householder (Orzechowski and Sepielli 2003; also see Angel et al. 1999; Smith 1995). The wealth gulf between native- and foreign-born Americans is also alarming; recent data show that the median wealth level of U.S.-born couples is 2.3 times the median of foreign-born couples, while the median wealth level of U.S.-born singles is three times that of foreign-born singles (Cobb-Clark and Hildebrand 2006).

Variations in wealth portfolio have intrinsic significance to differences in life chances and standard of living. A closer look at the distinct assets held by whites and the two largest economically disadvantaged minority groups—blacks and Hispanics—reveals substantial variations in asset portfolios (Terrell 1971: 366–68; Sobol 1979; Oliver and Shapiro 1989, 1995: 104–8). Compared to white households, the amount of wealth held in financial and income-producing assets (e.g. bonds, stocks, and businesses) is significantly smaller among minority households. In 2000, the average white household held 31 percent of its net worth in home equity, whereas the comparable figures for black and Hispanic households were 61.8 and 50.8, respectively (Orzechowski and Sepielli 2003, table G: 13; see also Sobol 1979; Blau and Graham 1990; Browne 1974; Schick and Schick 1991).[3] The determinants of asset holdings and portfolio composition also vary across asset categories. Residential segregation, redlining, and inequality in mortgage lending influence the accumulation of home equity but have no *direct* effect on the accumulation of wealth from financial and income-producing investments (Krivo and Kaufman 2004). As seen in table 14, the racial/ethnic variation in asset portfolio is visible among members of the pivot generation, who are entering the "third age." Whereas racial/ethnic differences in homeownership and functional assets have received much attention in the literature, the data suggest that, while considerable, the white-minority gaps in ownership of a main residence, vehicle, and liquid assets are smaller when compared to observed disparities in financial assets. White households are about five times more likely to own stocks or mutual funds than Hispanic households are, and about three times more likely to own a business than is the average black household.

These disparities in wealth portfolio have a significant effect on racial/ethnic inequality in income.[4] Data on income sources among the middle-aged

Table 14. Ownership Rates by Racial/Ethnic Origin and Asset Type

	Housing	Liquid	IRA/Keogh	Stocks/Mutual Funds	Business	Bonds	Other	Real Estate	Vehicle
White	.83	.89	.49	.35	.16	.082	.19	.34	.94
Black	.58	.57	.14	.085	.050	.013	.061	.16	.66
Hispanic	.56	.49	.11	.069	.065	.014	.053	.19	.74
Ratio:									
White/Black	1.43	1.56	3.4	4.1	3.20	6.3	3.11	2.12	1.42
White/Hispanic	1.48	1.89	4.3	5.0	2.46	5.8	3.8	1.78	1.27

Source: HRS-92

and elderly (table C.1 in appendix C) reveal that whites are more likely to report property-income than either Blacks or Hispanics and these racial gaps are widest among the older age group (sixty-five and older); while almost two-thirds of white families receive income from assets, the comparable figures for blacks and Hispanics are about one-third. The racial/ethnic income gaps are visible across the various categories of marital status but married couples in all three racial groups are more likely to report income from property.

Why Are Whites Wealthier?

Attempts to explicate the sources of racial and ethnic variation in household net worth and asset composition include a spectrum of theories, ranging from cultural Darwinism to institutional and demographic explanations. One of the early attempts to explain racial/ethnic gaps in wealth links wealth accumulation to cultural differentials in investment preferences and posits that racial gaps in asset holdings result from motivational differences and saving behavior. According to the model of cultural Darwinism, some racial and ethnic minorities are more successful than others because they place greater importance on education and share a particular set of cultural values emphasizing frugality, diligence, foresight, perseverance, ingenuity, and the like (Steinberg 1989). These characteristics translate into wealth disparities; some minority groups, such as "the Jews, the Japanese-Americans, and the West Indian Negroes" tend to sacrifice present comfort and enjoyment while saving, whereas "high value on 'fun,' 'excitement' and emotionalism has characterized the less successful minorities" (Sowell 1975: 144–46 in Mason 1996: 785). Consequently, cultural values and not class position are viewed as responsible for the gaps in both composition and magnitude of household wealth (see Clignet 1998; Thernstrom 1973).

Copious evidence on the black-white divide, however, rules out cultural distinctiveness in the propensity to save as an explanation for racial gaps in asset holdings (see, for example, Blau and Graham 1990; Mason 1996). Data from the Federal Reserve Board's 1998 Survey of Consumer Finances reveal substantial racial variation in saving behavior; whereas 23 percent of Americans report that they do not save and 39 percent say they save regularly, the comparable figures for black families are 32 percent and 34 percent, respectively. These behavioral differences, however, are largely explained by wealth differences; when the saving patterns of black Americans and all Americans with net wealth below $10,000 are compared, black and nonblack American households tend to exhibit similar financial behavior. In fact, some studies on saving patterns suggest that within comparable income categories, blacks tend to save more than whites. The relative income theory of consumption postulates that since, relative to whites, blacks are poorer, and spatially segregated, they tend to save more out of their income (Galenson 1972). Empirical analysis that specifically addressed saving behavior shows that African Americans at all income levels tend to save more and spend less than their white counterparts (see Mason 1996; Smith 1997), leading scholars to reject cultural explanations for wealth disparities.

> In spite of the talk about distinct cultural histories that may explain why some ethnic or racial groups do not save, there is little evidence in favor of such a view. Instead, the fundamental question is why low-income people save so little no matter what their race or ethnic background (Smith 1997: 78).

Explanations for the low wealth level accumulated by immigrant minorities also tend not to support the cultural explanation (Carroll, Rhee, and Rhee 1994), focusing instead on immigrant selectivity and length of residence in the host society (Cobb-Clark and Hildebrand 2006). Research on business ownership reports that immigrants with a high propensity for entrepreneurship, such as Cubans and Koreans, did not have prior histories of entrepreneurship in other regions in the world, including their country of origin. A propensity for self-employment is often attributed to discrimination faced by newcomers in the labor market and interpreted as an alternative path to socioeconomic mobility (Portes and Zhou 1995).[5] Light and Rosenstein (1995: 19) state: "Also, where entrepreneurship is legally available on an equal basis to immigrants and nonimmigrants, immigrant self-employment normally exceeds nonimmigrant self-employment. Because the foreign born outperform the native born, we cannot turn to unique cultural traditions for explanations."

The lack of explanatory power of cultural differences in financial behavior related to investments preferences, saving habits, propensity for self-employment, and risk aversion requires a more careful analysis of structural explanations for the white-minority wealth gap. Regardless of racial/ethnic origin, while asset holders in the same wealth bracket tend to behave similarly in terms of saving rates and asset portfolio, the likelihood of distinct racial groups to enter the commodity market and own desirable property differs. Growing evidence supports the significant role that structural and institutional explanations play in shaping racial and ethnic variations in household net worth. According to this line of research, the economic well-being of racial/ethnic minority groups is substantially different from that of whites, because many immigrant and minority households face more limited opportunity structure in the market.

Differential access to assets involves two stages. First, distinct opportunity structure in education and the labor market restricts mobility to prestigious occupations with high remuneration (American Sociological Association 2005). In 2005, non-Hispanic whites had the highest proportion of adults with a high school diploma or higher (90 percent), followed by Asians (88 percent), blacks (81 percent) and Hispanics (59 percent) (U.S. Department of Commerce 2006). The median income of black households was only 60 percent of the median for non-Hispanic white households ($30,858 and $50,784, respectively). Median income for Hispanic households was $35,967, which was 71 percent of the median for non-Hispanic white households. Second, minority households are more likely to encounter unfavorable opportunities in the commodity market when trying to convert their income into assets such as business and housing (Alba and Logan 1992; Bates and Howell 1997; Bianchi, Farley, and Spain 1982; Dymski 1997; Henretta 1984; Jackman and Jackman 1980; Kain and Quigley 1975; Krivo 1995; Parcel 1982; Krivo and Kaufman 2004; Shapiro 2004). Empirical evidence on trajectories to homeownership—the single most important source of wealth buildup for most middle-class Americans—shows that the racial/ethnic gaps remain significant even after controlling for income and labor market differentials (Alba and Logan 1992; Krivo 1995; Elmelech 2004), and account for a major part of racial/ethnic inequality in wealth (Henretta 1984; Jackman and Jackman 1980; Parcel 1982; Krivo 1995; Lewin-Epstein, Elmelech, and Semyonov 1997).

The remaining gaps in homeownership and home equity are typically attributed to institutional discrimination toward minority clients on the part of real estate agents, homeowners, and federal and local authorities (Oliver and Shapiro 1995; Page 1995; Dymski 2006). Research shows that despite the 1968 Fair Housing Act, black and Hispanic households are very likely to encounter discrimination when they search for housing, and that discriminatory practices such as steering and redlining in mortgage lending occur throughout the country (Yinger 1995). These practices severely limit the information households receive about the local housing market and in turn restrict minority households' access to desirable units. Indeed, housing, even for middle-class minority households, remains relatively segregated, and appreciation of minority home equity typically increases at a slower pace (Sherraden 1991: 137; Patillo-McCoy 1999).

Whereas time of migration is positively correlated with the likelihood of homeownership many recent immigrants do not simply enter at the bottom of the housing market and reside in the poorer neighborhoods, but rather occupy a distinct position in the housing market because of stigmatization and discrimination (Rosenbaum 1996). The concentration of some immigrant minorities in distinct residential areas and neighborhoods suppress the likelihood of homeownership (Krivo 1995), which is often seen as an important step toward social and economic assimilation: "Probably nothing is more central to the assimilation process than becoming a homeowner" (Clark 1998: 95). Comparing Hispanics and non-Hispanic whites in the United States, Krivo (1995: 613) found that living in a heavily immigrant milieu—defined by duration of residence, knowledge of the language, and ethnic residential concentration—constrains the housing opportunities of Hispanics. These distinct spatial conditions contribute to the low-level of home ownership and home equity of minority households and enhance residential segregation along racial and ethnic lines (see also Bolton and Rosenthal 2005), a process that contributes to white-minority gaps in education and labor market opportunities (Wenglinsky 1997; Kozol 1991).

Whereas homeownership is an important path to wealth accumulation and an indicator of a group's assimilation into the host society, business ownership is often seen as the most effective form of economic advancement for disadvantaged groups who face discrimination in the labor market (Glazer and Moynahan 1970). Oliver and Shapiro (1995) coined the term "economic detour" to describe the institutional restrictions that many blacks face in the free market, which affect their ability to build and maintain successful enterprises. Data from the National Survey of Small Business Finances (NSSBF) reveal that black and Hispanic business owners report greater difficulties in obtaining credit than white business owners (Cavalluzzo and Cavalluzzo 1998; Blanchflower et al. 2003). Econometric analysis of loans to small businesses found that black-owned businesses are about twice as likely to be denied credit even after taking into account racial variation in an extensive array of measures of creditworthiness and other attributes, leading the authors to conclude that "the racial disparity in credit availability is likely caused by discrimination" (Blanchflower, Levine, and Zimmerman 2003: 930). In addition, the black-white differences in start-up capital decreases the likelihood of business ownership among blacks, appears to limit the ability of black business owners to succeed, and contributes to higher failure rates, lower profits, less employment, and overall less survivability of the business (Robb and Fairlie 2007; Browne 1974). The picture that emerges from the institutional discrimination literature portrays a process of stratification involving multiple circles of exclusionary mechanisms faced by minority households in both the labor and the commodity markets:

Racial discrimination in the labor market has kept wage income so low as to preclude any significant savings by black laborers. Racial discrimination in credit markets has excluded blacks from the business sector, where most savings originate. Racial discrimination in the real estate market has kept the income of black landlords low, so savings from this sector also have been negligible. This low income directly inhibits savings. (Browne 1974: 30–31)

The Race-Class Debate

The rejection of cultural explanations—which are seen as an inaccurate, or at least insufficient, description of saving and wealth accumulation processes—combined with civil rights legislation, increasing economic polarization in the 1980s and 1990s, and the weight given to institutional and structural explanations, have led some scholars to question the validity of race as an explanatory variable in stratification analysis. This line of study asserts that class, not race, should be the focal point of the literature on social inequality

The race/class debate receives much attention in the context of the "declining significance of race" thesis, which describes a historical transition from racial barriers to class inequality as the key factor determining the life chances of blacks in contemporary U.S. society. This argument is most clearly and systematically presented by Wilson (1980), who contends that, in contrast to the plantation economy and early postbellum period, and the industrial expansion in the first half of the twentieth century, the third phase of American race relations—the industrial era, which peaked during the 1960s and 1970s—is characterized by gradual transition from race-based inequalities to class-based inequalities. The unprecedented economic growth and rising prosperity after World War II, along with the social and political pressures of the civil rights movement and civil rights legislation, greatly expanded the opportunities for economic advancement among the black middle class in the 1950s and 1960s: "Predominantly white educational institutions were admitting black students in large numbers, businesses were recruiting at black colleges and unions yielded to the pressure of their formerly excluded black workers" (Patillo-McCoy 1999: 99). The growth in the number of educated and professional minorities during the second part of the twentieth century is often seen as another proof of the changing balance between ascriptive characteristics (race, ethnicity) and achieved attributes (education, occupation) as determinants of location in the stratification system. Wilson (1980) argues that because the racial barriers of the past are less important than present-day economic attributes, class has become more detrimental than race in determining the labor market status of black men.

To say that race is declining in significance, therefore, is not only to argue that the life chances of blacks have less to do with race than with economic class affiliation, but also to maintain that racial conflict and competition in the economic sector—the most important historical factors in the subjugation of blacks—have been substantially reduced (Wilson 1980: 152).

Attempts to extend Wilson's thesis to other minority groups were justified on the ground that the post–World War II period—in particular the 1960s and 1970s, when legislation banning employment discrimination was passed—has also benefited nonblack minority workers, including Hispanics and Asians, whose numbers have increased rapidly since the mid-1960s. Studying trends in labor market characteristics of blacks, Native Americans, Chinese Americans, Latinos, whites, and Japanese Americans, the team of Sakamoto, Wu, and Tzeng (2000) found that, with the exception of Hispanic workers, the net disadvantage in the labor market was reduced for other minority group males (see also Cancio, Evans, and Maume Jr. 1996).

The declining-significance-of-race thesis has been contested on grounds that individual and institutional discrimination continues to play an important role in shaping the life chances of blacks and Hispanics. This line of research highlights the persistent effect of race and ethnicity in constraining individual choices and affecting chances of socioeconomic success and mobility. Reports by the American Sociological Association (2005) describe substantial white-minority differentials in labor market characteristics at the turn of the twenty-first century. The ratio of white-black unemployment rates, for example, continues to be 2 to 1, and Hispanics and blacks are also more likely to be unemployed for longer periods of time. Whereas about one-third of white men and nearly one-half of Asian men are employed in managerial, professional, and related occupations, only one-fifth of African American men and one-seventh of Hispanic men are employed in these prestigious occupations. Recent data show that the median annual earnings of Hispanic men as a percentage of white men's earnings have declined from 72.1 percent in 1975 to 61.6 percent in 1998, indicating an increase in white-Hispanic inequality. The comparable white-black figure varied from 69.7 percent in 1985 to 80 percent in 1996 and declined to 74.9 percent in 1998 (National Committee on Pay Equity 2001, figure 14.4: 214). Drawing on myriad studies on racial/ethnic gaps in the labor market based on the 1980 and 1990 censuses, research concludes that "race and ethnicity accounted for more of the earnings gaps between whites and minorities than differences in education and work experience" (American Sociological Association 2005: 7).

Wealth and the Race-Class Nexus

The theoretical models and empirical evidence presented by both proponents and opponents of the declining significance of race thesis remain confined within the boundaries of production-based processes and labor market outcomes, while treating the individual man as the unit of analysis. However, as mentioned above, the independence of the commodity market from labor market processes is a principal feature of the contemporary, modern, capitalist economy. Accordingly, emphasis on labor market outcomes in the race-class debate results in a partial and lopsided image of racial and ethnic stratification processes. Racial and ethnic disparity in annual earnings does not capture the full scale of socioeconomic inequality, because analysis of labor market outcomes overlooks the distinct and unequal opportunity structure in the commodity market, excludes property income, ignores financial transfers from family and kin, and underestimates the functional link between labor and commodity market processes; even a small annual gap in earnings accumulates over the years, leading to a significant gap in wealth. Moreover, whereas the civil rights movement targeted education and labor market equality, and mainly benefited the black middle class, it has had only a marginal impact on asset-building policies. In fact, according to some studies, prior to civil rights legislation, business ownership in the black community, particularly service businesses such as hotels, restaurants, grocery stores, laundries, insurance companies, and small banks was relatively high, and the 1920s have often been labeled as the "golden era" of black-owned enterprise growth (see Sherraden 1991: 138). The economic prosperity of the post–World War II period, combined with the government's assistance provided to veterans to establish business enterprises, further boosted business ownership in the black community (Coles 1973). With civil rights legislation, and as a result of the emphasis on desegregation, many black entrepreneurs faced increasing difficulties in competing with the more strongly established white businesses, and more blacks moved into management and government employment (Sherraden 1991: 138).

The strong emphasis on education and labor market remuneration in the literature on racial/ethnic inequality portray a partial and, under particular and transitory historical circumstances, more positive picture of closing economic gaps than the one seen in commodity market measures and total household wealth. Indeed, data from the Federal Reserve Board's Survey of Consumer Finances (SCF) indicate that the wealth gap is more than three times the income gap between African Americans and whites (Aizcorbe, Kennickell, and Moore 2003 in Nembhard and Chiteji 2006). The ostensible differences between slow but observable gains in education and labor market outcomes of minority men and women, and the persistent racial inequality in the commodity market—in terms of homeownership, stock ownership, and net worth—may be erroneously interpreted as a cultural deficit and a lack of long-term saving plans by minority groups. This conclusion, which is in line with the cultural Darwinism thesis, is often used to justify limited governmental intervention.

Family Formation and Economic Well-Being

Because wealth analysis treats the household as the unit of analysis, and because various racial and ethnic groups have distinctive patterns of family structure and intergenerational support systems, the economic circumstances of families and households are more appropriate for analysis of racial stratification than individual measures of economic success. In the United States, as in other multiethnic societies, kin relations, familial obligations, and family structures vary across racial and ethnic lines, and are likely to foster inequalities in asset holdings and household net worth.[6]

Black-white differences in marital status are persistent and substantial; black adults tend to postpone marriage longer than young adults of other races; and, since the 1970s, there has been an acceleration in the extent of marital disruption (separation or divorce) among blacks (Glick 1997: 126). The breakup of the husband-wife family has been cited as a major factor in differing rates of poverty and wealth between blacks and whites (Farley 1984; Bianchi 1999; Rodgers 1987; Smith and Ward 1980; Conley 1999). Black women are not only more likely than white women to experience divorce, but among divorced women with children, whites are more likely to receive child support and other financial assets as part of a divorce settlement (Cherlin 1992; Glick 1997). Consequently households headed by black women are falling further behind husband-wife black families in both absolute and relative terms.[7] As seen in table 15, in 1999, the marriage rate among blacks was relatively low (41.4 percent) and the proportion of adults who never married was substantially higher (39.2 percent), in comparison to whites and Hispanics.

The Hispanic family is relatively stable, although, between 1980 and 1999, the marriage rate of Hispanics declined and the proportion of those who never married increased. While most studies link immigrants' assimilation to socioeconomic mobility, length of residence in the United States is associated with an increasing likelihood of divorce among minority immigrant families

Table 15.   Marital Status of the Population by Ethnic Origin: 1980 and 1999 (Age 18 and Over)

	Total		White		Black		Hispanic	
	1980	1999	1980	1999	1980	1999	1980	1999
Total								
Never married	20.3	23.9	18.9	21.4	30.5	39.2	24.1	29.0
Married	65.5	59.5	67.2	62.0	51.4	41.4	65.6	59.4
Widowed	8.0	6.7	7.8	6.8	9.8	7.6	4.4	4.0
Divorced	6.2	9.9	6.0	9.8	8.4	11.9	5.8	7.6

Source: U.S. Bureau of Census 2000

(Elmelech and Lu 2004). Indeed, evidence shows that Hispanic families in the United States experience a substantial rise in divorce and separation rates (Bean and Tienda 1987, table 6.1: 183; see Gratton 1987). Hispanic families tend to be larger than white and black families and are typically characterized by high fertility rates. In 2000, the average number of children born to black and white women was fairly consistent; white women had a total fertility rate of 2.1, and black women had a total fertility rate of 2.2. Among Hispanic women, the total fertility rate was 3.1, with the highest rates reported for Mexican women (3.3) and Puerto Rican women (2.6) and the lowest for Cuban women (1.9) (NCHS 2002). Since having a low number of children is associated with more substantial intergenerational transmission of wealth (Atkinson 1975; McNamee and Miller 1998: 205–6; Keister 2000; Smith and Ward 1980), the relatively high fertility rate of Hispanic women is likely to increase future white-Hispanic wealth differentials (Jaffe, Cullen, and Boswell 1980: 40–41; Tidwell 1997).

Transmitting Advantage

Neglect of intergenerational transmission of material advantage is becoming harder to justify in the literature on racial and ethnic wealth inequality (Shapiro 2004; Conley 1999; Oliver and Shapiro 1995; Orr 2002). In comparison to white households, black and Hispanic households have more limited financial resources to pass on to adult children. Weighing various explanations for racial disparities in the magnitude and composition of assets, Blau and Graham (1990) postulate that the differences in intergenerational transfers in the form of bequests and inter vivos gifts are the most likely explanations. Because the grandparents and parents of middle-aged African Americans toiled under segregation, in which education and access to rewarding jobs and decent wages were severely restricted, they were unable to accumulate and transfer much, if any, wealth (Oliver and Shapiro 1995: 6–7).[8] It is estimated that inheritances account for 19.3 percent of the average difference in the black-white wealth gap for married couples and 11.6 percent of the average gap for single households, and that black-white differences in the receipt of financial inheritances help to explain why the average difference in wealth between black and white households is larger than the average difference in income (Menchik and Jianakopolos 1997; see also Avery and Randell 2002). Analysis of the sociodemographic determinants of business ownership among blacks and whites reveals that the racial differences in the probability of having a self-employed father and the lower level of assets among blacks explain a large portion of the gap, leading the author to conclude that the "lack of self-employment among previous generations of blacks is partly responsible for the low entry rate among the current generation of blacks" (Fairlie 1999: 97).[9]

In addition to inheritance, exchanges of goods and services are vital to the economic well-being of black households. More than two-thirds of participants in the National Survey of Black Americans (NSBA) reported receiving some assistance from family members, including financial support, child care, goods and services, and help during sickness. Financial assistance and child care were the most frequent types of support reported by the younger respondents, whereas goods and services were the major types reported by older family members (Taylor 2005a: 407). Using a snowball sampling and conducting in-depth interviews with families with young children, Shapiro (2004: 99) found that the less economically secure middle-class black families reported more extensive provision of financial support to parents, relatives, and friends than their white counterparts, and that the assistance provided involved transfer of money. Because low- and middle-class minority households are more likely than white households with similar economic resources to have family members in need, the flows of financial resources to poor members of the extended family drain the already limited resources of many minority families (Chiteji and Hamilton 2005; Jarrett 1994).

The historical and cross-generational dimension of familial resources is also critical to the economic well-being of non-black minorities and foreign-born immigrants. As of 2000, about one in five children in the United States had at least one foreign-born parent; more than three-fifths of these children were Hispanic (Hernandez 2004). Since the mid-1960s, the vast majority of immigrants in the United States come from developing countries that have a significantly lower level of wealth and income. For example, while in 2004 the GDP per capita in the United States was $40,100, the figures for those countries that send immigrants to the United States—for example China,

Mexico, and India—were substantially smaller ($5,600, $9,600, and $3,100, respectively). These immigrants are less likely to receive large sums of financial assistance from family members living abroad. In fact, one factor that hinders wealth accumulation among immigrant communities is remittance flows to family members and relatives living abroad. Although scarce, evidence indicates that millions of Hispanic and Asian immigrants transfer money to families and relatives abroad. A recent World Bank report titled "Global Development Finance 2003" lists India, Mexico, and the Philippines as the developing countries receiving the most substantial remittances from migrant workers.[10] It is estimated that some six million immigrants from Latin America living in the United States provide financial assistance to families abroad on a regular basis. According to a study released by the Pew Hispanic Center and the Multilateral Investment Fund of the Inter-American Development Bank, the total remittance flow from the United States to Latin America and the Caribbean is estimated at about $30 billion, making it the "most substantial single remittance channel in the world."[11]

Theorizing Racial/Ethnic Inequality in Asset Holdings

Because the structure and socioeconomic functions of the household vary across racial/ethnic lines, the theoretical framework developed in this book—the Family Transactions Model, which incorporates household-level mechanisms, family structure, and the inclusion of intergenerational transfers as factors determining standards of living and economic well-being—is particularly relevant to an understanding of race and ethnic stratification in wealth.

As seen in figure 17, the cumulative effect of racial/ethnic differences in individual characteristics (human capital and labor market attainment), family-based transfers of wealth, and institutionalized practices of exclusion is key to an understanding of why household net worth is unevenly distributed across racial and ethnic lines. Within this framework, marriage patterns and intergenerational transfers are central mechanisms of exclusion.

Table 16 displays data on middle-aged householders and provides statistics on demographic and labor market characteristics, as well as intergenerational transfers and marital history by racial and ethnic origin (see also appendix C). This age group is particularly interesting for wealth analysis. First, a lack of sufficient assets, particularly financial and income-producing assets, is especially critical for black and Hispanic households on the verge of retirement (see chapter 1); since blacks and Hispanics earn far less on average than whites, they more often rely primarily on Social Security as a source of post-retirement income and the amount they receive from this source is insufficient and often

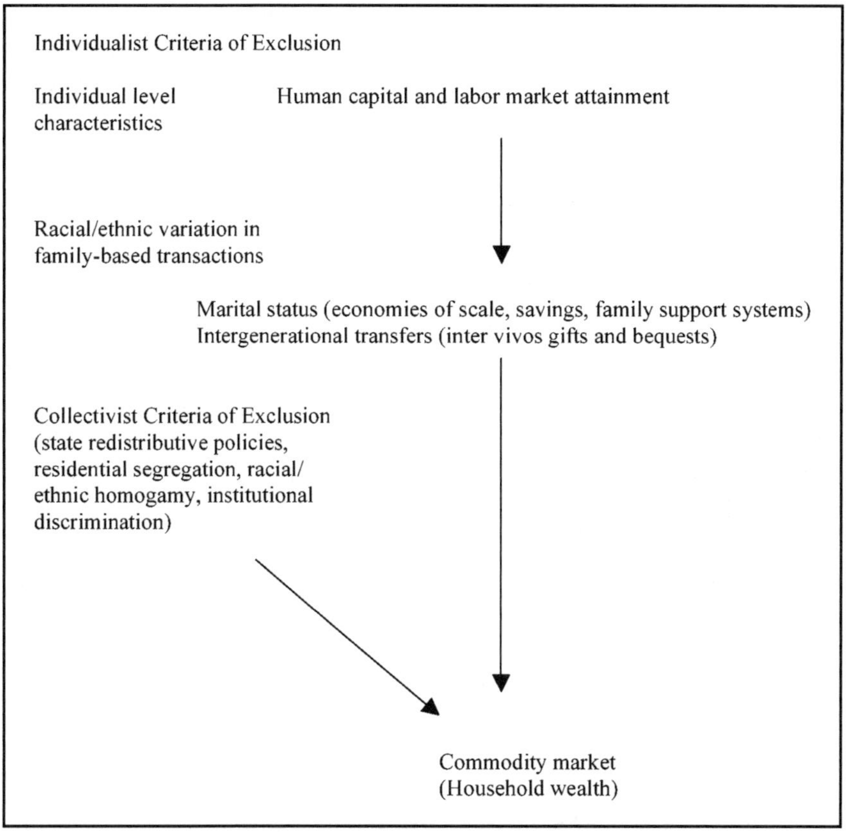

Individualist Criteria of Exclusion

Individual level   Human capital and labor market attainment
characteristics

Racial/ethnic variation in
family-based transactions

Marital status (economies of scale, savings, family support systems)
Intergenerational transfers (inter vivos gifts and bequests)

Collectivist Criteria of Exclusion
(state redistributive policies,
residential segregation, racial/
ethnic homogamy, institutional
discrimination)

Commodity market
(Household wealth)

Figure 17.   Family Transactions Model: Racial and Ethnic Wealth Stratification

leaves them very close to poverty (Angel and Angel 1997: 50). Second, this age group includes members of the pivot generation who entered the labor market in the 1950s and 1960s—a period of increasing white-collar opportunities for more educated minority workers. Finally, the parents of these middle-aged minority households have benefited from the post–World War II period of economic expansion and the rapid increase in homeownership and home equity and have transmitted some of these resources to their offspring (Shapiro 1994 in Miller and McNamee 1998).

The data presented in table 16 reveal extreme white-minority gaps in total household net worth. Whereas about one-tenth of the white households in the sample are asset-poor, that is, placed in the lower quintile of the wealth distribution, the figures for black and Hispanic households reach 40 percent. These figures are particularly alarming because these mid-life adults are on the verge of retirement, a stage in which prospects for economic mobility are slim,

Table 16. Mean Characteristics (Standard Deviation) of Households by Racial/Ethnic Origin (Weighted)

	Whites	Blacks	Hispanics
Net worth (in thousand $)	277.8	83.5	105.3
	(560.0)	(243.5)	(403.3)
Median Net worth (in thousand $)	127.0	28.5	31.5
Labor income (in thousand $)	41.8	24.9	21.3
	(47.7)	(27.8)	(28.9)
Asset poverty (lowest quintile)	12.3	40.3	38.0
Family transfers:			
Received inheritance (%)	24.5	4.7	5.0
Received gifts (%)	9.4	2.2	2.0
Life insurance (%)	5.7	4.3	3.1
Total transfers (%)	35.6	10.7	10.0
Marital status:			
Currently Married:	69.9	41.5	59.0
Intact marriage	48.9	28.7	44.8
Married before	21.0	12.8	14.2
Divorced	14.6	19.0	15.0
Widowed	7.1	14.9	8.8
Other (Cohabit/Never married/Separated)	7.9	24.0	17.2
Children	2.9	3.5	3.7
	(1.9)	(2.5)	(2.7)
Education and Labor Market Characteristics:			
Education (years)	12.9	11.4	8.9
	(2.7)	(3.2)	(4.5)
Parental education (years)	10.7	8.8	6.2
	(3.3)	(3.4)	(4.5)
Parental education missing (%)	4.9	11.7	9.1
Occupation:			
Managerial/professional	33.6	15.8	12.1
Currently employed	69.4	58.7	52.9
Native-born	95.5	95.3	47.0
Gender (Male)	55.0	40.7	51.2
N=7605	5297	1424	714

Source: HRS-92

and expectations and demands for financial support to elderly parents and younger children are expected to grow. Note, however, that while black and Hispanic households have similar levels of net worth, their sociodemographic characteristics differ. The educational level of minority respondents and their parents is substantially lower than whites' educational attainment, but the white-Hispanic gap exceeds the white-black differentials: while the average years of education among whites is 12.9 years, the figures for black and Hispanic householders are 11.4 and 8.9, respectively. Two particularly pertinent observations can be made regarding the data on marriage and family transfers. First, while about 70 percent of whites and 60 percent of Hispanics are married, less than half of black respondents in this sample are married. Hispanics are more likely than whites and blacks to live in larger households and to be in sustained stable marriages; about three-fourths of married middle-aged Hispanics live in intact families. Second, intergenerational transfers of wealth are distributed unequally across racial and ethnic lines. About one-quarter of the white households have received inheritances, but only 5 percent of the minority households in the sample report the receipt of an inheritance. Another 9.4 percent of white households and 2 percent of minority households have received financial assistance in the form of gifts from relatives. The racial gaps in life insurance benefits are relatively small.

Decomposing the Racial/Ethnic Gap in Asset Holdings

In order to assess the extent to which racial differences in socioeconomic and demographic composition explain differences in race-ethnic ownership among the pivot generation, I utilized a standardization technique that decomposes the racial-ethnic gaps in asset poverty and ownership of various assets (see Casper, McLanahan and Garfinkel 1994).[12] The results presented in table 17 are based on a series of logistic regression equations that were analyzed for each group separately (black, Hispanic, white). Column A describes results for the white-minority gap in asset poverty. The results suggest that racial differences in marital status strongly contribute to the black-white gap in asset poverty. Private transfers, in the form of bequests, inter vivos gifts, and life insurance benefits, also play an important role in shaping the white-minority gap in asset poverty and are particularly detrimental to the economic well-being of black households. Lastly, the relatively high number of foreign-born Hispanics seems to be critical to the understanding of lower rates of ownership of housing and financial assets.[13] This finding reiterates previous studies that emphasize the more limited knowledge and access to credit and housing faced by Hispanic immigrants (Krivo 1995). Columns B through D display results from analysis of the racial-ethnic gap in ownership of three fundamental categories: financial assets (stocks, bonds, business, and real estate); homeownership (primary residence); and liquid assets. White-black differentials in marital status, and the relatively low rates of intact marriage among blacks, are detrimental to the homeownership rates of minority, particularly black, households.[14] Intergenerational transfers of material resources have a much smaller contribution to racial gaps in ownership of housing and liquid assets, but seem particularly detrimental to the economic well-being of black

Table 17. Summary of Results from Decomposition Analysis: Comparison to white households assuming the same sample characteristics (Xs) as whites: Percent reduction in racial/ethnic gaps in asset ownership

	Asset Poverty	Financial	Housing	Liquid
Blacks:				
Family transfers	.18	−.11	−.05	−.09
Marital status	.25	−.08	−.20	−.10
Family transfers & marital status	.40	−.20	−.24	−.19
Education	.17	−.14	−.07	−.08
Occupation	.10	−.20	−.06	−.06
Children	.00	−.03	−.00	−.01
Nativity	.00	.00	.00	.00
Hispanics:				
Family transfers	.21	−.13	−.10	−.09
Marital status	.11	−.03	−.06	−.05
Family transfers & marital status	.31	−.16	−.16	−.14
Education	.03	−.02	−.05	−.16
Occupation	.11	−.25	−.03	−.09
Children	−.01	.01	−.01	−.02
Nativity	.28	−.22	−.19	−.03

Source: HRS 92

households.[15] Human capital and labor market differentials play a key role in shaping the racial-ethnic gap in ownership of financial assets. Educational differentials between Hispanics and whites have a relatively strong negative impact on Hispanic ownership of liquid assets, while ethnic differentials in occupational attainment have a strong effect on the ethnic gaps in financial assets.[16] Lastly, immigration explains a large portion of the white-Hispanic gap in ownership of tangible assets; the high proportion of foreign-born Hispanics is detrimental to the low level of asset holdings—particularly homes and financial assets—among this ethnic group.

As indicated by the Family Transactions Model (figure 17), racial-ethnic differences in family structure and intergenerational transfers are likely to have a strong mediating effect between racial-ethnic variation in labor market characteristics and household net worth. Findings from multivariate (Tobit) analysis of the logged net worth (appendix C) reveals that, in comparison to the black-white wealth gap, a more substantial portion of the gap between whites and Hispanics is explained by differentials in human capital and labor market attributes (baseline model).[17] As expected, educational attainment is positively associated with net worth. In accordance with the expectations, racial differentials in marital status explain a substantial portion of the white-minority gap in wealth. Moreover, net of human capital and labor market attributes (for example, labor income, employment status, education, parental education, and occupation), as well as demographic differentials, marital status (particularly intact marriage), and receipt of financial transfers in the form of inter vivos gifts and bequests have strong positive effects on total household net worth.[18] Racial-ethnic differences in these attributes substantially enhance minority-white wealth differentials. The analysis also shows that compared with the foreign born, native-born householders have a significant advantage in terms of accumulated resources.

The findings from the analysis presented above elucidate the important role that white-minority differences in education, labor market variables, marriage patterns, and intergenerational transfers play in shaping the minority-white differentials in wealth and asset holdings among the pivot generation. However, the pooled-sample analysis assumes the same subgroup returns on demographic and socioeconomic attributes among whites and minority groups. Indeed, it is likely that the effects of economic and demographic factors would vary substantially across racial and ethnic lines. Differential returns on education and employment are said to be due to differences in quality of human capital (areas such as school quality and language proficiency) (Bratsberg and Dek 2002; Chiswick 1978), as well as differences in opportunity structure and discrimination, both individual and institutional (see Borjas and Tienda 1993; Butcher 1994; Phillips and Massey 1999).[19] Although some minority group members have relatively high levels of education and labor force participation, differential returns on education may accentuate white-minority gaps in economic status (Barringer, Takeuchi, and Xenos 1990). Finally, returns on marital status are likely to vary by racial and ethnic origin (Butcher 1994), as the economic advantages associated with two-parent families relative to single-parent families vary across racial and ethnic lines (Elmelech 2005). With few exceptions, models that analyze inequality between groups tend to ignore intragroup inequality within racial and ethnic groups. The next chapter focuses on the social and demographic determinants of intragroup wealth inequality and explores the potential effect of the persistent homogamy in the marriage market on the distribution of wealth across racial and ethnic lines.

CHAPTER SEVEN

∼

Intragroup Inequality and Social Closure

The situation *was* this:

All white
_____
All colored

It is *now* this:

White	*Colored*
Professional occupation	Professional occupation
Business occupation	Business occupation
Labor	Labor

—Robert E. Park, *The Bases of Race Prejudice*

Intragroup Polarization: Double Disadvantage?

Research on internal economic divisions among minority groups has mainly focused on blacks. The emergence of the black middle class and the growing number of educated and professional minority men and women is often seen as another proof of the declining significance of ascriptive characteristics (race, ethnicity) and the increasing importance of achieved attributes (education, occupation) as determinants of location in the contemporary stratification system. The existence of class divisions within the black community is not a new phenomenon; intragroup distinctions among the black population were documented during slavery and were based on differential positions between skilled servants and the majority of adult slaves who were field hands. These divisions overlapped with skin color; dark-skinned slaves were treated more harshly by overseers than the "mulatto elite," who, by virtue of their light skin and blood connection to whites, benefited from training in skilled occupations and more choice in work tasks (Frazier 1930, 1939; Keith and Herring 1991; Rockquemore 2002; Patillo-McCoy 1999: 98; Cole and Omari 2003). After the Civil War, light-skinned blacks attempted to sustain their privileged status by maintaining a proximity to whites, attending elite educational institutions, concentrating in economic activities such as entrepreneurship and banking, "and belonging to certain exclusive social clubs and organizations" (see Cole and Omari 2003: 787). The migration of blacks from the South to northern cities at the turn of the twentieth century led to changes in this population's occupational structure and resulted in the rise of the "new black middle class" whose members were professionals and entrepreneurs; Landry (1987: 39) asserts that in contrast to the old elite, entrance into the new middle class was based on economic achievement rather than on family background, skin color, or white approval. The most drastic growth in the size of the black middle class, which was accompanied by rising intragroup economic divisions, became visible in the second half of the twentieth century.

The civil rights movement has opened up opportunities in education and the labor market. While a growing number of minority group members have taken advantage of these new opportunities and experienced upward economic mobility, many others stayed trapped within inner-city ghettos, where education and employment opportunities are limited (Patillo-McCoy 1999). Since the mid-1970s, deindustrialization and economic restructuring, as well as the increase in temporary and part-time jobs, has had a particularly detrimental effect on the economic circumstances of black men, who were traditionally overrepresented in manufacturing and in the central cities (Kasarda 1995; Wilson 1987). These structural changes in the economy effectively intensified the internal economic polarization between the haves and have-nots in the black community (see Nembhard, Pitts, and Mason 2005). Consequently, the recently observed internal class divisions within communities of color are, at least partially, a function of the economic progress made by some minority group members and the deteriorating economic and social circumstances experienced by the economically vulnerable segments of the population.

While acknowledging the visible changes in the economic circumstances and the increasing economic polarization, both between and within racial lines, students of social inequality have debated both the form and the magnitude of the economic hardship endured by poor minority families. The conjunction between class and race/ethnicity can occur in two different forms. The *unidimensional economic* form suggests that the economic hardship that minority families experience as members of a minority group does not differ significantly from the disadvantages suffered by lower-class white families. The more complex type of inequality takes a *multidimensional* or *interactive* form whereby the disadvantages associated with economic hardship are augmented by being a minority group member. This perspective suggests that the relationships between class and race can be understood only from a position of intersectionality, that is, the notion that racial minorities struggle both for upward economic mobility and freedom from the structural racial and ethnic restrictions imposed by the wider society (Ogbu 1987; Cole and Omari 2003).[1] In the context of wealth, two findings on intragroup disparities within communities of color merit attention. First, the intersection of race/ethnicity and class is pertinent not only to the economic conditions of poor minorities, but also to the living standards of the better-off segments of the minority population; by contrast to other measures of inequality, racial/ethnic gaps in wealth illuminate the distinct historical and intergenerational economic circumstances of minority households, relative to whites, even among the middle-class ranges. Oliver and Shapiro (1995: 7) report that middle-class blacks earn 70 cents for every dollar earned by middle-class whites, but they possess only 15 cents for every dollar of wealth held by middle-class whites. The authors conclude:

> For the most part, the economic foundation of the black middle class lacks one of the pillars that provide stability and security to middle-class whites—assets. The black middle class position is precarious and fragile with insubstantial wealth resources. This analysis means it is entirely premature to celebrate the rise of the black middle class.

Second, while minority households have lower net worth than white counterparts in the same income bracket, wealth is more unequally distributed among black and Hispanic households than among whites, and this pattern is likely to be perpetuated across generations. Using data from the Survey of Consumer Finance (SCF) at three points in time—1962, 1983, and 1989—and comparing the mean and median value of wealth of whites and nonwhites, Wolff (1994) concludes that the distribution of wealth is more unequal among nonwhites than whites and that the gaps have increased over time. National figures indicate that the median net worth held by white households at the highest income quintile is 16.2 times greater than the median net worth of the wealth held by households at the lowest income quintile, and is 3.3 times greater than the amount held by the middle (third) quintile. The comparable figures are 180.0 and 5.3 among blacks, and 112.0

and 8.8 among Hispanics (U.S. Department of Commerce 1995a). While these findings corroborate the copious empirical evidence on the increasing polarization in education and labor market remuneration among minority populations, we know very little about the demographic and socioeconomic determinants of intragroup wealth inequality.

Do Family Transfers Widen Intragroup Socioeconomic Inequality?

Multivariate (Tobit) regression predicting the distinct effect that labor market attainment, marital status, and intergenerational transfers have on household net worth among each of the three groups under study—black, white, and Hispanic—reveals that intergenerational transmission of financial resources enhances intragroup wealth inequality within all three groups (appendix D).[2] However, in the two minority populations, within which wealth is more highly concentrated, private transfers of wealth have a particularly strong and significant effect on household net worth, thus contributing to intergenerational reproduction of intragroup inequality.[3] In addition, being married is strongly associated with the level of a household's net worth, and marriage (relative to widowhood) is a particularly strong predictor of wealth for black and Hispanic households. Divorce is associated with a significant financial disadvantage among Hispanics, whereas the category "Other" (which includes those never married and separated) has a strong negative effect on intragroup inequality among the two minority populations.[4] One possible explanation for these effects of marital status is that among relatively poor ethnic minorities, in which family and kin relations are highly valued and family support systems play an important role in determining economic well-being (Aleman 1997; McAdoo 1997; Mutran 1985; Shapiro 2006), the status of not being married carries a higher financial cost and disconnection from social and economic resources.

The analysis also reiterates the vulnerable status of foreign-born Hispanics in the American commodity market; net of labor market and demographic characteristics, foreign-born Hispanics are more likely to be excluded from one of the main sources of social and economic security in the United States: command over material resources.[5] Thus, immigration status substantially contributes to intragroup wealth polarization among Hispanics on the verge of retirement. Finally, in accordance with the literature on the increasing effect that labor market characteristics have on intragroup economic polarization, the analysis shows that labor income and employment status exert strong effects on net worth, particularly among the black sample.

Sharing the Wealth?
Social Closure in the Marriage Market

As mentioned above, racial and ethnic endogamy in marriage is crucial to an understanding of the white-minority wealth gap. Public opinion polls show a steady decline in the number of Americans who object to interracial marriages: those who favor laws against interracial marriage dropped from almost 40 percent in 1972 to about 10 percent thirty years later (figure 18). While interracial marriages have become more prevalent in recent decades, racial endogamy remains strong, especially among blacks (Qian 1997; Waters and Eschbach 1995) and interracial couples have a greater probability of family disruption than do same-race couples (Glick 1997). Moreover, recent evidence on social networks in the United States observed a shift from larger structures that attach individuals to communities and neighborhoods to smaller, tighter, kin-based ties, that make the interpersonal environment more homogenous with regard to race (McPherson, Smith-Lovin, and Brashears 2006: 371), a transition that decreases interracial and interethnic contacts.

Social scientists view interracial and interethnic marriages as a measure of assimilation and often study the extent to which intermarriage patterns blur racial-ethnic distinctions and shape the racial-ethnic identity of children of

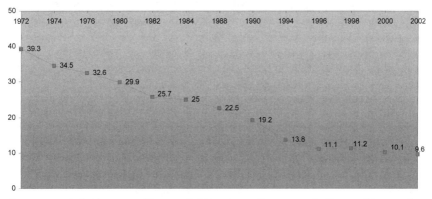

Figure 18. Attitudes toward Interracial Marriages: Percentage in Favor of Law against Racial Intermarriage, 1972–2002
Source: General Social Survey (GSS), 1972–2002

mixed-race couples. The socioeconomic consequences of racial and ethnic intermarriage and homogamy should not be underestimated. Interracial and interethnic marriages, particularly between whites and nonwhites, are likely to have a significant impact on the distribution of wealth; one can expect that high rates of intermarriage will be associated with smaller wealth gaps across racial-ethnic lines, even if the overall wealth inequality remains high. Explanations for intermarriage focus on demographic characteristics and cultural distinctiveness. Because mate selection depends on opportunities for social contacts between potential mates, in-group marriage depends, in part, on the size of the racial-ethnic group and the prevalence of homogamous marriages tends to increase with the size of the racial group; the probability of dating and marrying someone with a similar racial-ethnic background is positively correlated with the proportion of the group in the community (Qian 1997). In addition, propinquity and the level of spatial segregation have a direct effect on interracial marriage patterns. The more segregated the group is, the lower the likelihood that its members will interact, date, and marry members of a different racial-ethnic group. These spatial structures are often used to explain why interracial marriage of whites occurs most frequently with Asian Americans, followed by Hispanics, and then by African Americans (Qian 1997). African American patterns of out-marriage are also distinct in the sense that African American women are less likely to marry white men than African American men are to marry white women.[6] This propensity to out-marry is especially strong among black men with high levels of education (Kalmijn 1993; Qian 1997) and is often explained within the social exchange theory (Merton 1941), according to which black men offset a lower racial status by obtaining human capital and high economic position that increase their marriageability and enable them to "marry up" to white women (see Jacobs and Labov 2002).

Research on mate selection processes also shows that the association between education and out-marriage is prevalent; higher education is typically associated with more liberal views and more opportunities to meet people of a different racial and ethnic background. This pattern enhances the replication of class-based disparities. Because the more educated individuals of a minority group are more likely to out-marry, "leave" the group, and experience upward mobility, class divisions between three marital status categories are likely to emerge: those who out-marry, those who in-marry, and those who remain single. The fact that among blacks, out-marriage rates are higher for the more educated men and lower for women may add to the feminization of poverty and the growing economic gaps between married and nonmarried minority households (Elmelech and Lu 2004).

In multiethnic societies, marriage patterns are also shaped by immigration and assimilation. Foreign nativity is associated with higher propensity to in-marry; immigrants tend to marry immigrants, and second-generation ethnics tend to marry others in the second generation (see Edmonston and Passel 1999; Pagnini and Philip 1990). This tendency is attributed in part to age structure and social assimilation of immigrant communities. Indeed, immi-grant groups with younger members show higher levels of intermarriage, which presumably reflect a lower likelihood of being married at the time of arrival, as well as social and economic assimilation that increases with dura-tion of residence in the host society (Edmonston and Passel 1999).

Due to the relative scarcity of black-white unions, these relationships have received more attention by American scholars. Qualitative data pro-vide an interesting glance into the rarity of black-white interracial marriages. Based on interviews with a sample of participants in the "A Better Chance" (ABC) scholarship program, which since the mid-1960s has sent more than ten thousand adolescents from low-income families (most of them black) to exclusive private high schools in the United States, Zweigenhaft and Domhoff (2003) conclude that, in the long run, interracial relationships are difficult to maintain.[7] Whereas interracial friendships were relatively com-mon and long lasting, interracial marriages were rare, leading the authors to conclude that class similarities cannot counteract racial differences, even at the top levels of the American social ladder, and that race continues to play a critical role in family formation and socioeconomic mobility. National sta-tistics on marriage patterns show that, despite an increasing number of in-terracial marriages, racial endogamy remains strong, especially between blacks and whites.

Table 18 displays data on same- and mixed-race marriage in 1980 and 1998. I use the ratio of in-marriage (marriage within the racial-ethnic group) to out-marriage (interracial and interethnic marriages) to summarize the main find-ings. These ratios reveal that, in 1980, for every white individual who was married to a black individual, there were about 270 in-married whites couples. In 1998, this ratio declined to 145. For blacks, the ratio was 20 in 1980 and 12 in 1998. The ratio of interethnic marriages among Hispanics was signifi-cantly lower: 2.1 in 1980 and 2.6 in 1998.

These figures raise two issues on current and future trends in interracial marriages and their impact on social and economic assimilation. The first is related to the relative size of the racial groups engaged in interracial or in-terethnic unions between majority and minority group members. Assuming that there are only two racial-ethnic groups and one is ten times greater than the other, the intermarriage rates of individuals belonging to the smaller

Table 18. Married Couples of Same or Mixed Races and Origins: 1980 and 1998 (in thousands)

	1980	1998
White/white	44,910	48,050
Black/black	3,354	3,839
Interracial marriages:		
Black/white	167	330
Black husband/white wife	122	210
White husband/black wife	45	120
White/other race (excluding white and black)	450	975
Black/other race (excluding white and black)	34	43
Interracial married couples total	651	1348
All other couples (excluding white and black)	799	2,068
Hispanic Origin:		
Hispanic/Hispanic	1,906	4,279
Hispanic/other origin (not Hispanic)	891	1,662
All other couples (not of Hispanic origin)	46,917	49,363
Ratio of white/white to black/white	268.9	145.6
Ratio of black/black to black/white	20.0	11.6
Ratio of Hispanic/Hispanic to Hispanic/not Hispanic	2.1	2.6

Persons 15 year old and over. Persons of Hispanic origin may be of any race.
Source: Author calculations based on Statistical Abstract of the US, 2000: Table 54. Page 51.

group would be ten times larger than the intermarriage rates among members of the larger group. For example, if one group has one hundred members and the second has only ten, and two members of the first group marry two members of the second group, the proportion of individual members of the first group that out-marry would be 2 percent (2/100*100=2), while the comparable figure among the smaller group would be 20 percent (2/10*100=20). Since in the United States there are more whites than minority group members, the out-marriage rates of a minority group with whites exceeds the out-marriage rate of whites with that minority group.

The second issue stems from the unit of analysis and the effect of intermarriage patterns on couples and families. This point is particularly relevant to wealth analysis where the household—not the individual—is the unit of analysis. Because those who in-marry find a spouse from within their racial-ethnic group and those who out-marry find a spouse from outside the group, the proportion of *couples* who out-marry is always larger than the rate at which *individuals* out-marry (Perlmann and Waters 2004). For example, if 8 out-marry among every 100 minority group members, while 92 in-marry, the number of interracial couples would be 8, while the number of couples formed from in-marriage would be 46 (92/2). Accordingly, while the in-marriage rate for *individuals* is 92 percent and the out-marriage rate for individuals is 8 percent, the proportion of mixed-origin *couples* amounts to 14.8 percent (8/8+46*100), and the proportion of couples who in-marry is 85.2 percent.

These numerical differences have important implications for the distribution of wealth across racial and ethnic lines. First, since the sharing and passing on of financial resources involves a wide network of kin and relatives, the distribution of wealth within interracial families is likely to cut across racial and ethnic lines; because a growing number of minority-status people have family members of more than one racial and ethnic origin, the racial-ethnic disparities in wealth are likely to diverge from those gaps seen in individual-level measures of inequality, such as education and employment. Second, as Perlmann and Waters (2004) note, since the ethnic origin of the next generation is a function of the rate at which couples form, not the rate at which individuals out-marry, assuming that fertility rates of same-race and mixed-race couples are similar, the number of mixed-race-ethnic children is likely to increase in the future. Note, however, that a large proportion of black adults never marry. This phenomenon, which is often attributed to lack of marriageable minority men because of high rates of incarceration and unemployment, is also used to explain the high number of black children who are born to nonmarried women. The number of black children who live in two-parent families has increased recently—from 33.3 percent in 1994 to 38.4 percent in 2002 (based on U.S. Census Bureau 2003), but the majority of black children today are born to unmarried mothers. Whereas data on the fathers' race are often unavailable for children born to unmarried couples, the prevalence of mixed-race couples is higher among cohabiting than among married couples. This reality implies that the figures presented in table 19 may underestimate the actual number of mixed race children in the United States.

Preliminary data on the extent to which increasing rates of intermarriage are likely to affect the distribution of household wealth in a multiethnic society is presented in table 19. The data come from the HRS 2002, which encompasses middle-aged and elderly households (HRS and AHEAD). The table reports the amount of household net worth held by same-race and mixed-race couples who are either married or cohabit. The data show clear hierarchy based on race-ethnic origin and union-formation patterns; same-race white couples have the highest level of net worth, followed by white-Hispanic couples and white-black couples, respectively. At the bottom are same race-ethnicity minority couples.

Table 19.   Mean Net Worth by Union (Marriage and Cohabitation) Status

	N	Net Worth/1,000
White-white	9,116	518
White-Hispanic	232	408
White-black	55	237
Black-Hispanic	24	210
Black-black	1,147	152
Hispanic-Hispanic	803	107

Source: HRS/AHEAD 2002
Data are weighted by Household weight.

Conclusions: Polarization and the Transmission of Inequality

During the past two decades, innovative research on racial inequality developed along two lines. The first focuses on wealth and its intergenerational transmission as a key factor determining disparities in life chances and standards of living across racial lines (Oliver and Shapiro 1995; Conley 1999). The second focuses on the race-class nexus and the debate over the declining significance of race. In chapters 7 and 8, an attempt was made to link these two lines of research. Applying the Family Transactions Model (FTM) to a study of racial and ethnic wealth inequality, the empirical analysis reveals that intergenerational transfers and marital status are detrimental in explaining white-minority disparities in asset holdings and accumulated wealth. One of the main conclusions from the findings on racial-ethnic inequality in the commodity market is that white-minority wealth differentials in the past are replicated across generations and contribute to persistent racial-ethnic economic divisions. Consequently, policies that aim to reduce racial-ethnic disparities in asset holding, by enhancing human capital and occupational mobility of less-privileged groups, will have only limited success. These policies need to take into account the different social and historical mechanisms responsible for the racial-ethnic inequality in private property, and to adopt specific strategies based on these considerations. For example, while both Hispanics and blacks have low levels of wealth and receive limited financial resources via intergenerational transfers of wealth, the large number of foreign-born Hispanics affects the relatively low level of wealth held by members of this group.

The net effect of immigration on wealth accumulation may be attributed to factors such as institutional discrimination and lack of language proficiency and information that hinder access to housing and other desirable assets. The hardships that immigrant minorities endure in the labor market tend to alleviate with time. However, the double disadvantage many immigrants face in both labor market remuneration and access to private property; the remittances many immigrants send to family members abroad; and the limited intergenerational transfers they receive from relatives living abroad reduce the ability of immigrant minorities to convert their human capital and labor market remuneration into a better position in the commodity market.

Although marriage is associated with economic well-being and high living standards, marriage may not be a feasible remedy to the racial-ethnic gap in asset holdings and wealth. Policies that advocate marriage as a way out of economic hardship for minority women should consider the growing class divisions within minority populations, the limited potential pool of minority men who can provide financial support to women and children, and the persistence of racial and class homogamy in mate-selection processes. Whereas the number of mixed marriage unions is small and data on wealth and interracial marriage are limited, any attempt to reduce the extreme white-minority gaps in wealth should investigate the association between social closure in family formation processes and the reproduction of wealth inequality along racial-ethnic lines.

The visible internal wealth disparities within the Hispanic and black populations are replicated across generations, further dividing the population between receivers and nonreceivers of family wealth. Because both blacks and Hispanics have, on average, lower levels of wealth than whites, even a small number of financial transfers results in substantial intragroup differentials in net worth. Thus, despite the racial differences in intergenerational transfers, inherited wealth accounts for a sizable share of the net worth held not only by white, but also black and Hispanic households (see also Wilhelm 2001). The fact that intergenerational transfers are playing an important role in shaping economic outcomes among minority groups suggests that the emergence of the black and Hispanic middle class is not a new phenomenon, but rather an acceleration of disparities that are passed on from previous generations.

CHAPTER EIGHT

~

Conclusions: Looking Ahead

The case for restoring the notion of property into the center of class analysis is that it is the most important single form of social closure common to industrial societies.

—Frank Parkin, *Marxism and Class Theory: A Bourgeois Critique*

Toward a Fresh Analysis of Social Inequality

Why do some people own valuable assets and are financially better off than others? What are the determinants of economic security and comfortable living standards? Common answers to these questions often include such attributes as formal education, personal character, work ethic, and relative risk aversion. The objective of this book is not to refute or undermine the significance of these individual-level explanations but, rather, to balance and expand the literature on social stratification by analyzing the relationships between three distinct levels of analysis that shape the distribution of private property and wealth: micro-level processes; macro-level processes that include the role of the state and the market, as well as cultural norms that underlie the accumulation and distribution of private property; and mezzo-level processes (family transfers and kin networks) that function as a link between individual attributes and commodity market inequality (figure 19).

The following assumptions have been made about the scope of social stratification and the mechanisms that shape it. First, as a measure of socioeconomic inequality, *stock* of material resources (private property, net worth) has

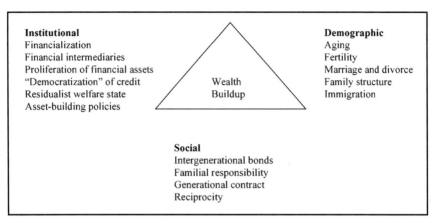

Figure 19.　Institutional, Demographic, and Social Determinants of Wealth Accumulation

precedence over *flow* of material resources (income, earnings). As such, wealth inequality is critical not only to an understanding of economic disparity, but also to the distribution and replication of power and status. Second, although *labor market* attainment represents an important gauge of social and economic achievement, it is, and should be primarily understood as, a means by which people improve standards of living, achieve economic security, and gain control over material resources. Third, *family-based transactions* of material resources are important mechanisms that determine position in the stratification system. The data presented in this book elucidate various institutional, demographic, and sociological variables that intertwine in the production and perpetuation of inequality and bring property and family into the forefront of the stratification system. I argue that in contemporary U.S. society, a combination of institutional conditions that protect property rights and enhance wealth buildup, changing demographic structure that increases social and financial interdependence between generations, and the prevalence of social and cultural norms that emphasize familial obligations, have not only enhanced the significance of property and wealth as determinants of inequality but also redefined the role the family plays in the stratification system.

While it is difficult to assess the form that these trends will take in the twenty-first century, and the impact they will have on future generations, the sound institutional foundations and the long-term effects of demographic transitions are likely to remain critical in shaping the life chances of individuals and families in the twenty-first century. In the following pages, I provide a general overview of the Family Transactions Model (FTM), which builds on findings from the previous chapters and draws on recent institutional, demographic, and social processes that are likely to continue to shape the property-family nexus in the future.

Past Trends and Future Outcomes

During the past three decades, the U.S. labor market has become increasingly volatile, due to economic restructuring, stagnation in wages and earnings, an increase in part-time, temporary jobs in the service sector, and a weakening of organized labor. With these changes, the United States's social welfare safety net for families in poverty has continued to wane, while the nonpoor benefit from durable policies that promote wealth buildup and provide favorable conditions for its intergenerational transmission. Consequently, a family's stock of asset holdings has become an increasingly important determinant of economic status, not only to the small propertied elite, but also to a growing number of middle-class families who now have access to housing, cars, corporate stocks, businesses, and pension wealth. These trends increased the autonomy of both the labor and the commodity markets and have changed the role family resources play in determining the life chances of individuals and families.

To characterize the family as an internal part of the stratification system is not to ignore the role of human capital and labor-market attainment, but to acknowledge the inter-relationship between them. As seen in the elaborated family transactions model (figure 20), the process of wealth stratification starts with individual position in the production processes. Human capital and labor-market attainments are determined by various socioeconomic and demographic factors that are exogenous to this model and include family resources, as well as age, gender, race, and ethnicity. Labor-market remuneration is based almost exclusively on economic principles of transactions between employers and employees, and these monetary rewards are used to purchase assets and accumulate wealth. In this context, there is a direct link between individual labor-market attainment and his/her household position in the commodity market. Moreover, those workers who occupy the more prestigious and rewarding positions in the labor market can not only save more out of their higher earnings, but also benefit from generous pension and retirement plans, with automatic enrollment and restricted withdrawals. These plans, which have become more popular in the past three decades, make saving and wealth accumulation easier, as they allow the individual to "save without exerting willpower" (Sherraden et al. 2005: 78). Those segments of the population that are unemployed or work in more volatile jobs and earn low wages have limited or no access to these means of wealth buildup.

During the past thirty years, however, many intervening variables emerged to disrupt the direct link between individual labor market remuneration and commodity market resources. Belief in the inviolability of property rights; democratization of credit; generous asset-based policies; tax breaks to homeowners; increase in two-earner families; emergence of financial intermediaries that expand asset holdings and diversify the wealth portfolio of middle-class households; and property income that is generated from financial assets—have broken the functions of a "pure" market relationship and the direct labor-property linkage. Moreover, while assets are not fungible, and there are substantial differences between asset categories in terms of revenues, liquidity, taxation, and ownership rights, the institutionalization of the commodity market has increased the connection between ownership of financial and functional assets. In the contemporary multi-asset market in which assets are frequently used as a collateral against loans, investment in one type of assets enhances access to other forms of saving and investment and contributes to the detachment between labor and commodity market resources. The asset-poor are largely excluded from these benefits. Contributing to this distinct opportunity structure in the commodity market is the persistently unequal access to assets due to such practices as steering and redlining in mortgage lending, and the exclusion from formal credit markets of many minority and immigrant households that tend to rely on family members, social networks, and rotating savings and credit associations (ROSCAS) to borrow the financial resources necessary for establishing businesses or purchasing homes.

In addition to the institutional conditions that shape the autonomy of the two markets, enhance wealth buildup, and determine its uneven distribution, the significance of demographic changes to the distribution of property and wealth should not be underestimated. As seen in figure 20, inequalities generated by property ownership are accentuated not only by the accumulation of modest wealth on the part of those in the well-rewarded occupations, or by the operations of the state and the market, but also through intra- and intergenerational transfers of wealth via marriage and inheritance. A major portion of the distributional mechanisms of private property and wealth takes place outside of the market. By connecting individuals and households, production and accumulation processes, individualist and collectivist practices of exclusion, and earnings and wealth, the family functions as a mediating pathway between the labor and the commodity markets. By forming a conversational-type link between individual attainment and accumulated resources, marriage patterns and intergenerational transfers establish a link between economic-based transactions in the labor and the commodity markets, and play an important role in the creation of opportunities for economic mobility and wealth accumulation.

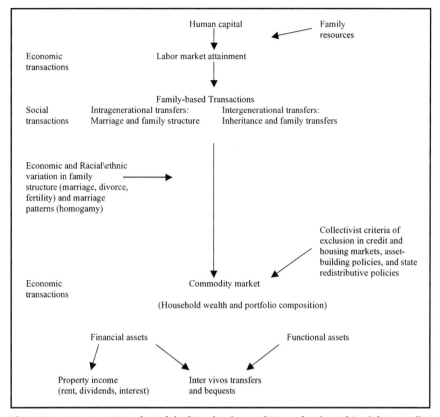

Figure 20. An Asset-Based Model of Production and Reproduction of Social Inequality

Consequently, substantial economic transactions of wealth take place in the private sphere and contribute to disparities in economic resources.

One of the key demographic changes likely to continue to affect the unequal distribution of wealth is aging. The aging of American society has altered intergenerational transfers in several areas: it has lengthened the duration of marriage and the number of years that the young know their grandparents and otherwise share lives with older generations; strengthened economic interdependence between generations; increased the role middle-aged households play in providing financial assistance to young adult children and elderly parents; and enhanced multigenerational kin support systems that can provide financial assistance in the form of inter vivos gifts and bequests (Bengston 1996; Bengston 2001; Bengston and Lowenstein 2003; Uhlenberg 1980, 1996 in Skolnick 2005: 32).[1] Family transfers across three and more generations are more common today than ever before and, although *parental* wealth is the most substantial source of transmitted economic advantage, parents-in-law, grand-parents, aunts, uncles, and other relatives also contribute to the economic well-being and life chances of younger generations.[2] While increased life expectancy is associated with longer years of productive life and financial independence, high eldercare costs and the growing financial needs of younger generations augment the financial burden faced by the pivot generation, the main provider of financial assistance to both ailing parents and young adults.

In addition to aging, the changing patterns of marriage, divorce, and fertility—as well as the persistent class and race-ethnic homogamy in the marriage market—have also brought the family to the forefront of the stratification system. Recent data on young Americans illuminate the strong correlation between family structure and economic status; as economic assortative mating continues to be widespread, marriage and inherited resources are likely to remain imperative as a mechanism of transmitted advantage in the coming decades. In comparison to European industrialized countries, family patterns in the United States are distinct. Americans are more likely to marry, but single motherhood is more common, partially due to high rates of divorce. And among young cohorts, there is a growing convergence between marital status and economic resources. This trend leads to two trajectories: (1) young women with low levels of education are increasingly more likely to face divorce, nonmarital childbearing, and single motherhood, and to have limited financial resources to pass on to children; whereas (2) college-educated women are more likely to delay marriage and childbearing, and are less likely to divorce than other women, a pattern associated with greater gains for their children in terms of parental time and financial resources (Cherlin 2005; McLanahan 2004).[3] In light of these strong relationships between economic resources and family structure, scholars and policymakers warn that the growing economic polarization in the United States may lead to circumstances in which the younger population will continue to "sort itself between those who are eligible for marriage and a growing number who are deemed ineligible to marry" (Furstenberg 2005: 195), a process that would further increase economic divisions by marital status.

Moreover, while fertility remains at or slightly above replacement level, birth rates have fallen faster for married women than for unmarried women (Cherlin 2005), a trend that will likely affect the role that familial resources play in the distribution and replication of wealth among future generations. Ample evidence shows an inverse correlation between number of children and accumulated wealth, as well as between the number of siblings that adult people have and the amount of material resources they own, at all levels of education. This finding is attributed to resource dilution, which occurs since the number of dependent children increases demands on parental financial resources (Keister 2005, figure 5.4: 120). Discussing the second demographic transition—a concept used to describe delays in fertility and marriage, increase in nonmarital unions and childbearing, and decline in fertility rates to below replacement level—and the potential impact of these emerging trends on future inequality, McLanahan (2004: 208) concludes:

> As a consequence, the second demographic transition is widening social-class disparities in children's resources . . . children who were born to mothers from the most-advantaged backgrounds are making substantial gains in resources . . . in contrast, children born to mothers from the most disadvantaged backgrounds are making smaller gains, and in some instances, even losing parental resources.

Given the marginal welfare provision, the relatively large number of single and economically disadvantaged young mothers and their children would continue to place strain on the limited resources of parents and grandparents. Indeed, during the past three decades, the pervasiveness of multigenerational living arrangements in which grandparents assist their adult children in raising grandchildren has risen. Between 1970 and 2003, the number of children living in their grandparents' homes increased by 73 percent (U.S. Census Bureau 2004b) and, in 2001, 6.2 million children lived in households with at least one grandparent present, comprising 9 percent of all children in the United States (Kreider and Fields 2005: 8). Of these, 77 percent of children living with a grandparent were also living with a parent in the household (Kreider and Fields 2005: 8).[4] Children living with grandparents more often live in poor households than children living in households with no grandparents present (Kreider and Fields 2005) and this multigenerational living arrangement is more visible among poor minority households, where the role of grandparents, particularly grandmothers, in caring for the grandchildren and other children of extended kin is more common.

The institutional arrangements and demographic structures that underlie the economic reality of persistent inequality, and reliance on private resources, coincide with strong normative support in familial obligation. Because families function as sociocultural units that often bring together individuals from three generations, the social relationships formed in this intergenerational context create unique opportunities for interactions, transmission of values, and social and economic exchanges across cohorts within the family (Jackson, Jayakody, and Antonucci 1997). In the United States, familial exchanges of goods and services and intergenerational transfers of financial resources are not only a necessary means of support in a liberal welfare regime, but are also guided by a strong normative structure that emphasizes familial responsibility to the economic well-being of family members. As social networks are becoming smaller, more closely interconnected, and center on family and kin members, the American family retains its role as the core of economic support to the young and the old (see also Logan and Spitze 1996).

In that respect, social and economic transfers are inseparable. The form and magnitude of intergenerational wealth transfers are shaped by the strength and quality of social bonds. Receipt of financial transfers, in turn, enhances positive attitudes toward familial obligation to the economic well-being of family and kin members. Through these reciprocal mechanisms, private property is shared, accumulated, divided, and transferred. Most of the evidence presented in earlier chapters of this book supports the generational contract thesis of increasing interdependence and support across generations. These demographic and normative structures, however, can also endure financial stress, particularly among asset-poor and minority households, and many Americans do not benefit from the social and economic advantages that stem from intergenerational networks. Drawing on Coleman and Hoffer (1987), we can observe asset accumulation and transfer processes in four "ideal-type" households that vary by economic resources, family structure, and intergenerational ties (figure 21).

Cell 1 represents affluent families with strong familial and intergenerational bonds. The transfer of wealth in these families is based on reciprocity and the receipt of wealth both enhances positive attitudes toward familial obligation and enables family members to engage in exchanges of financial resources. Cell 4 represents the asset poor, who are more likely to be single and/or experience marital disruption early in life and have relatives and kin who have limited resources to share. The feminization and juvenilization of poverty are associated with this form of financial deprivation within families. In these cases, reliance on extended family and kin members, particularly parents, may further drain the limited resources of these families leading to a

		Social Capital (strong vs. weak family network)	
		YES	NO
Tangible Capital	YES	1	2
(high vs. low wealth level)	NO	3	4

Figure 21. Four Types of Social Capital and Wealth Transfers

growing economic polarization by family structure. Cell 2 represents those families with significant material assets but weak social capital (intergenerational ties), as a result of structural and/or functional deficiency, and cell 3 represents households with limited financial resources but strong family support systems; some ethnic and racial minorities who are relatively poor, but are inclined to rely on family support system and family networks as a source of credit and financial assistance, characterize this form of social capital and wealth transfers.

Reducing Inequality

The complex amalgamation of institutional and intergenerational components of wealth buildup implies that prospects for closing racial and ethnic gaps in wealth in the near future are unlikely. In recent years, there has been a growing recognition, both in the United States and in other countries, that income transfer programs are limited and offer a short-term solution to poverty and economic hardship (Midgley 2005). The need to provide long-term solutions to wealth inequality—through the expansion of business ownership, homeownership, and savings among asset-poor households—has recently received more attention. These proposals involve inclusive asset-building policies that would benefit the nonpoor and poor alike. One example currently in play is Individual Development Accounts (IDAs) that provide matches for savings by low-income families; these funds can be used for home purchase and maintenance, business startup or expansion, retirement, and/or investment in human capital (Sherraden 1990, 2005; Schreiner 2004).[5] Recent evidence shows that for the most part, participants in IDAs report positive psychological and financial effects, including an increase in confidence about the future, growing economic security and control of life, and greater consumption efficiency (Sherraden et al. 2004).

Expansion of private ownership is strongly embedded in the "ownership society" initiative,[6] driven by the idea that private ownership empowers people and should be promoted; families should be given incentives for owning homes and businesses and for controlling their own savings and health and retirement benefits (Brown, Kuttner, and Shapiro 2005).[7] Whereas the idea of spreading private ownership resonates very well in a country founded on individualism and property ownership, this initiative also sharpens the debate over the appropriate means to achieve this goal (Brown, Kuttner, and Shapiro 2005), and in particular, the definition of the target population to which these policies should be applied. Whereas for the better-off segments of the population, individual ownership translates into financial security and command over resources that can be transferred to younger generations, for the asset-poor, the shift of more responsibility—from the society back to individuals and their families—may result in greater financial debt and vulnerability.[8] Indeed, a growing number of first-time homebuyers face increasing affordability problems and mortgage and credit debt among the poor is on the rise. While it is too early to determine the depth of the current crisis in the housing market, and academic research on the topic is primarily anecdotal, preliminary data show that a disproportionate number of low income and minority households face increasing financial difficulties in keeping up the mortgage payments on houses which were recently purchased with financial assistance in the form of subprime mortgages (Dymski 2006; Hearing before the Subcommittee on Financial Institutions and Consumer Credit 2006).

The evidence presented in this book illustrates the need to adopt social policies that both promote asset accumulation and reduce wealth inequality. For long-term asset-based policies to succeed, existing structural constraints in the labor market and the commodity market should be addressed. Institutional discrimination in the labor market, the formal credit market, and the housing markets—as evidenced in such practices as steering and redlining—limits access to desirable assets, affects price appreciation and rates of return, and should be eliminated. For example, the large number of foreign-born Hispanic householders who are likely to endure distinct opportunity structures in the credit and housing market affect both the relatively overall low amount of wealth held by this ethnic group, and the high level of intragroup wealth polarization between immigrants and native-born Hispanics. Eliminating collectivist exclusionary practices is likely to decrease economic disparities both between and within racial and ethnic groups. Furthermore, asset-based policies should take into account the familial and intergenerational nature of wealth accumulation. Since intergenerational transfers perpetuate inequalities arising originally from other sources, wealth accumulation in one generation could improve the living standards and life chances of future generations. In contrast to income-based policies, enhancing asset accumulation among the poor could benefit not only individuals and nuclear families but also the extended family, relatives, and kin members. Whereas not all parental wealth is transferred to children, and family structure and marital history evidently affect the amount and form of these transfers, inter vivos gifts and bequests come almost exclusively from family members. As more family members, particularly mid-life adults in the pivot generation, face growing demands from younger and older relatives to provide financial support, promoting wealth buildup among the asset-poor may not only improve the living standards of poor nuclear families, but could ease the pressure on extended families, relatives, and racial and ethnic communities (Chiteji and Hamilton 2005). Evidence also indicates that one of the main obstacles to growing wealth equality is the persistent homogamy in marriage across class, race, ethnicity, and nationality. As mentioned above, propinquity and the level of residential segregation tend to constrain interracial and interethnic marriage and cohabitation patterns.[9] The more segregated and socially isolated the group is, the lower the likelihood that its members will interact, date, and marry members of other racial and ethnic groups. Without breaking the social boundaries of class, race, and ethnicity in a nation that is not only economically polarized and racially diverse, but in which class and race are deeply intertwined, growing wealth gaps are likely to stimulate public resentment and political polarization.

The findings reported in this book also indicate that a shift is needed toward a new social agenda for reducing inequality that, rather than blaming the poor for their economic circumstances, acknowledges the structural and extra-individual mechanisms of stratification. Analysis of wealth inequality highlights the complex nature of social inequality and its intergenerational perpetuation; the study of commodity market structure more sharply illuminates the multifaceted nature of social stratification—which involves institutional, cultural, legal, familial, and demographic variables that determine living standards and life chances. A better understanding of these extra-individual sources of inequality could produce noticeably different public views on this issue and encourage a growing acceptance for the need to adopt policies that take into account both the distinct risks and widespread benefits of asset-based programs.[10] I hope that the conceptual framework and empirical evidence presented in this book will contribute to this effort.

~

Appendix A

Table A.1. Description of HRS-92 Variables Used in the Various Analyses

Variable	*Description*
Race/ethnicity	Four dummy variables: White, Black, Hispanic, and Other.
Household net worth	Total sum of wealth held by the household net of households' debts. The measure includes marketable wealth (Wolff 1993) and includes: home, real estate, business, IRA and Keough account, other sources, vehicle, bank accounts, stocks, bonds, mutual funds.
Houshold Labor income	Annual income of the respondent and spouse from earnings, pension and annuity income.
Transfers received	Measures whether the respondent received (1) inheritance (2) other transfers from relatives in the amount of $10,000 or more (3) life insurance payments. Coded 1 if received transfers and 0 if not.
Age	Measured in years.
Sex	Sex (male) of primary respondent (versus female).
Education	Years of formal education.
Parental education	Years of parental education.
Marital status:	Dummy variables: Married (intact), Married (remarried), Divorced, Widow, Cohabit, Separated, Never married.
Employment status	Coded 1 if the respondent is currently working.
Occupation:	A set of dummy variables; coded 1 if respondent in specific occupational category.
Managerial/ Professional	Managerial or professional and technical occupation.
Sales/clerical	Sales/ Clerical and administrative support.

(continued)

Table A.1. (*continued*)

Variable	Description
Service	Private households, cleaning, protection, food preparation, health, personal.
Other	Machines and repair, construction trade, precision production, operators (machines, transport, armed forces, farming forestry, missing)
Religion	Three dummy variables: Catholic, Protestant, and Other.
Church Attendance	Coded 1 if attend more than once a month, and 0 if other.
Household size	Number of additional members, except for respondent and spouse/partner, aged 15 and older.
Number of children	Number of children born.
Region (South)	1- live in the southern region of the US; 0-Other.
Metropolitan area	1- live in metropolitan area; 0-Other.
Immigration status	1- native born; 0-foreign born.

Source: HRS 92

Table A.2. Coefficients from Regression Analysis: Percentage of Wealth Held in Financial Assets

	% Financial	
	Base 1a	Full 1b
Marital Status:		
Married (Intact)	4.839***	3.512**
	(1.260)	(1.152)
Married (Remarried)	5.195***	5.211***
	(1.395)	(1.275)
Cohabit	11.166***	9.627***
	(2.711)	(2.478)
Separated	8.790**	7.930**
	(2.624)	(2.398)
Widow	1.463	1.182
	(1.864)	(1.704)
Never Married	−.200	−.674
	(2.203)	(2.013)
Family Transfers:		
Inheritance	6.082***	4.118***
	(.880)	(.806)
Gift	9.281***	5.239**
	(1.270)	(1.166)
Life insurance	.493	.453
	(1.719)	(1.571)
Employment	2.067*	3.035***
	(.829)	(.758)
Education	.707***	.539***
	(.149)	(.136)

	% Financial	
	Base 1a	Full 1b
Labor-income(/1000)	.032***	−.039***
	(.009)	(.009)
Native-born	−5.936***	−4.148**
	(1.366)	(1.249)
Net worth	—	.00***
	(.00)	
Constant	13.796***	20.748***
	(5.299)	(4.847)
N	6068	
R square	.071	.221

*p<0.05, **p<0.01, ***p<0.001
Note: Additional variables were included in the analysis but not displayed in
the Table. These include: occupation, presence of children, gender, metro-
politan area, race, size of household, and region.
Employment: Omitted term is for 'Unemployed/not in labor force'
Native-born: Omitted term is for 'Foreign born'
Marital Status: Omitted term is for 'Divorced'
Family Transfers: Omitted term is for 'No transfers received'
Source: HRS-92

**Table A.3. Coefficients from Logistic Regression Analysis:
Ownership of Financial Assets and Main Residence for Low (20–60
percentile) and High (60–100 percentile) Net Worth Categories
(standard errors in parentheses)**

	Financial Assets (1a)	Homeownership (1b)
20–60 Percentile of the net worth distribution		
Marital Status:		
Married (intact)	0.82	2.00***
	(.135)	(.304)
Married (remarried)	.308*	1.076***
	(.150)	(.318)
Cohabit	−.121	.320
	(.317)	(.495)
Separated	.037	−1.184**
	(.271)	(.422)
Widowed	−.062	1.276**
	(.198)	(.494)
Never married	.252	.043
	(.220)	(.403)
Family Transfers:		
Inheritance	.431**	−.039
	(.112)	(.218)

(*continued*)

Table A.3. (*continued*)

	Financial Assets (1a)	Homeownership (1b)
Gift	.195	−.342
	(.180)	(.267)
Life insurance	.054	−.431
	(.202)	(.386)

N=3942

	Financial Assets (2a)	Homeownership (2b)
60–100 Percentile of the net worth distribution		
Marital Status:		
Married (Intact)	.236	1.315***
	(.185)	(.177)
Married (Remarried)	.358	.755***
	(.204)	(.192)
Cohabit	.483	.005
	(.386)	(.348)
Separated	−.162	−.154
	(.419)	(.285)
Widowed	−.006	−.026
	(.269)	(.226)
Never Married	−.228	−.439
	(.316)	(.231)
Family Transfers:		
Inheritance	.480**	−.242
	(.113)	(.151)
Gift	.377*	−.076
	(.159)	(.256)
Life insurance	−.029	.401
	(.224)	(.283)

*p<0.05, **p<0.01, ***p<0.001
N=3027
Control variables include: Region, age, occupation, labor-income, employment, education, gender, native-born, number of persons in the household, race, metropolitan area, number of children.
Source: HRS-92

Table A.4. Coefficients from Logistic Regression Analysis: Asset-Poverty

	Asset-Poverty	Exp.
Marital Status:		
Married (Intact)	−1.6***	.20
	(.11)	
Married (Remarried)	−.97***	.38
	(.12)	

	Asset-Poverty	Exp.
Cohabit	−.06	
	(.19)	
Separated	.04	
	(.15)	
Widowed	−.35**	.70
	(.13)	
Never Married	.05	
	(.15)	
Family Transfers:		
Inheritance	−.72***	.48
	(.12)	
Gift	−1.0***	.35
	(.29)	
Life insurance	−1.1	.31
	(.20)	
Race (White)	−.50***	.60
	(.07)	
Employment	−.35***	.70
	(.08)	
Education	−.09***	.91
	(.01)	
Labor-income(/1000)	−.03***	.96
	(.00)	
Native-born	−.25*	.78
	(.11)	
Constant	5.8***	
	(.50)	
N	7605	
-2 Log likelihood	5303	

*p<0.05, **p<0.01, ***p<0.001
Note: Additional variables were included in the analysis but not displayed in the Table. These include: marital status, presence of children, gender, region, metropolitan area, size of household, and region.
Occupation: Omitted term is for 'Service occupations'
Employment: Omitted term is for 'Unemployed/not in labor force'
Native-born: Omitted term is for 'Foreign born'
Race (White): Omitted term is for 'Other'
Marital Status: Omitted term is for 'Divorced'
Family Transfers: Omitted term is for 'No transfers received'
Source: HRS-92

~

Appendix B

Table B.1.   Descriptions of Variables Used in the Analyses: The Generations Survey, 1995

			Mean
Dependent Variables			
Assistance to Children: Education			4.7
Transfers to Children: Inheritance			3.2
Transfers to Parents: Financial Assistance			2.5
Independent Variables			
Age (Categories)			43.3
18-35			39.5
36-45			20.8
46-55			12.8
56-65			11.6
65+			14.5
Married	Versus non-married		56.3
Sex	Male versus female		49
Children (Yes)	Whether has children		71.1
Education:			
Less than college			51.7
Some college			40.6
Graduate School			8.7
Religion:			
Protestant			55.2
Catholic			28.8
Other			16.0

(*continued*)

Table B.1. (*continued*)

		Mean
Religiosity	Scale from 1 (not religious) to 4 (religious)	3.4
Religiosity (Missing)	Dummy variables for missing information on religiosity.	9.6
Income	Family income in the past year (in $1000)	32.2
Inherited	Inherited property (versus not): land, house, real estate, financial assets, non-financial assets (e.g. jewelry, furniture, and paintings).	22.9
Expect inheritance	Expect to receive inherited assets (versus not).	29.6
Contact with parents	'Opportunities to have some conversation or contact between parents and children in your family when you were about 10 years old' ('Often' versus 'Else').	67.9
N		1500

Source: The Generations Survey 1995

Table B.2.   Determinants of Attitudinal Support for Family Transfers to Elderly Parents: OLR and OLS Regression (Standard Errors in Parentheses)

	1A	1B
Age 36-45[1]	−.110	−.080
	(.140)	(.150)
Age 46-55	−.272	−.223
	(.165)	(.177)
Age 56-65	**−.500****	**−.410***
	(.171)	(.186)
Age 65+	**−1.007*****	**−.891*****
	(.162)	(.183)
Education: College[2]		.219
		(.117)
Education: More than college		.247
		(.210)
Income ($)		.000
		(.000)
Inherited (Yes)		−.145
		(.128)
Expect inheritance (Yes)		**.260***
		(.126)
Religiosity		**.376*****
		(.079)
Race (white)		−.133
		(.125)
Frequent contacts with parents		**.234***
		(.114)
−2LL	−1179.6	−1156.4

	1A	1B
N		1473	
chi2 (Proportional odds)	.771	.675

*p<.05, **p<.01, ***p<.001
Note: Additional variables were included in the analysis but not displayed in the table. These include: marital status, presence of children, religion, and gender.
[1]Omitted term is for "Age: 18-35"
[2]Omitted term is for "Education: High school and less"
Dummy variables were included for missing values for income and religiosity.
Source: The Generations Survey 1995

Table B.3. Determinants of Attitudinal Support for Family Transfers: OLR and OLS Regression (Standard Errors in Parentheses)

	(1-B) OLS Model Transfers to Children: Education		(2-B) OLR Model Transfers to Children: Property	
Age 36-45[1]	.002	−.041	−.480***	−.294*
	(.034)	(.036)	(.130)	(.138)
Age 46-55	−.065	−.119*	−.773***	−.590***
	(.041)	(.042)	(.157)	(.164)
Age 56-65	−.025	−.075	−.470**	−.357*
	(.042)	(.045)	(.158)	(.172)
Age 65+	−.006	−.038	.124	.174
	(.039)	(.043)	(.147)	(.162)
Education: College[2]		.050		−.180
		(.028)		(.108)
Education: More than college		.013		−.520**
		(.050)		(.191)
Income		.000**		−.000
		(.000)		(.000)
Inherited (Yes)		.068*		.259*
		(.031)		(.117)
Expect inheritance (Yes)		.000		.257*
		(.030)		(.116)
Religiosity		.078***		.134
		(.018)		(.071)
Race (white)		.044		−.545***
		(.030)		(.116)
requent contacts with parents				
Constant	3.74	3.31		
	(.020)	(.093)		
R square	.002	.033		
−2LL			−1853.2	−1819
N		1488	1425	
chi2 (Proportional odds)			0.850	.321

*p<.05, **p<.01, ***p<.001
Note: Additional variables were included in the analysis but not displayed in the table. These include: marital status, presence of children, religion, and gender.
[1]Omitted term is for "Age: 18-35"
[2]Omitted term is for "Education: High school and less"
Source: The Generations Survey 1995

Appendix C

Table C.1. Income of the Population 55 or Older, Percentage with Income from Specified Source, by Age, Marital Status, Sex of Nonmarried Persons, Race, and Hispanic Origin, 2000

| | All Units | | | Married Couples | | | Nonmarried Persons | | | | | | | | |
| | | | | | | | Total | | | Men | | | Women | | |
	55–61	62–64	65 or Older	55–61	62–64	65 or Older	55–61	62–64	65 or Older	55–61	62–64	65 or Older	55–61	62–64	65 or Older
Whites															
Income from assets	65	64	63	75	73	72	51	52	57	45	45	54	55	56	58
Interest	61	61	61	71	70	69	47	48	55	40	42	52	53	52	56
Other income from assets	41	39	31	49	48	40	29	26	24	27	21	24	31	28	24
Dividends	37	34	26	44	43	34	26	23	20	23	19	20	28	25	20
Rent or royalties	11	11	10	14	15	13	8	5	7	10	5	7	7	6	7
Estates or trusts	0	0	0	0	0	0	0	0	0	1	1	0	0	0	0
Blacks															
Income from assets	34	33	29	49	44	44	27	28	22	25	21	29	27	32	20
Interest	32	31	27	47	40	42	24	27	21	23	21	28	25	30	19
Other income from assets	15	11	9	21	14	17	11	10	5	10	12	7	12	8	5
Dividends	12	9	6	18	8	13	9	9	3	9	12	3	9	7	3
Rent or royalties	5	2	4	7	6	6	3	1	3	1	0	4	4	1	2
Estates or trusts	0	0	0	0	0	0	0	0	0	0	0	0	0	0	0
Hispanics															
Income from assets	30	29	28	39	31	38	21	29	23	17	c	24	24	25	23
Interest	27	27	26	35	29	35	19	27	21	14	c	23	23	24	20
Other income from assets	13	15	9	18	20	13	7	11	7	8	c	4	7	9	7
Dividends	10	10	6	13	15	8	6	7	4	6	c	3	7	5	5
Rent or royalties	4	7	5	7	10	7	1	5	3	2	c	3	1	4	4
Estates or trusts	0	0	0	0	0	0	0	0	0	1	c	0	0	0	0

Source: Social Security Online 2002

Table C.2. Mean Characteristics (Standard Deviation) of Households by Racial/Ethnic Origin (Weighted)

	Whites	Blacks	Hispanics
Net worth (/1000)	277.8	83.5	105.3
	(560.0)	(243.5)	(403.3)
Median Net Worth (/1000)	127.0	28.5	31.5
Labor income (/1000)	41.8	24.9	21.3
	(47.7)	(27.8)	(28.9)
Asset poverty (lowest quintile)	12.3	40.3	38.0
Family Transfers and Marital Status			
Received inheritance (%)	24.5	4.7	5.0
Received gifts (%)	9.4	2.2	2.0
Life insurance benefits (%)	5.7	4.3	3.1
Total transfers (%)	35.6	10.7	10.0
Marital Status			
Married	69.9	41.5	59.0
Intact marriage	48.9	28.7	44.8
Married before	21.0	12.8	14.2
Divorced	14.6	19.0	15.0
Widowed	7.1	14.9	8.8
Other (Par/Nev/Sep)	7.9	24.0	17.2
Children	2.9	3.5	3.7
	(1.9)	(2.5)	(2.7)
Education and Labor Market Characteristics of Household Head			
Education (years)	12.9	11.4	8.9
	(2.7)	(3.2)	(4.5)
Parental education	10.7	8.8	6.2
	(3.3)	(3.4)	(4.5)
Parental education missing (%)	4.9	11.7	9.1
Occupation			
Managerial/professional	33.6	15.8	12.1
Sales/clerical/support	25.8	14.7	15.4
Service	11.2	30.3	19.3
Other (no occupation/farming)	18.1	17.9	30.5
Operators	11.1	21.1	22.5
Currently employed	69.4	58.7	52.9
Native-born	95.5	95.3	47.0
Other Demographic and Social Characteristics			
Gender (male)	55.0	40.7	51.2
Age	56.1	55.8	55.9
	(4.9)	(4.6)	(5.1)
Household size	2.4	2.5	3.3
	(1.1)	(2.6)	(1.9)
Region (South)	32.2	49.8	39.3

(*continued*)

Table C.2. (*continued*)

	Whites	Blacks	Hispanics
Religion:			
Attend (>Once a month)	44.6	66.0	64.3
Protestant	61.0	86.1	16.7
Catholic	27.8	6.3	78.4
Metropolitan area	72.1	86.9	83.8
N=7605	5297	1424	714

Source: HRS-92

Table C.3. **Unstandardized Regression Coefficients from Tobit Analysis Predicting Logged Total Household Net Worth**

	(1)	(2)	(3)
	Human Capital	Marital Status	Family Transfers
Race:			
Black	−2.340***	−1.658***	−1.473***
	(.118)	(.117)	(.117)
Hispanic	−1.108***	−.738***	−.656***
	(.180)	(.173)	(.172)
Other race	−1.231**	−.978***	−.843**
	(.291)	(.279)	(.277)
Marital:			
Married (intact)	—	2.599***	2.553***
	(.129)	(.129)	
Married (remarried)	—	2.178***	2.113***
	(.145)	(.144)	
Cohabit	—	1.054***	.980***
	(.266)	(.264)	
Separated	—	−.850***	−.916***
	(.225)	(.223)	
Widowed	—	.614***	.134
	(.174)	(.182)	
Never married	—	−.290	−.333
	(.212)	(.210)	
Employed	1.001***	1.096***	1.087***
	(.092)	(.089)	(.088)
Native-born	.503**	.511**	.462**
	(.162)	(.155)	(.154)
Total Household Income (/1000)	.015***	.008***	.008***
	(.001)	(.001)	(.001)
Religiosity (attendance)	.473***	.322***	.302***
	(.085)	(.082)	(.081)
Received Family Transfers:			
Inheritance	—	—	.601***
			(.102)

	(1) Human Capital	(2) Marital Status	(3) Family Transfers
Gift	—	—	.770***
			(.150)
Life insurance	—	—	1.545***
			(.192)
Constant	−.204	−.261	−.035
	(.614)	(.596)	(.591)
log-likelihood	−19431	−19111	−19049

*p>.05, **p>.01, ***p>.001
N censored = 743
Total N=7605
Note: Additional variables were included in the analysis but not displayed in the table. These include: presence of children, religion, religiosity, sex, region, metropolitan area, size of household, parental education, occupation.
Region: Omitted term is for "Other regions"
Occupation: Omitted term is for "Service occupations"
Employed: Omitted term is for "Unemployed/not in labor force"
Native-born: Omitted term is for "Foreign born"
Race: Omitted term is for "White"
Marital status: Omitted term is for 'Divorced'
Family transfers: Omitted term is for "No transfers received"
Religion: Omitted term is "Other"
Source: HRS-92

Appendix D

Table D.1. Unstandardized Regression Coefficients from Tobit Analysis Predicting
Logged Total Household Net Worth by Racial Category

	Net Worth Whites	Net Worth Blacks	Net Worth Hispanics
Marital status:			
Married, intact	1.62***	2.88***	2.84***
	(.152)	(.472)	(.690)
Married, married before	1.21***	2.22***	2.86***
	(.166)	(.539)	(.781)
Divorced	−.652***	.166	−1.01
	(.183)	(.489)	(.767)
Other	−.016	−1.00*	−1.15
	(.206)	(.469)	(.760)
Received family transfers	.783***	2.33***	2.13***
	(.079)	(.434)	(.574)
Employed	.550***	2.19***	1.43***
	(.086)	(.305)	(.366)
Income (/1000)	.008***	.042***	.018*
	(.000)	(.006)	(.008)
Native-born	−.380*	.692	1.96***
	(.190)	(.632)	(.359)
Metropolitan area	−.105	−1.03*	.099
	(.084)	(.424)	(.459)
Constant	4.97	−5.32	.506
	(.538)	(1.91)	(2.00)

(*continued*)

175

Table D.1. (*continued*)

	Net Worth Whites	Net Worth Blacks	Net Worth Hispanics
log-likelihood	−12619	−3629	−1830
N censored	256	332	132
Total N	5297	1424	714

*p>.05, **p>.01, ***p>.001
Note: Additional variables were included in the analysis but not displayed in the table. These include: gender, presence of children, region, metropolitan area, size of household, education, occupation, sex.
Marital status: Omitted term is for "Widowed"
Family transfers: Omitted term is for "No transfers received"
Employment: Omitted term is for "Unemployed/not in labor force"
Native-born: Omitted term is for "Foreign born"
Metropolitan area: Omitted term is for "Nonmetropolitan area"
Source: HRS-92

~

Notes

Introduction

1. Using data from 2000 and estimating wealth in purchasing power Davies et al. (2006: 12) report that with *per capita* wealth of $143,727, the United States ranks first, followed by Australia at $121,597 and Japan at $91,856.

2. The terms *wealth* and *net worth* are used interchangeably to refer to the total value of household assets, net of liabilities.

3. Data reported exclude missing cases (3 percent of the cases), that is, respondents whose answers to the question were not reported.

4. The U.S. Census Bureau uses a set of money-income thresholds that vary by family size and composition to determine who is poor. The official poverty definition counts money income before taxes and does not include capital gains and noncash benefits (such as public housing, Medicaid, and food stamps).

5. Whereas the vast majority of families below the official poverty line have low levels of wealth, about one-tenth of those families own a significant amount of wealth. Of those, approximately 4–5 percent have significant wealth holdings in real estate and unincorporated business equity and their poverty income is based on substantial income losses associated with these assets (Wolff 1994: 161; see also Sherraden 1995).

6. Some scholars argue that, whether deliberately or not, the emphasis on income-based inequality directs attention away from how enormously unequal the distribution of wealth is (Haslett 1986).

7. Family businesses account for 40 percent of the U.S. gross domestic product (GDP) and 60 percent of its workforce (Bhattacharya and Ravikumar 2001).

Chapter One

1. Sherraden (1991: 100–5) makes a distinction between tangible and intangible assets, which are based on individual characteristics (human capital) or social or economic relations such as cultural capital and political capital. The current study focuses on the first category.

2. The French sociologist Emile Durkheim (1992: 126) notes that the equity held in private property "depends on opinion and is a matter of opinion;" as such, it can increase or decrease based on the value that people assign to the property (rather than the amount of labor associated with its production). One example used to demonstrate the significance of public views to the monetary value of assets focuses on housing equity: "If I build a house in a spot that suddenly becomes sought after for its qualities of charm or some other reason, its value becomes much enhanced. If, on the contrary, favor turns against it, it may reach the point of having no value at all . . . my property, or what I own, might double its market value, without my lifting a finger" (Durkheim 1992: 126).

3. The authors estimate that in 2000, the total amount of cash required to mount winning political campaigns "topped out at $193 million for the presidency (not counting indirect party funding), $7.2 million for a Senate seat, and $837,083 for a House seat . . . in the 2000 Senate races, candidates from both major parties raised a total of $250.3 million from individual contributors" (Perruci and Wysong 2003: 126–27).

4. Attempts to fill the scholarly gap on intergenerational mobility by analyzing occupational mobility across three generations are rare; Warren and Hauser (1997) found that only a few significant and direct effects of grandparents' characteristics on grandchildren's educational attainment or occupational status once parents' characteristics are held constant.

5. Dick (1970 in Shanks 2005: 24) notes that whereas the property holder could vote and hold office, the propertyless man "was practically on the same political level as the indentured or slave."

6. John Adams, another important public figure of the postrevolutionary period, agreed: "Power always follows property . . . the balance of power in a society accompanies the balance of property in land. The only possible way, then, of preserving the balance of power on the side of equal liberty and virtue is to make the acquisition of land easy to every member of society, to make a division of land into small quantities, so that the multitude may be possessed of landed estates. If the multitude is possessed of the balance of real estate, the multitude will have the balance of power, and in that case the multitude will take care of the liberty, virtue and interest of the multitude, in all acts of government" (Taylor 1979: 210 in Price 2003: 37–38).

7. Those men who did not work in farming—such as merchants, artisans, and craftsmen—were generally self-employed (Ruggles 2006: 111).

8. In order to claim a maximum parcel of 160 public acres, a homesteader had to be the head of a family over the age of twenty-one and a citizen of the United States

or had "filed his declaration of intention to become such . . . and who has never borne arms against the United States Government or given aid and comfort to its enemies" (U.S. Department of the Interior).

9. Rather than protecting the propertyless sectors of the population from the power of the propertied elite, the Federalists envisioned a potential danger for the welfare of property owners from the hands of the propertyless mass. This rationale led the government to develop a clear and publicly stated set of mechanisms to safeguard the rights of the property owners:

> Property arose as a problem for government because this inequality required protection; those with property had to be protected from those who had less or none. Without security, property lost its value. And the threat to security was inevitable, for (the Federalists presumed) it was the very nature of a productive system of private property that many, perhaps most, would have none. (Nedelsky 1990: 205)

10. The sharp expansion in homeownership during the post–World War II period has led to a small industry of academic research that emphasizes the need to incorporate asset holdings and consumption behavior into the stratification processes. This line of research contends that homeownership should be studied as a principal source of financial rewards (e.g. tax deductions, long-term amortized mortgages) and personal wealth, unrelated to production processes (see Rex and Moore 1967; Saunders 1978, 1990; Thorns 1981).

11. In addition to these factors, sociologists Morris and Western (1999) attribute the stagnation in earnings and the increasing polarization in income to the changing sociodemographic characteristics (age, gender, immigration status, and education) of the labor force, the role of political context, and institutions (for example, the freezing of the federal minimum wage and the declining power of labor union organization).

12. In 1996, manufacturing accounted for 15 percent of nonfarm employment, while the service industry accounted for 29 percent (Meisenheimer 1998).

13. Analyzing data from the Current Population Surveys (CPS) from the mid-1990s, Meisenheimer (1998 table 6: 34) reports that in 1993, 35 percent of workers in private service industries participated in an employer-sponsored retirement plan, whereas the comparable figures of participation in mining, manufacturing, and transportation and public utilities were 69.1, 64.2, and 61.8 percent, respectively.

14. The one hundred largest U.S. multinational corporations—such as IBM, Colgate-Palmolive, Coca-Cola, Pepsi-Cola, and Procter & Gamble—reported foreign revenue in 1994 that ranged from 30 to 70 percent of their total revenue ("The 100 Largest U.S. Multinationals," *Forbes*, July 17, 1995, 274–76, in Perrucci and Wysong 2003).

15. Shammas, Salmon, and Dahlen (1997: 5) attribute the almost exclusive reliance on land and the limited ownership of stocks, bonds, and other financial and income-producing assets during the colonial period to the absence of financial institutions and private corporations. After the Revolution, however, the emergence of

financial institutions and the increasing opportunities to invest in assets that were only remotely linked to one's occupation and labor market participation ameliorated the wealth portfolio of the well-off sectors of the population

16. Consequently, the proportion of children in working families living in owner-occupied housing declined 8 percent over the last twenty-five years (Center for Housing Policy 2004).

17. The booming housing market in the late twentieth century was fueled by low mortgage rates and speculation, as more people purchased real estate as rental property with the expectation that housing prices would continue to rise. According to the National Association of Realtors, about one-third of all single-family homes purchased in 2004–2005 were second-home purchases, mostly for investment purposes.

18. The increase in stock prices by 170 percent between 1989 and 2001 (Wolff 2004: 1) has drastically boosted the proportion of wealth held in financial assets (Keister 2000).

19. At the end of August 2000, mutual funds held about $7.5 trillion in assets, making them the largest type of financial institution (as measured by assets under management), even larger than commercial banks (Kennickell 2003).

20. As the number of retired people is expected to continue to grow in the next decade, pension rights are becoming a major component of household wealth (OECD 1988; Kinsella and Gist 1995; Smith 1995; Angel and Angel 1997, chap. 3; Gale 1998: 706; Wolff 2004; Belcher 1994; for a similar trend in Britain, see Lowe 1988).

21. Using data from the Survey of Consumer Finances (SCF), Kennickell (2003, table 11: 23) estimates the percent of net worth held in principal residences in 2001 as 27.1; the share of family net worth held in financial assets was 42.2 percent.

22. Wolff's (2007: 19) analysis also shows that when the value of total stocks owned through mutual funds, trusts, and retirement accounts are included in the analysis, the value of total stocks owned by households more than doubled, from 11.3 percent in 1983 to 24.5 percent in 2001, and then dropped to 17.5 percent in 2004. This trend reflects the bull market in corporate equities during the 1990s, which was followed by a decline in the stock market and the decline in stock ownership. For more information on the datasets mentioned in this section and the definition of wealth in the SIPP and the SCF data, see Wolff (1997: 5–8) and Orzechowski and Sepielli (2003: 3–5).

23. Clignet (1992: 81) proposes a parallel between theories of labor market segmentation, which view the labor market as an entity composed of several segments with distinct structures and opportunities with regard to mobility, income, and job security, and the increasingly distinct forms of capital accumulation mechanisms.

24. Between 1983 and 1995 the wealthiest 1 percent of households experienced a 17 percent growth in net worth, whereas the proportion of households with negative or zero net worth increased from 15.5 percent to 18.5 percent (Mishel, Bernstein, and Schmitt 1999: 259 in Spilerman 2000). This sharp increase was followed by a more modest rise during the 1990s.

25. Lenski (1984) asserts that income derives from three sources or systems: (1) the *welfare system*, in which claims to benefits are based on citizenship and need and in which benefits take the form of free public education, Medicare and Medicaid, unemployment compensation, disability benefits, and welfare benefits; (2) the *labor market system*, in which rewards are compensation for work (wages and salaries); and (3) the *capitalist* or *property system*, in which rewards are based on the type and amount of property one owns and take the form of capital gains, dividends, interests, and rent (see also Browne 1974; Pryor 1973: 6–7).

26. Karoly (1994) reports that capital income and other income sources, combined, have increased their relative share in total income from about 5 percent in 1970 to nearly 13 percent in 1990. In addition, since the early 1970s, the percent of American households that reported having no capital income fell from 62 in 1970 to 36 in 1980, and remained at that level through 1990.

27. In contrast to property income, the wealth-adjusted measure of income also reflects the "stock" dimension of income inequality, and includes the sum of income from home and nonhome wealth. The sum of income from home was calculated as the imputed rent assigned to each household minus the annuitized value of mortgage debt, while income from nonhome wealth is the imputed lifetime annuity from nonhome wealth minus the annuitized values of other debt (Wolff and Zacharias 2006).

Chapter Two

1. Light and Gold (2000: 110) describe how ethnic minority groups often provide their members with financial capital through rotating savings and credit associations (ROSCAS) and other cooperative endeavors, all of which "rely on reputation and enduring relationships as collateral."

2. Townsand's (2005) analysis of social network and finance patterns in ethnic neighborhoods reports that use of informal credit among Hispanic residents is inversely correlated with use of the formal banking sector, and that assistance from relatives and friends tends to decline with labor market assimilation and language proficiency.

3. Wright (1997) states:

Class exploitation is defined by three principal criteria: (A) The material welfare of one group of people causally depends on the material deprivations of another. (B) The causal relation in (a) involves the asymmetrical exclusion of the exploited from access to certain productive resources. Typically this exclusion is backed by force in the form of property rights, but in special cases it may not be. The causal mechanism which translates exclusion (b) into differential welfare (a) involves the appropriation of the fruit of labor of the exploited by those who control the relevant productive resources. . . . The welfare of the exploiter depends upon the effort of the exploited, not merely the deprivations of the exploited.

4. According to Laslett (1991), increasing life expectancy and retirement practice necessitate a Fresh Map of Life, according to which—after the First Age of im-
maturity, dependence, and education and the Second Age of maturity, independence, and earning—comes the Third Age, a stage of self-fulfillment, followed by the
Fourth Age of final dependence, decrepitude, and death.

5. Whereas the median is the middle category in the distribution, the mean
value is sensitive to extreme values. When the data is not symmetrical, as in the case
of household net worth, the mean tends to be larger than the median.

6. Property tax reductions, which are granted in all states for elderly persons,
have also contributed to the increasing share of income derived from asset holdings
(Schultz 1988: 36).

7. Two main approaches—the *mobility tables* approach, which analyzes occupational mobility by focusing on the distribution of cases across the cells of cross-
classification tables, and the *regression* approach which estimates the respondent's position in a social hierarchy as a function of his/her family of origin and other intervening variables, are commonly used to study intergenerational mobility (Warren
and Hauser 1997).

8. In contrast to a "natural" division of labor, which is determined by diversity of
talents and abilities, hereditary transmission of wealth is defined as an "abnormal"
form of division of labor that renders the external conditions for competition very
unequal, since it gives to some the benefit of advantages that "do not necessarily correspond to their personal value" (Durkheim 1984: 312–14).

9. In the *Gospel of Wealth*, industrialist Andrew Carnegie (1998: 17) asserts that
the best mode of disposing of wealth is when it is administered by its owners during
their lives. In this way, "the surplus wealth of the few will become, in the best sense,
the property of the many." Carnegie also argues that bequeathing great sums of
wealth to relatives "often work(s) more for the injury than for the good of the recipients" and the leaving of inheritance for public uses indicates that the owner of such
wealth "is content to wait until he is dead before he becomes of much good in the
world" (Carnegie 1998: 13–15).

10. Sorokin's (1925) work on the sources of wealth held by millionaires found that
42 percent came from wealthy families (see also Mills 1956 in Jaher 1980: 224).
Thurow (1981: 171) estimates that about 50 percent of the great fortunes are acquired through inheritance.

11. As Soltow (1976: 164) notes, the mechanism of wealth transmission from one
generation to the next "is complex, if one considers the fertility and wealth of the
parents, the marriage of children among wealth groups, and the inheritance and
length of life of each person."

12. Kotlikoff and Morris (1989 in Kohli and Künemund 2003) propose that parents transfer wealth to children as an active incentive to get their children to provide them with services (see also Cox and Raines 1985; Stark and Falk 1998; Mc-
Garry and Schoeni 1995). Additional reasons that underlie such transfers include
power over family members and relatives with fewer financial resources (Thurow

1975), social status, or compliance with external norms pertaining to such transfers (Kohli and Künemund 2003: 130).

13. The data come from the first wave of the Health and Retirement Study (HRS-92). The data were collected in 1992 and include a sample of more than 12,600 people in 7,600 households for the 1931–1941 birth cohort (and their spouses, if married, regardless of age). The HRS core sample design is a multistage area probability sample of households, with an oversample of Hispanics, blacks, and Florida residents. The HRS is an exceptional source of data, suitable for the current analyses, because it contains detailed information on wealth, asset portfolio, type and timing of intergenerational transfers, and the marital history of white, black, and Hispanic households. Measures of family transfers include the receipt of (1) inheritance, (2) other transfers from relatives in the amount of $10,000 or more, and (3) life insurance payment. (See also Appendix A.)

The variable "total household net worth" includes the value of nine main components:

1. Housing: farm, ranch, mobile home, or home/apartment
2. Vehicle: vehicle and recreational vehicle
3. Real estate: other real estate that is not the main residence
4. Bonds: bonds and bond funds
5. Stocks: stocks, mutual funds, investment trusts
6. Retirement: individual retirement accounts (IRA) and Keogh accounts
7. Liquid asset: checking/saving accounts, money market funds, CDs, government saving bonds, and T-bills
8. Business
9. Other assets: all other assets in addition to those reported, including other investments, money owed to the respondents by others, and valuable collection for investment purposes

14. While rates of first marriage in the United States are 715 per 1,000 women, the comparable figures for other European and developed countries are substantially lower: for example, 670 in Italy, 631 in Canada, and about 560 in France and Sweden (Cherlin 2005: figure 3: 43).

15. The labor force participation rates of mothers who had a birth in the previous year has also gone up drastically, from less than one-third (31 percent) in 1976 to 55 percent in 2004, after reaching a high of 59 percent in 1998 (Dye 2005). Labor force participation rates among this population were slightly higher for married mothers in comparison to nonmarried mothers.

16. While marriage penalties in the tax system were reduced in 2001, cohabiting couples may still end up owing more in taxes together than they would if they were married (Thomas and Sawhill 2005: 61). However, in contrast to European nations, cohabitation in the United States is unusually unstable (Elwood and Jencks 2004). In addition, cohabitation is more common today among the less affluent and less well

educated (those with less than college education) and is more prevalent today before remarriage than before a first marriage (Bumpass and Sweet 1989).

17. According to the Census definition, a *household* consists of all the persons who occupy a housing unit. A household includes the related family members and all the unrelated persons, if any, such as lodgers, foster children, wards, or employees who share the unit. The census defines *family household* as a household maintained by a family, and any unrelated persons (unrelated subfamily members, other individuals, or both) who may be residing there.

18. The poverty rate for children under 18 in 2005 was 17.6, far exceeding the rate for adults (18 to 64 years) and the elderly (65 years and older) (11.1 percent and 10.1 percent, respectively) (DeNavas-Walt, Proctor, and Lee 2006, figure 5: 16).

19. Congress recently passed a bill that aims to assist family members who need a break to pay for substitute care for ailing family members and provides tax credit for long-term care for family members (*New York Times*, December 30, 2006).

20. Viewing the household as a mediating pathway between production and consumption processes was suggested by Randolph (1991) in his analysis of the relationship between labor and housing market processes. The author proposes an analytical framework that aims to explain the connection between the two markets and views the household as the "missing link" that connects labor and housing processes at the local level.

21. Tilly (2000) describes two images of the processes that produce social inequality. According to the "queue" image, inequality is seen as a process in which individuals line up "to pass a checkpoint where a monitor scans them, matches their various attributes with well-established templates, then shunts them into different channels, where they join other people having similar attributes." In contrast to this individualistic perspective that characterizes the human capital and status attainment perspectives, there exists another image, labeled "conversation," according to which inequality is seen as a "relation between persons or sets of persons in which interaction generates greater advantages for one than for another."

Chapter Three

1. Atkinson (1972) states that, from the two main types of life-cycle accumulation—steady saving out of income and "self-made fortune"—the great "new" fortunes of the wealthiest families grew out of the second process (Atkinson 1972; see also Brittain 1978, 9). Thurow (1975: 129) adds: "Large fortunes are passed from generation to generation, and great fortunes occur suddenly."

2. The names and some other identifying details have been changed.

3. Tilly (1998: 155) mentions four conditions that define opportunity hoarding: (1) a distinctive network; (2) valuable, renewable resources that are enhanced by the network's modus operandi; (3) sequestering of those resources by network members; and (4) creation of beliefs and practices that sustain network control of the resources.

4. While the membership rate of government employees increased between 1975 and 2004 from 25 to 36 percent, the percent in the private sector decreased from 21.5 to 8 percent in 2004, with the sharpest declines seen in the areas of construction, manufacturing, and transportation.

5. Tilly (1996) attributes this trend to the overall shift from full-time to part-time work, as well as to the shift from manufacturing to the service industries, which have long depended on a large number of part-time workers.

6. Friedrich Engels (1969) offers an interesting interpretation, making the distinction between rights of accumulation and rights of use as two separate types of property; he states that although it does not constitute ownership of capital, home-ownership does play an independent part in class formation, and can be viewed as "one criterion by means of which a distinct middle class may be identified" (Saunders 1978: 241).

7. Under market conditions, both homeownership and the type of housing (for example, public, private, mortgaged) determine the household class position. British scholars Rex and Moore (1967), for example, identify six classes, ranging from outright owner of the whole house, to that of the owner of a mortgaged whole house, and to that of the tenant of rooms in a lodging house.

8. British scholar Peter Saunders later explains (1978; 1984) that because home-ownership belongs in the domain of consumption—rather than production-based social cleavages—it cannot be treated as a sole basis for class formation. Housing inequality, however, remains an important arena in the stratification research:

> Because such cleavages are no less important than class divisions in understanding contemporary social stratification, and because housing plays such a key role in affecting life chances, in expressing social identity and (by virtue of the capital gains accruing to owners-occupiers) in modifying patterns of resource distribution and economic inequality, it follows that the question of home ownership must remain as central to other analysis of social divisions and political conflicts (Saunders 1984: 207).

9. While economists tend to define financial wealth as the total net worth minus net equity in owner-occupied housing, the focal point of the current analysis is in identifying specific forms of financial assets that are "central to the definition and operation of the capitalist economy" (Turner and Starnes 1976).

To measure this variable, the amount of net worth held in business, stocks, mutual funds, bonds, and real estate (excluding main residence) was divided by the total household net worth and was multiplied by 100; the upper level of the distribution was set on 100 percent. The analysis includes two sets of variables: a baseline model and a full model that includes the independent variable "household net worth."

I also calculated the percentage of wealth held in functional assets, that is, the equity held in home (main residence) and vehicle. The amount was divided by the total net worth and was multiplied by 100. The findings overall were consistent with the patterns reported in Appendix A. The exclusion of the asset poor from this analysis is appropriate for both theoretical and empirical reasons because they are virtually excluded from the commodity market.

An alternative method to estimate the distinct effect that demographic and socio-economic characteristics have on asset composition involves the prediction of the probability of asset ownership for different net worth brackets. Table A.3 in Appendix A displays the main results from four logistic regression equations predicting ownership of financial assets and homeownership for households at 20–60 percent of the net worth distribution (Models 1a, 1b respectively) and households at 60–100 percent of the distribution (Models 2a, 2b, respectively). On the one hand, the results indicate that marriage, especially intact marriage, is positively and strongly associated with ownership of functional assets (homeownership), but has a weak effect on possession of financial assets. On the other hand, whereas family transfers in the form of inheritance and gifts are strongly and positively associated with ownership of financial assets, these private transfers have a much smaller effect on homeownership. This pattern is interesting, as it suggests distinct trajectories to asset holdings; whereas being married is positively correlated with homeownership, intergenerational transfers are associated with the holdings of financial and income-producing assets.

10. Analysis also reveals that, consistent with expectations, when compared with householders in service occupations, householders in managerial and professional occupations are likely to hold a higher percentage of their wealth in financial assets (not shown).

11. Economists Caner and Wolff (2004; see also Haveman and Wolff 2001) define asset poverty as a condition in which access to "wealth-type resources" is insufficient to meet the basic needs for a limited period of time. The authors propose three measures of wealth-type resources (net worth, net worth minus home equity, and liquid wealth) and use poverty thresholds that were proposed by the National Academy of Sciences panel to assess the proportion of households that would be unable to live at the poverty level for three months if forced to liquidate their wealth and consume the proceeds. Empirical analysis reveals that the asset-poverty gap rose during the 1990s, and that nonelderly (younger than sixty-five years old) female-headed households with children have the highest rates of asset poverty, whereas married couples with children have higher rates of asset poverty than married couples with no children (Caner and Wolff 2004). This last finding is in line with the evidence on the growing economic burden that children have on the limited resources of parents and grandparents.

12. The lowest quintile in this survey includes households with net worth ranging from a negative value to $18,500. All things being equal, the probability that inheritors will be asset poor is 50 percent (Exp. b=.48) that of noninheritors. The effect of inter vivos gifts on asset poverty is even stronger, suggesting that the probability of middle aged households that received financial gifts from family members is 35 percent (Exp. b=.35) of that of households who have not received family transfers in the form of inter vivos gifts.

13. In addition, the effect of the coefficient estimate "attendance at religious services" (not shown) implies that attachment to community is inversely associated

with asset poverty (see Keister 2005 on the association between religion and wealth).

14. According to Weber, "A uniform class situation prevails only when completely unskilled and propertyless persons are dependent on irregular employment" (1958).

15. While definitions of the underclass vary over issues of race and ethnicity, gender, employment, family structure, and crime (see review in Marks 1991), there is a consensus in the literature that a key characteristic of the underclass is exclusion from the labor force and dependency on the welfare system. This definition of the underclass ignores the third subsystem of stratification, the property system (Lenski 1984).

16. In the current sample, this category includes households with net worth of $299,500 and higher.

Chapter Four

1. Studies on the top wealth holders conclude that one of the main ways to join the top strata of the wealth distribution is by becoming an active and successful entrepreneur. Atkinson (1972) states that self-made fortunes may derive from various strategies, such as the invention or development of a new technique or product; the ability to forecast future consumer needs; ownership of natural resources (but also the impact of government restrictions and the gains that can be made by those who are able to circumvent the restrictions); the creation and expansion of a company in new areas that become a growth industry; as well as pure luck.

2. According to Bollier (2002), some of the consequences of the exploitation of the commons include the siphoning of billions of dollars away from the public purse, the fostering of market concentration, and the reduction of competition.

3. An editorial in *Business Week* that discusses the debate over the proposal to repeal the estate tax reports that very few Americans currently pay estate taxes: "Of all Americans who died in 1998, only 46,000 of their estates paid any tax; 44,000 had estates of $4 million or less, and 2,000 paid about half the total. Estate tax insurance policies were used by many small-business heirs to pay their share and all estates were passed on without paying capital-gains taxes" (Gleckman 2001).

4. The data presented in figures 9–14 come from the Social Inequality III module (1999), the most recent social inequality module conducted by the International Social Survey Program (ISSP). The data reported exclude missing values and are unweighted. In the survey, which was conducted during years of increasing economic disparities in income and wealth and at the peak of the booming stock market, Americans were asked a series of questions on the factors that determine individual mobility, on the sources of social inequality, and on government's role in reducing economic inequality. The ISSP is a continuing annual program of cross-national collaboration on surveys covering topics important for social science research, such as work orientation, family and changing gender roles, national identity, and religion.

Each year, more than thirty countries participate in the ISSP, in which the same module of questions is asked cross-nationally. The ISSP representative in the United States is the National Opinion Research Center (NORC) at the University of Chicago.

5. Nathan Glazer (2003 in Bartles 2004a: 5) has argued that, unlike the citizens of other countries, Americans do not seem to care much about inequality in general and tend to channel their "outrage against those who do not play fair—not outrage over inequality as such."

6. People seem to agree with this interpretation; about 45 percent of the respondents in the General Social Survey (GSS) either agree or strongly agree with the view that "inequality continues to exist because ordinary people don't join together to get rid of it."

7. Analysis not shown revealed that those identifying themselves as belonging to the working, middle, or upper class were more likely to express support in this statement than those identifying themselves as lower class; this pattern suggests that the narrative of success by one's own effort correlates with his/her subjective class status.

8. Sociologists Davis and Moore (1945) argue that certain positions in society, such as doctors or lawyers, carry different degrees of prestige than others, because they have greater functional importance for the society, and require more talent and specialized skills than other positions. Because only a limited number of individuals have the talent and skills to fill these important positions, and because the conversion of talent into skills involves a long and, in most cases, expensive training period, the only way to persuade the talented persons to undergo these sacrifices and to insure that these positions will be filled competently is to offer sufficient social and economic incentives for them to acquire the necessary training.

9. This popular view on the sources of economic status is in line with the "culture of poverty" thesis that views the poor as a subculture whose values and work ethics differ from those shared by the nonpoor. These values, the literature contends, are transmitted to children, who internalize them, and through this socialization process the "culture of poverty" is reproduced across generations (Kerbo 2000). Research examining cultural differences between the poor and nonpoor, however, fails to provide convincing evidence in support of the view that the poor adhere to a distinct value system (see Iceland 2003a).

Chapter Five

1. Indeed, the "family decline" view has been criticized on grounds that it is largely based on demographic changes in family structure, but sidesteps the question of whether variation in kinship forms actually represents a weakening of the family (Furstenberg 2005).

2. The authors (Sandberg and Hofferth 2001) report that these changes are largely attributed to behavioral, rather than structural, elements such as family structure, maternal labor force participation, and maternal education.

3. Research on married women suggests that individualism and familial bonds should not be viewed as two contrasting values.

> For married women, individualism can be a tool to resist old and enforce new terms of marital commitment, including nurturance, commitment, and relational responsibility shared by both spouses. When mothers use the power of individualism for relational ends—by working to provide, by removing children from violent households, or by refusing to be subordinated—individualism is neither an end in itself nor easily severed from committed responsibility. (Hackstaff 2005: 208)

4. Goldscheider and Goldscheider (1994: 35) report: "The likelihood that young adults in the U.S. return home for four months or more after having been away for at least that length of time increased from 22% to about 40% between the 1920s and the 1980s."

5. About 30 percent of those in the 65–74 age group work for pay, about one-third engage in formal volunteering for an organization, more than half engage in informal volunteering, and more than one-third provide care for family members (including spouses, grandchildren, and parents). (See Johnson and Schaner 2005.)

6. Studying intergenerational contacts in Japan, a society that is characterized by strong intergenerational transfers of social and financial support, Peng (2000: 91) asserts that, whereas the practice of family support seen in Japan might be rooted in tradition, its continuing existence is reinforced by the legal framework that holds family members legally responsible for one another's welfare.

7. One of the key potential challenges of cross-national attitude research is how to establish cross-national validity of indicators; specifically, how to ensure that the variation seen in the data reflects actual differences in attitudes rather than differences in the meaning and connotations of the concepts measured in the study. As Svallfors (1997) notes, this problem has been dealt with as far as possible within the ISSP. The ISSP questionnaire design is a product of cross-national collaboration, involving drafting groups composed of researchers from all the participating nations to ensure clarity and comparability of meaning between the versions.

8. Analysis of attitudes on whether children should care for old parents by age categories (not shown), revealed strong support for such familial obligation among the younger age category (18–30); 42.7 percent of the respondents in this age group strongly agreed with the statement and 35.9 percent agreed. The lowest level of support was documented among the oldest category (61 years and older); only 23.9 percent strongly agreed with the statement and 32.5 agreed with it.

9. The data for this analysis come from The Generations Survey. The data were collected in 1995 under the sponsorship of the International Longevity Center, Mount Sinai School of Medicine, New York. The survey was based on a national random sample of men and women 18 years and older (N=1500) (see Silver and Muller 1997).

10. I utilized ordered logit regression (OLR) involving a proportional-odds model to test the determinants of attitudes about assistance to elderly parents and about inherited property to children. The OLR models take the ordered nature of

ordinal variables and provide one set of coefficients for each independent variable. The models assume that the effects of the independent variables are constant across the comparisons—that is, that the slope (coefficients) for the variables in the equations would not vary significantly if they were estimated separately. I tested the proportional-odds assumption, and the results suggest that that the assumption is reasonable for the full models (prob. chi^2 > .05) (see Elmelech 2005).

11. Logan and Spitze (1996) suggest that such age differences in attitudes toward filial obligations actually highlight intergenerational solidarity: older people's attitudes seem to give greater weight to the needs of younger generations and vice versa (Bengston and Lowenstein 2003: 13).

12. Because the number of respondents that disagreed with the statement about family obligations for children's education is small—a pattern that might lead to biased results (see King and Zeng 2001)—I used ordered-least-square (OLS) regression to predict this attitudinal variable (see, for example, Loftus 2001; Burr and Mutchler 1999). To assess whether the "not sure/don't know" category in the dependent variables indicates a lack of clear opinion on the subject matter (Fazio 1990), a condition that could violate the ordered nature of the variables, I tested two sets of models—one that included the respondents who answered "not sure/don't know" to the statements, and one that excluded them. Although the two sets of models led to identical substantive conclusions, the inclusion of the category "not sure/don't know" in one of the models tested has led to a violation of the parallel regression assumption. For this reason, table 3 reports results from models that exclude the category "not sure/don't know."

13. Among the twenty-nine countries that participated in the ISSP survey, and with only one exception (Israel), the U.S. data show the highest proportion of people expressing reliance on parents as a source of money in times of need. The Israeli pattern is partially attributed to the high percentage of the Arab respondents who expressed a greater reliance on their fathers to provide such assistance. This ethnic minority comprises about 20 percent of all Israeli citizens and is characterized by traditional familial values.

14. Due to the sample size, it is impossible to derive reliable data by age and marital category, even when the variable age is operationalized to include a limited number of categories. Analysis by gender categories revealed no substantial gender differences vis-à-vis the dependent variables.

Chapter Six

1. The terms African Americans and blacks and the terms Hispanics and Latinos are used interchangeably depending on the terms used in the cited sources and primary data utilized in this chapter.

2. Analyzing the schooling level among the foreign-born population in the United States, Chiswick (1986) reports two patterns among recent immigrants: a declining level of education for the growing Hispanic population, offset by the high

level of education among the increasing Asian population. Both high-skilled and low-skilled immigrants face the changing labor market, which resulted in their significantly lower wage rates compared with both former cohorts of immigrants (Borjas 1994), and with similarly educated white counterparts (Waldinger and Bozorgmehr 1996).

3. Four decades ago, Terrell (1967) reported that blacks invest almost two-thirds of their wealth (64 percent) in "functional assets" (homes and vehicles), while 36 percent was held in income-producing and financial assets. By contrast, white households held only 37 percent of their wealth in functional assets, while 63 percent was held in income-producing and financial assets (in Oliver and Shapiro 1995: 105). Two decades later, these figures remained almost intact; Oliver and Shapiro (1995, table 5.3: 106) report that black households held 72.5 percent of their wealth in functional assets and only 27.5 percent in financial assets, whereas whites held 49 percent of their wealth in functional assets and 51 percent in financial assets.

4. Browne (1974) discusses the limitations of income as a gauge of blacks' economic well-being by stressing that income sources, rather than the annual amount of income, need to be taken into consideration when studying the economic well-being of blacks: "In comparing the income of blacks with that of other groups, all income dollars are treated as identical, whether earned or unearned. Yet, for the U.S. as a whole, nearly a quarter of the national income originates from property or wealth; in contrast, virtually the entire income of the black community originates from wages, transfer payments, and self-employment in marginal enterprises—a fact which may be nearly as significant as the income figures themselves" (Browne 1974: 29). The proportion of income that the elderly (65 years and over) generate from financial and income-producing assets is larger in the United States than in European countries.

5. The cultural explanations for racial inequality were also criticized on the grounds that they involve circular reasoning in tending to inaccurately "infer group values and norms from group socioeconomic outcomes and then pointing to such values as causal factors, while ignoring structural constraints" (see Taylor 2002).

6. Studies on business ownership among racial-ethnic groups found that marital status and length of residence in the United States are the principal characteristics differentiating workers and entrepreneurs: "In all groups, the self-employed are much more likely to be married and much less likely to be recent immigrants" (Portes and Zhou 1995: 508).

7. As Wilson (1980: 158–61) acknowledges, the increase in the income gap between whites and blacks occurs, to a large extent, as a result of the increase in the proportion of black families with female heads during the 1960s and 1970s.

8. Oliver and Shapiro (1995, 6–7) state: "Inherited wealth is a very special kind of money imbued with the shadows of race. Racial difference in inheritance is a key feature of our story. For the most part, blacks will not partake in divvying up the baby boom bounty."

9. This finding is consistent with the argument on lack of traditions in business ownership (Frazier 1939). In the same vein, Chiteji and Stafford (1999) postulate

that portfolio choices are influenced by a "social learning process" whereby "parental decisions to hold certain kinds of assets influence the subsequent choices of their children."

10. Based on data from 2001, India topped the list with $10 billion, Mexico followed with $9.9 billion, and the Philippines was third with $6.4 billion. The three countries' remittances accounted for about 36 percent of total workers' remittance receipts of developing countries (some $72.3 billion) (GlobalNation 2003; Pew 2003).

11. About 18 percent of all adults in Mexico and 28 percent in El Salvador are remittance receivers—and the impact is no longer limited to rural or poor communities (Pew 2003).

12. Our goal here is to estimate the extent to which racial-ethnic-specific differentials in each of the distinct factors emphasized in this study—human capital, family structure, and intergenerational transfers—shapes asset-based inequality across racial and ethnic lines. Based on the racial-ethnic-specific demographic and socioeconomic attributes, the question examined is: What would the racial ownership gap between minority and white households be if minority households had the same demographic and socioeconomic characteristics as whites have? This procedure involves three stages. First, I produce the weighted mean values and specify separate logistic regression equations by racial-ethnic origin. Second, I estimate the predicted racial-ethnic specific ownership rates for white, black, and Hispanic households by using the following formula:

$$\text{Prob (ownership)} = \frac{1}{1 + e^{-(\hat{\beta}_0 + \sum_{i=1}^{l} \hat{\beta}_i \bar{X}_i)}}$$

Where $\hat{\beta}_0$ is the estimated intercept of the model; $\hat{\beta}_i$ is the estimated coefficient of the model and the sub-is indicate explanatory variables included in the logistic regression models; $\bar{X}_i$ is the sample mean for the corresponding variable (see Elmelech 2002). In order to estimate the predicted ownership rate, I imputed the sample mean for each variable i, $\bar{X}_i$, and, based on the logistic regression models, apply the estimated coefficient, $\hat{\beta}_i$.

Third, a standardization technique is used to assess the extent to which racial-ethnic differences in demographic and socioeconomic background explain differences in portfolio.

13. If Hispanic households had the same nativity composition as white households, the Hispanic-white differences in homeownership and in ownership of financial assets would go down by approximately 20 percent.

14. The relatively high rates of marriage in the white population, compared with the lower rate of marriage in the African American population, explain about 20 percent of the racial gap in homeownership In other words, if African Americans have had the same marital status characteristics as whites, the racial gap in homeownership rate—measured as the racial ownership ratio—would have been smaller by 20 percent. Racial variations in marital status contribute to the racial gap in ownership

of financial and liquid assets as well, reducing the race-ownership ratio by 8 percent and 10 percent, respectively.

15. Intergenerational transfers explain approximately 11 percent of the black-white gaps in financial assets. For example, white-black occupation and education differentials account for 20 percent and 14 percent, respectively, of the race-ownership ratio in financial wealth. Racial variation in the number of children and nativity status has no effect on the racial ownership gap among middle-aged households.

16. For example, if middle-aged Hispanics have had the same occupational characteristics as whites, the ethnic ownership gap in financial assets would have been smaller by 25 percent.

17. Because the right-hand skew of net worth distribution creates complications in regression analysis, the dependent variable (net worth) was transformed by taking natural logarithms. However, the log transformation cannot be applied to those households with zero or negative net worth. Furthermore, the least squares estimation of a regression model for a truncated sample, which includes only those households with positive net worth, or a censored sample in which an arbitrary zero value is used for those households with a nonpositive value, leads to biased and inconsistent regression estimators (Amemiya 1985: chap. 10; Land and Russell 1996; Long 1997). For these reasons, the multivariate analysis presented in the following tables is based on a lower-bound Tobit regression model.

The Tobit model is appropriate for samples that have information on the independent variables for the entire sample, but have only limited information about the dependent variable. The Tobit regression model can be described as:

$$y^*i = xiB + ui$$

Where

$$
\begin{aligned}
yi &= y^*i & \text{if} & & y^*i > 0 \\
&= 0 & \text{if} & & y^*i < 0
\end{aligned}
$$

Where the xs are observed for all cases, y^* is a latent variable (net worth) that is observed for values greater than 0 and is censored for values less than or equal to zero. The Tobit model yields estimates of the effects of the regressors that have good statistical properties in the presence of all observations (i.e., households with positive, zero, and negative net worth) (see Amemiya 1985; Long 1997; Land and Russell 1996).

Appendix C-3 presents the results of a multivariate (Tobit) analysis of logged net worth. Three models are displayed. The baseline model includes human capital (education and parental education), labor market characteristics (labor income, occupation), as well as control variables: religion and religiosity, geographical characteristics (residence in metropolitan area and residence in the south region), and demographic characteristics (age, gender, native-born, age, size of household, number of children).

Findings from the baseline model (column 1) reveal that compared with white house-holders, black and Hispanic households have a lower level of wealth, net of labor market, and demographic attributes. The results also show that the effect of being Hispanic is much weaker than the effect of black origin when compared with white (B=-1.1 and B=-2.3, respectively). This pattern suggests that a substantial portion of the gap between whites and Hispanics is explained by differentials in human capital and labor market attributes. As expected, educational attainment is positively associated with net worth.

In model 2, to which marital status is added, it becomes apparent that although the predictive capability of race-ethnicity is still significant, the effect of racial-ethnic origin has declined substantially (from b=-2.3 to b=-1.6 for blacks, and fromb=-1.1 to b=-.73 for Hispanics). This finding suggests that for both blacks and Hispanics, racial differentials in marital status explain a substantial portion (about 30 percent) of the racial gap in wealth. Compared with the reference category "divorced," married couples—especially those who never experienced family disruption—are likely to have higher levels of wealth. In the full model (3), measures of intergenerational transfers were added to model 2. The results show that the inclusion of family transfers further reduces the coefficient estimates of the race-ethnic variables by approximately 10 percent (from b=-1.65 to b=-1.47 for blacks and from b=-.73 to b=-.65 for Hispanics). Net of human capital and labor market attributes (e.g. labor income, employment status, education, parental education, and occupation), as well as demographic differentials and marital status, receipt of financial transfers in the form of inter vivos gifts, and bequests have strong positive effects on household total net worth.

18. The results show that the inclusion of family transfers further reduces the coefficient estimates of the race-ethnic variables by approximately 10 percent (from b=-1.65 to b=-1.47 for blacks and from b=-.73 to b=-.65 for Hispanics).

19. In a recent study on labor market remuneration of Mexican immigrants in the United States, Phillips and Massey (1999) found decreasing returns on labor market participation since the passage of the Immigration Control and Reform Act (IRCA) in 1986.

Chapter Seven

1. Ogbu (1987), for example, states that while both whites and nonwhites have internal class divisions, their respective class structures differ in both development and attributes, and the economic problems endured by minority poor do not result merely from lower-class status:

> Instead they are consequences of the double stratification of class and racial caste. As a result, lower-class blacks share certain attributes common to all lower-class people everywhere, but they also have distinctive attributes because they belong to subordinate racial caste. (Ogbu 1987: 239–40)

2. Because the dependent variable is the natural logarithm of net worth, the coefficients can be transformed using the natural logarithm to indicate a percentage increase in net worth. For example, in the white model, the effect of being employed is 1.73 times that of unemployed (Exp 0.55=1.73). Applying the McDonald and Moffit correction factor (1980; see also Roncek 1992) enables us to illustrate the differential effects that the independent variables have on wealth for cases with positive net worth.

3. For example, within the white population, the effect of receipt of family transfers on wealth is 1.9. That is, all things being equal, the amount of net worth held by white households who received family transfers is 90 percent higher than the amount held by white households who have not received family transfers. The comparable effects for blacks and Hispanics are greater—3.6 and 3.5, respectively. These findings are in line with previous evidence on black-white differences in business ownership. Whereas having a self-employed father increases the probability of self-employment among both whites and blacks, the effect of parental self-employment varies: "the intergenerational link in self-employment appears to be stronger for blacks than for whites" (Fairlie 1999: 92).

4. This pattern was also evident in models that included three categories of marriage: "Married, intact"; "Married, married before"; and the omitted term "Other (divorced, never married, separated, widowed)." In these models the coefficient for "marriage intact" was B=1.9 for whites, B=3.3 for blacks, and B=3.6 for Hispanics (all statistically significant at the P>.001 level). The comparable effect for "Married, married before" was B=1.5, B=2.6, and B=3.6, respectively (all statistically significant at the P>.001 level) (Elmelech 2002).

5. The net worth held by native-born Hispanics is about three times greater than the amount held by foreign-born Hispanics, even after controlling for education and labor market characteristics.

6. Gender differentials in intermarriage among other racial and ethnic groups reveal a different pattern; for most Asian groups, women's out-marriage substantially surpasses that of their male counterparts, whereas insignificant gender differences in intermarriage are observed among Mexican Americans and Puerto Ricans (Jacobs and Labov 2002, table 1: 631).

7. Though many participants in the ABC program "indicated that they continued to date whites as well as blacks in college, by the time they left college, relatively few black ABC graduates continued to date whites. Some attributed this to less tolerance of interracial relationships in their working environments than in their college environment" (Zweigenhaft and Domhoff 2003: 92).

Chapter Eight

1. The aging of American society has led economists and policymakers to raise concerns about what most acknowledge will be a shortage in the Social Security program's

funding in the coming decades, and to propose plans that aim to increase saving and reliance on private resources (Bernanke 2006).

2. Some economists now predict that the amount of bequests the baby boomers receive will be overall more modest than earlier assessments, but highly unequal; the modest inheritance transfer to the baby boom generation is attributed to longer life expectancy and soaring health-care costs of elderly parents, and the distinctively large size of the baby boomer cohort, which affects the total sum of wealth that each sibling receives:

> Although baby boomers will inherit more as a group than their parents did, inheritances will be roughly the same as those of their parents when considered relative to labor earn-ings. Our estimates show that the size of the aggregate flow of U.S. bequests, measured relative to labor compensation, has not changed much in the last 35 years and is likely to remain near its current level for the next decade and a half. (Gokhale and Kotlikoff 2000: 3)

3. While in 1960, about 14 percent of the mothers in the bottom quartile of edu-cation and 4.5 percent of women in the top quartile were single, the comparable fig-ures for 2000 were 43 percent and 7 percent, respectively (McLanahan 2004, figure 2: 611; see also Ellwood and Jencks 2004, figures 1.4 and 1.5: 13–14).

4. Kreider and Fields (2005: 9–10) report that children living with grandparents more often live in poor households than children living in households with no grand-parents present (23 percent and 17 percent, respectively). Among children living with their mother only, those living in households with a grandparent present, the poverty rate was 24 percent, but the rate was higher for black children (28 percent) than white or Hispanic children (19 and 18 percent, respectively). And while these multigenerational living arrangements often involve positive social outcomes for children and their elderly caregivers, they are also associated with greater financial stress for the elderly (see Jarrett 1994).

5. Other programs include enhancing homeownership for the poor, electronic banking, and children's trust funds (Sherraden 2005).

6. The CATO Institute, a strong supporter of initiative, defines *ownership society* as a society that values responsibility, liberty, and property: "Individuals are empow-ered by freeing them from dependence on government handouts and making them owners instead, and in control of their own lives and destinies. In the ownership so-ciety, patients control their own health care, parents control their own childrens' ed-ucation, and workers control their retirement savings" (Boaz 2005).

7. In 2005, at a lecture given at the Indiana Black Expo, President Bush (U.S. Office of the Press Secretary, July 14, 2005) describes his vision of the ownership so-ciety:

> To ensure that the promise of America reaches all our citizens, we're working to build an ownership society in which more of our citizens have a personal stake in the future of our country. When you own something, your life is more secure. When you own something,

you have more dignity. When you own something, you have greater independence. The more people who own something in America means this country is better off. So we've been working to promote an ownership society. I want more people from all walks of life, including African Americans, to have a chance to own their own business.

8. Brown, Kuttner, and Shapiro (2005) provide examples that demonstrate the shifting of risks from the public to the private sphere during the past quarter century; these include, among other things, the shifting of pension coverage from the corporate sector to the individual, in the form of 401(k), and the shutdown of federal subsidies for rental housing (see also Wray 2005).

9. Studies have shown that residential segregation is high in metropolitan areas where the concentration of poverty is severe, and tends to undermine the well-being of minority groups in both the labor and the commodity markets; employment opportunities, educational attainment, homeownership, business ownership, and access to credit, as well as interracial cohabitation and marriage, are affected by an exceedingly high levels of social and spatial segregation (Massey, Gross, and Shibuya 1994; Quillian and Campbell 2003).

10. As survey data showed (chapter 2), people who are less likely to accept the equal opportunity ethos and more likely to believe in extra-individual determinants of mobility are also more likely to view inequality as extreme and are inclined to support government redistributive policies.

References

Aizcorbe, Ana M., Arthur B. Kennickell, and Kevin B. Moore. 2003. Recent Changes in U.S. Family Finances: Evidence from the 1998 and 2001 Survey of Consumer Finances. *Federal Reserve Bulletin*.

Ajzen, Icek, and Martin Fishbein. 1980. *Understanding Attitudes and Predicting Social Behavior*. Englewood Cliffs, NJ: Prentice-Hall.

Alba, Richard D., and John R. Logan. 1992. Assimilation and Stratification in the Homeownership Patterns of Racial and Ethnic Groups. *International Migration Review* 26 (1992): 1314–41.

Aleman, Sara. 1997. *Hispanic Elders and Human Services*. New York: Garland Publications.

Allen, John, and Chris Hamnett. 1990. *Housing and Labour Markets: Building the Connections*. London: Unwin Hayman.

Allen, Michael P. 1989. *The Founding Fortunes: A New Anatomy of the Super-Rich Families in America*. New York: Truman Talley Books.

Alwin, Duane F. 1996. Coresidence Beliefs in American Society, 1973 to 1991. *Journal of Marriage and the Family* 58, no. 2: 393–403.

Alwin, Duane F., and Arland Thornton. 1984. Family Origins and the Schooling Process: Early Versus Late Influence of Parental Characteristics. *American Sociological Review* 49, no. 6: 784–802.

American Sociological Association. 2005. *Race, Ethnicity, and the American Labor Market: What's at Work?* Sydney S. Spivack Program in Applied Social Research and Social Policy. June. www.asanet.org/galleries/default-file/RaceEthnicity_LaborMarket.pdf.

Amemiya, Takeshi, 1985. Advanced Econometrics. Harvard University Press.

Angel Ronald J., Jacqueline L. Angel, Geum-Yon Lee, and Kyriakos S. Markides. 1999. Age at Migration and Family Dependency among Older Mexican American Immigrants: Recent Evidence from the Mexican American EPESE. *The Gerontologist* 39, no. 1: 59–65.

Angel, Ronald J., and Jacqueline L. Angel. 1997. *Who Will Care for Us? Aging and Long-Term Care in Multicultural America.* New York: New York University Press.

Antonucci, Toni C., and J. S. Jackson. 1990. The Role of Reciprocity in Social Support. In *Social Support: An Interactional View*, ed. I. G. Sarason, B. R. Sarason, and G. R. Pierce. New York: Wiley, 111–28.

Aponte, Robert. 1991. Urban Hispanic Poverty: Disaggregations and Explanations. *Social Problems* 38, no. 4: 516–28.

Arber, Sara, and Claudine Attias-Donfut, eds. 2000. *The Myth of Generational Conflict: The Family and State in Ageing Societies.* London: Routledge.

Arrondel, Luc, and Andre Masson. 2006. Altruism, Exchange or Indirect Reciprocity? What Do the Data on Family Transfers Show? In *Handbook of the Economics of Giving, Altruism and Reciprocity*, vol. 2, ed. Serge-Christophe Kolm and Jean Mercier Ythier. Amsterdam: Elsevier/North-Holland.

Atkinson, A. B. 1975. *The Economics of Inequality.* Oxford: Clarendon Press.

———. 1972. *Unequal Shares: Wealth in Britain.* London: Penguin.

Attias-Donfut, Claudine, and Sara Arber. 2000. Equity and Solidarity Across the Generations. In *The Myth of Generational Conflict: The Family and State in Ageing Societies*, ed. Sara Arber and Claudine Attias-Donfut. London: Routledge, 1–22.

Attias-Donfut, Claudine, and F. C. Wolff. 2000. The Redistributive Effects of Generational Transfers. In *The Myth of Generational Conflict: The Family and State in Ageing Societies*, ed. Sara Arber and Claudine Attias-Donfut. London: Routledge, 22–46.

Avery, Robert B. and Rendall, Michael S. 1994. Estimating the Size and Distribution of the Baby Boomers' Prospective Inheritances. Mimeo, Cornell University.

Avery, Robert B., and Michael S. Rendall. 2002. Lifetime Inheritances of Three Generations of Whites and Blacks. *American Journal of Sociology* 107, no. 5: 1300–46.

Axinn, William, Greg J. Duncan, and Arland Thornton. 1997. The Effects of Parents' Income, Wealth, and Attitudes on Children's Completed Schooling and Self-Esteem. In *Consequences of Growing Up Poor*, ed. Greg J. Duncan and Jeanne Brooks-Gunn. New York: Russell Sage, 518–40.

Bachu, Amara, and Martin O'Connell. 2001. Fertility of American Women: June 2000. Current Population Reports. U.S. Department of Commerce. P20–543RV.

Bahchieva, Raisa, Susan M. Wachter, and Elizabeth Warren. 2005. Mortgage Debt, Bankruptcy and the Sustainability of Homeownership. In *Credit Markets for the Poor*, ed. Patrick Bolton and Howard Rosenthal. New York: Russell Sage, 73–113.

Barber, Bernard. 1957. *Social Stratification: A Comparative Analysis of Structure and Process.* New York: Harcourt Brace.

Barber, Jennifer S. 2001. Ideational Influences on the Transition to Parenthood: Attitudes toward Childbearing and Competing Alternatives. *Social Psychology Quarterly* 64, no. 2: 101–27.

Barlett, Donald L., and James B. Steele. 1992. *America: What Went Wrong.* Kansas City, MO: Andrews and McMeel.

Barlow, James, and Simon Duncan. 1994. *Success and Failure in Housing Provision.* London: Pergamon.

Barringer, Herbert R., David T. Takeuchi, and Peter Xenos. 1990. Education, Occupational Prestige and Income of Asian Americans. *Sociology of Education* 63, no. 1: 27–43.

Bartels, Larry M. 2004a. Homer Gets a Tax Cut: Inequality and Public Policy in the American Mind. Paper prepared for the annual meeting of the American Political Science Association, Philadelphia, PA. www.princeton.edu/csdp/research/pdfs/homer.pdf, accessed November 20, 2006.

———. 2004b. Unenlightened Self-Interest: The Strange Appeal of Estate-Tax Repeal. *The American Prospect*, Online Edition. Issued 06.07.04 www.prospect.org/web/page.ww?section=root&name=ViewPrint&articleId=7754, accessed November 20, 2006.

Barzel, Yoram. 1997. *Economic Analysis of Property Rights.* Cambridge, UK: Cambridge University Press.

Bassett, William F., Michael J. Fleming, and Anothony P. Rodriques. 1998. How Workers Use 401(k) Plans: The Participation, Contribution and Withdrawal Decisions. *National Tax Journal* 51, no. 2: 263–89.

Bates, Timothy, and David Howell. 1997. Status of Self-Employed and Employee African Americans in the New York City Construction Industry. In *Race, Markets, and Social Outcomes*, ed. Patrick L. Mason and Rhonda Michele Williams. Boston: Kluwer Academic Publishers, 15–31.

Bean, Frank D., and Marta Tienda. 1987. *The Hispanic Population of the United States.* New York: Russell Sage.

Becker, Gary S. 1991. *A Treatise on the Family.* Cambridge, MA: Harvard University Press.

Belcher, John R. 1994. How to Help the Working Poor Develop Assets. *Journal of Sociology and Social Welfare* 21, no. 4: 57–75.

Bellah, Robert N., Richard Madsen, William H. Sullivan, Ann Swidler, and Steven M. Tipton. 1985. *Habits of the Heart: Individualism and Commitment in American Life.* Berkeley, CA: University of California Press.

Bengston, Vern L. 2001. Beyond the Nuclear Family: The Increasing Importance of Multigenerational Bonds (The Burgess Award Lecture). *Journal of Marriage and the Family* 63, no. 1: 1–15.

———. 1996. Continuities and Discontinuities in Intergenerational Relationships over time. In V. L. Bengston (ed.) *Adulthood and Aging: Research on Continuities and Discontinuities.* New York: Springer.

―――. 1996. *Adulthood and Aging: Research on Continuities and Discontinuities.* New York: Springer Publishing.

Bengtson, Vern L., and Ariela Lowenstein, eds. 2003. *Global Aging and Its Challenges to Families.* Hawthorne, NY: Aldine de Gruyter.

Bengston Vern, Ariella Lowenstein, Norella M. Putney, and Daphna Gans. 2003. Global Aging and the Challenge to Families. In Global Aging and Challenges to Families. Bengston V. and A Lowenstein (eds.). New York: Walter de Gruyter. Pp. 1-27.

Berglof, Erik, and Patrick Bolton. 2002. The Great Divide and Beyond: Financial Architecture in Transition. *The Journal of Economic Perspectives* 16, no. 1: 77–100.

Bergstrom, Theodore C. 1996. Economics in a Family Way. *Journal of Economic Literature* 34, no. 4: 1903–34.

Bernanke, Ben S. 2006. The Coming Demographic Transition: Will We Treat Future Generations Fairly? Remarks by Chairman Bernanke before the Washington Economic Club, Washington, DC, October 4. www.federalreserve.gov/newsevents/speech/bernanke20061004a.htm.

―――. 2003. Balance Sheets and the Recovery. Remarks by Governor Ben S. Bernanke at the 41st Annual Winter Institute, St. Cloud State University, St. Cloud, Minnesota, February 21, 2003. www.federalreserve.gov/Boarddocs/Speeches/2003/20030221/default.htm.

Bernheim, B. Douglas. 1991. How Strong are Bequest Motives? Evidence Based on Estimates of the Demand for Life Insurance and Annuities. *Journal of Political Economy* 99, no. 5: 899–927.

Bernstein, Robert. 1995. Sixty-Five Plus in the United States. Bureau of the Census, Statistical Brief. www.census.gov/population/socdemo/statbriefs/agebrief.html, accessed October 28, 2006.

Bhattacharya, Uptel, and B. Ravikumar. 2001. Capital Markets and the Evolution of Family Businesses. *The Journal of Business* 74, no. 2: 187–219.

Bianchi, Suzanne M. 2000. Maternal Employment and Time with Children: Dramatic Change or Surprising Continuity? *Demography* 37, no. 4: 401–14.

―――. 1999. Feminization and Juvenalization of Poverty: Trends, Relative Risks, Causes and Consequences. *Annual Review of Sociology* 25: 307–33.

Bianchi, Suzanne M., Reynolds Farley, and Daphne Spain. 1982. Racial Inequalities in Housing: An Examination of Recent Trends. *Demography* 19, no. 1: 37–51.

Blackwell, James E. 2005. *The Black Community: Diversity and Unity.* New York: HarperCollins.

Blanchflower, David G., Philip B. Levine, and David J. Zimmerman. 2003. Discrimination in the Small-Business Credit Market. *Review of Economics and Statistics* 85, no. 4: 930–43.

Blanchflower, David G., and Andrew J. Oswald. 1998. What Makes an Entrepreneur? *Journal of Labor Economics* 16, no. 1: 26–60.

Blau, Francine D., and John W. Graham. 1990. Black-White Differences in Wealth and Asset Composition. *The Quarterly Journal of Economics* 105, no. 2: 321–39.

Blau, Peter, and Otis D. Duncan. 1967. *The American Occupational Structure*. New York: Wiley.

Blinder, Alan S. 1988. Comments on Chapter 1 and Chapter 2. In *Modelling the Accumulation and Distribution of Wealth*, ed. D. Kessler and A. Masson. Oxford: Clarendon Press, 68–77.

Bluestone, Barry, and Bennett Harrison. 1982. *The Deindustrialization of America*. New York: Basic Books.

Blumstein, P., and P. Schwartz. 1983. *American Couples*. New York: William Morrow.

Boaz, David. 2005. Defining an Ownership Society. Washington, DC: Cato Institute. www.cato.org/special/ownership_society/boaz.html.

Bollier, David. 2002. *Silent Theft: The Private Plunder of Our Common Wealth*. New York: Routledge.

Bolton, Patrick, and Howard Rosenthal, eds. 2005. *Credit Markets for the Poor*. New York: Russell Sage.

Borjas, George J. 1994. The Economics of Immigration. *Journal of Economic Literature* 32, no. 4: 1667–1717.

Borjas, George J., and Marta Tienda, eds. 1993. The Employment and Wages of Legalized Immigrants. *International Migration Review* 27, no. 4: 712–47.

Boulding, Kenneth. 2003. Kenneth Boulding on Possible Consequences of Increased Life Expectancy. *Population and Development Review* 29, no. 3: 493–504.

Brady, Peter J., Glenn B. Canner, and Dean M. Maki. 2000. The Effects of Recent Mortgage Refinancing. (July) *Federal Reserve Bulletin*, 441–50.

Bratsberg, Bernt, and Terrell Dek. 2002. School Quality and Returns to Education of U.S. Immigrants. *Economic Inquiry* 40, no. 2: 177–98.

Braun, Dennis D. 1997. *The Rich Get Richer: The Rise of Income Inequality in the United States and the World*. Chicago: Nelson-Hall.

Breen, Richard. 2005. Foundations of a Neo-Weberian Class Analysis. In *Approaches to Class Analysis*, ed. E. O. Wright. Cambridge, UK: Cambridge University Press.

Brittain, John A. 1978. *Inheritance and the Inequality of Material Wealth*. Washington, DC: Brookings Institution.

Brown, J. D. 1956. The American Philosophy of Social Insurance. *Social Service Review* 39: 1-8.

Brown, J. Larry, Robert Kuttner, and Thomas M. Shapiro. 2005. *Building a Real Ownership Society*. New York: The Century Foundation Press.

Browne, Robert S. 1974. Wealth Distribution and Its Impact on Minorities. *Review of Black Political Economy* 4: 27–39.

Brudner, Lilyan A., and Douglas R. White. 1997. Class, Property, and Structural Endogemy: Visualizing Networked Histories. *Theory and Society* 26, no. 2/3: 161–208.

Bucks Brian K., Arthur K. Kennickell, and Kevin B. Moore. 2006. Recent Changes in U.S. Family Finances: Evidence from the 2001 and 2004 Survey of Consumer Finances. *Federal Reserve Bulletin*, March.

Bumpass, Larry. 1990. What's Happening to the Family? Interactions Between Demographic and Institutional Change. *Demography* 27, no. 4: 483–98.

Bumpass, Larry, and Hsien-Hen Lu. 2000. Trends in Cohabitation and Implications for Children's Family Contexts in the U.S. *Population Studies* 54, no. 1: 29–41.

Bumpass, Larry, and J. Sweet. 1989. National Estimates of Cohabitation. *Demography* 26, no. 4: 615–25.

Burr, Jeffrey A., and Jan E. Mutchler. 1999. Racial and Ethnic Variation in Norms of Filial Responsibility among Older Persons. *Journal of Marriage and the Family* 61, no. 3: 674–87.

Burrows, Roger, and Catherine Marsh, eds. 1992. *Consumption and Class: Divisions and Change.* Basingstoke, UK: Macmillan.

Burstein, Paul. 1998. Bringing the Public Back In: Should Sociologists Consider the Impact of Public Opinion on Public Policy? *Social Forces* 77, no. 1: 27–62.

Butcher, Kristin F. 1994. Black Immigrants in the United States: A Comparison with Native Blacks and Other Immigrants. *Industrial and Labor Relations Review* 47, no. 2: 265–84.

Caldwell, John. 1978. A Theory of Fertility: From High Plateau to Destabilization. *Population Development Review* 4, no. 4: 553–77.

Cancio, A. Silvia, T. David Evans, and David J. Maume Jr. 1996. Reconsidering the Declining Significance of Race: Racial Differences in Early Career Wages. *American Sociological Review* 61: 541–56.

Caner, Asena, and Edward Wolff. 2004. Asset Poverty in the United States: Its Persistence in an Expansionary Economy. The Levy Economics Institute, Public Policy Brief 76.

Carnegie, Andrew. 1998. *The Gospel of Wealth.* Bedford, MA: Applewood Books.

———. 1968 [1885]. The Road to Business Success. In *The American Gospel of Success: Individualism and Beyond,* ed. M. Raschin. Chicago: Quadrangle, 91–97.

Carroll, Christopher D., Changyong Rhee, and Byungkun Rhee 1994. Are There Cultural Effects on Savings? Some Cross-Sectional Evidence. *Quarterly Journal of Economics,* 109, no. 3: 685–99.

Casper, Lynne M., Sara S. McLanahan, and Irwin Garfinkel. 1994. The Gender-Poverty Gap: What We Can Learn from Other Countries. *American Sociological Review* 59, no. 4: 594–605.

Castells, Manuel. 1975. Advanced Capitalism: Collective Consumption and Urban Contradictions. In *Stress and Contradiction in Modern Capitalism,* ed. L. Lindberg et al. London: Lexington Books, 423–24.

Castles, Francis G. 1998. *Comparative Public Policy: Patterns of Post-War Transformation.* Cheltenham, UK: Edward Elgar.

Cavalluzzo, Ken S., and Linda C. Cavalluzzo. 1998. Market Structure and Discrimination: The Case of Small Businesses. *Journal of Money, Credit and Banking* 30, no. 4: 771–92.

Center for Housing Policy. 2004. Working Families With Children: A Closer Look at Homeownership Trends. Release date: May 2004, www.nhc.org/pdf/.

Chang, Mariko. 2003. With a Little Help from My Friends (and My Financial Planner): How Socioeconomic Status and Race Influence the Search for Financial Information. Paper presented to the session on culture and economy at the 2003 annual meeting of the American Sociological Association, Atlanta, GA.

Cherlin, Andrew J. 2005. American Marriage in the Early Twenty-First Century. *The Future of Children* 15, no. 2: 33–55.

———. 1992. *Marriage, Divorce, Remarriage*. Cambridge, MA: Harvard University Press.

———. 1983. Changing Family and Household: Contemporary Lessons from Historical Research. *Annual Review of Sociology* 9: 51–66.

Chester, Ronald. 1982. *Inheritance, Wealth and Society*. Bloomington: Indiana University Press.

Chiswick, Barry R. 1986. Is the New Immigration Less Skilled than the Old? *Journal of Labor Economics*, April 1986, 4, 168–92.

———. 1982. The Economic Progress of Immigrants; Some Apparently Universal Patterns. In *The Gateway: U.S. Immigration Issues and Policies*, ed. B. Chiswick. Washington, DC: American Enterprise Institute for Public Policy Research, 119–58.

———. 1978. The Effect of Americanization on the Earnings of Foreign-Born Men. *Journal of Political Economy* 86: 897–922.

Chiswick, Barry R., and Teresa A. Sullivan. 1995. The New Immigrants. In *State of the Union: America in the 1990s*, ed. R. Farley, vol. 2. New York: Russell Sage, 211–70.

Chiteji, Ngina S., and Frank P. Stafford. 1999. Portfolio Choices of Parents and Their Children as Young Adults: Asset Accumulation by African-American Families *The American Economic Review*. 89 (2): 377–380.

Chiteji, Ngina, and Darrick Hamilton. 2005. Kin Networks and Asset Accumulation. In *Inclusion in the American Dream: Assets, Poverty, and Public Policy*, ed. Michael Sherraden. Oxford: Oxford University Press.

Clark, Simon, and Norman Ginsberg. 1975. Political Economy and the Housing Questions. Paper presented at the housing workshop of the Conference of Socialist Economics. London: Political Economy of Housing Workshop.

Clark, William A. V. 1998. *The California Cauldron: Immigration and the Fortunes of Local Communities*. New York: Guilford Press.

Clignet, Remi P. 1999. *Death, Deeds, and Descendants: Inheritance in Modern America*. Hawthorne, NY: Aldine De Gruyter.

———. 1998. Ethnicity and Inheritance. In *Inheritance and Wealth in America*, ed. R. K. Miller and S. J. McNamee. New York: Plenum Press, 119–38.

———. 1992. *Death, Deeds, and Descendents: Inheritance in Modern America*. Hawthorne, New York: Aldine de Gruyter.

Coale, Ansley J., and Susan Cotts Watkins. 1986. *The Decline of Fertility in Europe*. Princeton, NJ: Princeton University Press.

Cobb-Clark, Deborah A., and Vincent A. Hildebrand. 2006. The Wealth and Asset Holdings of U.S.-Born and Foreign-Born Households: Evidence from the SIPP Data (with Vincent Hildebrand). *Review of Income and Wealth* 52, no. 1: 17–42.

Cole, Elizabeth R., and Safiya R. Omari. 2003. Race, Class and the Dilemmas of Upward Mobility for African Americans. *Journal of Social Issues* 59, no. 4: 785–802.

Coleman, James S., and Thomas Hoffer. 1987. *Public and Private High Schools: The Impact of Communities.* New York: Basic Books.

Coles, Flournoy A. Jr. 1973. Financial Institutions and Black Entrepreneurship. *Journal of Black Studies*, Vol. 3 (3): 329–349.

Collins, Chuck, Mike Lapham, and Scott Klinger. 2004. I Didn't Do It Alone: Society's Contribution to Individual Wealth and Success. United for a Fair Economy. www.responsiblewealth.org/press/2004/notalonereportfinal.pdf.

Conley, Dalton. 2001. Capital for College: Parental Assets and Postsecondary Schooling. *Sociology of Education* 74: 59–72.

———. 1999. *Being Black, Living in the Red: Race, Wealth, and Social Policy in America.* Berkeley: University of California Press.

Conley, Dalton, and Miriam Ryvicker. 2005. The Price of Female Headship: Gender, Inheritance, and Wealth Accumulation in the United States. *Journal of Income Distribution* 13: 41–56.

Coontz, Stephanie. 2006. Historical Perspectives on Family Diversity. In *American Families Past and Present: Social Perspectives on Transformation,* ed. S. M. Ross. New Brunswick, NJ: Rutgers University Press, 65–81.

———. 1995. The American Family and the Nostalgia Trap (attributing Americans' social problems to the breakdown of the traditional family) (KAPPAN Special Report). *Phi Delta Kappan* 76, no. 7: K1–K20.

Cowell, Frank A. 1977. *Measuring Inequality.* Oxford: Philip Allen.

Cox, Donald, and Fredric Raines. 1985. Interfamily Transfers and Income Redistribution. In *Horizontal Equity, Uncertainty and Measures of Economic Well-Being,* ed. Martin David and Timothy Smeeding. Chicago: University of Chicago Press.

Cox, Donald, and Mark R. Rank. 1992. Inter vivos Transfers and Intergenerational Exchange. *Review of Economics and Statistics* 74, no. 2: 305–14.

Curtis, Richard F. 1986. Household and Family in Theory on Inequality. *American Sociological Review* 51, no. 2: 168–83.

Dalaker, Joseph. 2001. Poverty in the United States: 2000. U.S. Census Bureau, Current Population Reports, series P60–201. Washington, DC: U.S. Government Printing Office.

D'Amico, Ronald, and Nan L. Maxwell. 1995. The Continuing Significance of Race in Minority Male Joblessness. *Social Forces* 73, no. 3: 969–91.

Davies, James B. 1982. The Relative Impact of Inheritance and Other Factors on Economic Inequality. *Quarterly Journal of Economics* 97, no. 3: 471–98.

Davies, James B., Susanna Sandstrom, Anthony Shorrocks, and Edward N. Wolff. 2006. The World Distribution of Household Wealth. www.iariw.org/papers/2006/davies.pdf.

Davis, Kingsley, and Wilbert E. Moore. 1945. Some Principles of Stratification. *American Sociological Review* 10, no. 2, 1944 Annual Meeting Papers: 242–49.

Dean, John P. 1945. *Home Ownership: Is It Sound?* New York: Harper and Row.

DeNavas-Walt, Carmen, Bernadette D. Proctor, and Cheryl Hill Lee. 2006. Income, Poverty and Health Insurance Coverage in the United States: 2005. U.S. Department of Commerce. Issued August 2006, P60-231.

Domhoff, G. William. 1998. *Who Rules America? Power and Politics in the Year 2000*, 3rd edition. Mountain View, CA: Mayfield.

Draut, Tamara, and Javier Silva. 2004. Generation Broke: The Growth of Debt Among Young Americans. Demos, Borrowing to Make Ends Meet, briefing paper #2. www.demos-usa.org/pubs/Generation_Broke.pdf.

Dreier, Peter. 1982. The Status of Tenants in the United States. *Social Problems* 30, no. 2: 179–98.

Dreier, Peter, John Mollenkopf, and Todd Swanstrom. 2001. *Place Matters: Metropolitics for the Twenty First Century.* Lawrence, KS: University Press of Kansas.

Dressel, Paula L. 1998. Gender, Race, and Class: Beyond the Feminization of Poverty in Later Life. *The Gerontologist* 28, no. 2: 177–80.

Duncan, Greg J., and Jeanne Brooks-Gunn, eds. 1997. *Consequences of Growing Up Poor.* New York: Russell Sage.

Duncan, Otis Dudley, and Peter M. Blau. 1967. *The American Occupational Structure.* New York: Wiley.

Duncan, Otis Dudley, David L. Featherman, and Beverly Duncan. 1972. *Socioeconomic Background and Achievement.* New York: Academic Press.

Dunn, Thomas A., and John W. Phillips. 1997. The Timing and Division of Parental Transfers to Children. *Economics Letters* 54, no. 2: 135–37.

Durkheim, Emile 1984. *The Division of Labor in Society.* New York: the Free Press.

Durkheim, Emile. 1992. *Professional Ethics and Civic Morals.* New York: Routledge.

Dwyer, Jeffrey, and Raymond T. Coward. 1992. Gender, Family and Long Term Care of the Elderly. In *Gender, Families and Elder Care*, ed. Jeffrey W. Dwyer and Raymond T. Coward. Thousand Oaks, CA: Sage Publications.

Dye, Jane Lawler. 2005. Fertility of American Women: June 2004. Population Characteristics P20–555. Current Population Reports. www.census.gov/prod/2005pubs/p20–555.pdf.

Dymski, Gary A. 2006. Discrimination in the Credit and Housing Markets: Findings and Challenges. In *Handbook on the Economics of Discrimination*, ed. William Rodgers. Northampton, MA, Cheltenham, UK: Edward Elgar.

———. 1997. Why Does Race Matter in Housing and Credit Markets? In *Race, Market and Social Outcomes*, ed. P. L. Mason and R. Williams. Norwell, MA: Kluwer Academic Publishers, 157–91.

Dynan K., K. Johnson, and K. Pence. 2003. Recent Changes to a Measure of U.S. Household Debt Service. *Federal Reserve Bulletin*, October.

Edmonston, Barry, and Jeffrey S. Passel. 1999. How Immigration and Intermarriage Affect the Racial and Ethnic Composition of the U.S. Population. In *Immigration and Opportunity: Race, Ethnicity, and Employment in the United States*, ed. Frank D. Bean and Stephanie Bell-Rose. New York: Russell Sage, 373–415.

Elwood, David T., and Christopher Jencks. 2004. The Uneven Spread of Single-Parent Families: What Do We Know? Where Do We Look for Answers? In *Social Inequality*, ed. Kathryn M. Neckerman. New York: Russell Sage, 3–79.

Elmelech, Yuval. 2005. Attitudes toward Familial Obligation in the United States and in Japan. *Sociological Inquiry* 75, no. 4: 497–526.

———. 2004. Housing Inequality in New York City. *Housing, Theory and Society* 21, no. 4: 163–75.

———. 2002. Transmitting Inequality: An Asset-Based Analysis of Racial and Ethnic Inequality and Its Intergenerational Transmission. Ph.D. dissertation. Columbia University.

Elmelech, Yuval, and Hsien Hen-Lu. 2004. Race, Ethnicity and the Gender Poverty Gap. *Social Science Research* 33, no. 1: 158–82.

Elmelech, Yuval, Katherine McCaskie, Mary Clare Lennon, and Hsien-Hen Lu. 2002. Children of Immigrants—A Statistical Profile. National Center for Children in Poverty (NCCP) www.nccp.org/publications/pub_475.html.

Engelhardt, Gary V., and Christopher J. Mayer. 1998. Intergenerational Transfers, Borrowing Constraints, and Saving Behavior: Evidence from the Housing Market. *Journal of Urban Economics* 44, no. 1: 135–57.

Engels, Friedrich [1935] 1975. *The Housing Question*. Progress Publishers.

Engen, Eric M., Andreas Lehnert, and Richard Kehoe. 2000. Mutual Funds and the U.S. Equity Market. *Federal Reserve Bulletin*.

England, Paula. 2004. More Mercenary Mate Selection? Comment on Sweeney and Cancian (2004) and Press (2004). *Journal of Marriage and Family* 66: 1034–37.

Epstein, Gerald. 2002. Financialization, Rentier Interests, and Central Bank Policy. Department of Economics and Political Economy Research Institute (PERI), University of Massachusetts, Amherst.

Esping-Andersen, Gosta. 1990. *The Three Worlds of Welfare Capitalism*. Princeton, NJ: Princeton University Press.

Fairlie, Robert W. 1999. The Absence of the African-American Owned Business: An Analysis of the Dynamics of Self-Employment. *Journal of Labor Economics* 17, no. 1: 80–108.

Farley, Reynolds. 1984. *Blacks and Whites: Narrowing the Gap?* Cambridge, MA: Harvard University Press.

Farley, Reynolds, and Richard Alba. 2002. The New Second Generation in the United States. *International Migration Review* 36, no. 3: 669–701.

Fazio, R. H. 1990. Multiple Processes by Which Attitudes Guide Behavior: The MODE Model as an Integrative Framework. In *Advances in Experimental Social Psychology* (vol. 23), ed. M. P. Zanna. San Diego, CA: Academic Press.

Ferrera, Maurizio. 1997. Welfare States and Social Safety Nets in Southern Europe: An Introduction. In *Welfare States Reform in Southern Europe: Fighting Poverty and Social Exclusion in Italy, Spain, Portugal, and Greece*, ed. Maurizio Ferrera. New York: Routledge.

Fields, Jason. 2001. Living Arrangements of Children: 2001. Household Economic Studies. P70–74. Issued April 2001. Current Population Reports. U.S. Department of Commerce. www.census.gov/prod/2001pubs/p70–74.pdf.

Fishbein, Martin, and Icek Ajzen. 1975. *Belief, Attitude, Intention and Behavior: An Introduction to Theory and Research*. Reading, MA: Addison-Wesley.

Fisher, Gordon M. 1992. The Development and History of the Poverty Thresholds. *Social Security Bulletin* 55, no. 4: 3–14, www.ssa.gov/history/fisheronpoverty.html.

Frazier, E. Franklin. 1939. *The Negro Family in the United States*. Chicago: University of Chicago Press.

———. 1930. Occupational Classes Among Negroes in Cities. *The American Journal of Sociology* 35, no. 5: 718–38.

Friedman, Milton. 1962. *Capitalism and Freedom*. Chicago: University of Chicago Press.

FRBSF (The Federal Reserve Bank of San Francisco) Economic Letter. 2006. The Rise in Homeownership. 2006-30.

Furstenberg, Frank F. 2005. The Future of Marriage. In *Family in Transition*, ed. A. S. Skolnick and J. H. Skolnick. Boston: Allyn and Bacon: 190–96.

Furstenberg, Frank F., Saul D. Hoffman, and Laura Shrestha. 1995. The Effect of Divorce on Intergenerational Transfers: New Evidence. *Demography* 32, no. 3: 319–33.

Gale, William G. 1998. The Effects of Pensions on Household Wealth: A Reevaluation of Theory and Evidence. *The Journal of Political Economy* 106, no. 4: 706–23.

Gale, William G., and John K. Scholz. 1994a. Intergenerational Transfers and the Accumulation of Wealth. *The Journal of Economic Perspectives* 8, no. 4 : 145–60.

———. 1994b. IRAs and Household Saving. *The American Economic Review* 84, no. 5: 1233–60.

Galenson, Marjorie. 1972. Do Blacks Save More? *The American Economic Review* 62, no. 1/2: 211–16.

Galster, George C. 1987. *Homeowners and Neighborhood Reinvestment*. Durham, NC: Duke University Press.

Ganong, Lawrence, Marylin Coleman, Annette K. McDaniel, and Tim Killian. 1998. Attitudes Regarding Obligations to Assists an Older Parents or Stepparent Following Later-Life Remarriage. *Journal of Marriage and the Family* 60, no. 3: 595–610.

Gauthier, Anne Hélène. 1996. *The State and the Family: A Comparative Analysis of Family Policies in Industrialized Countries*. Oxford: Clarendon Press.

Giddens, Anthony. 1981. *The Class Structure of the Advanced Societies*. New York: Harper and Row.

———. 1971. *Capitalism and Modern Social Theory. An Analysis of the Writings of Marx, Durkheim and Max Weber*. Cambridge, UK: Cambridge University Press.

Gilderbloom, John I., and John P. Markham. 1995. The Impact of Homeownership on Political Beliefs. *Social Forces* 73, no. 4: 1589–1607.

Glazer, Nathan. 2003. On Americans and Inequality. *Daedalus* 132 (Summer): 111–15.

Glazer, Nathan, and Daniel Moynahan. 1970. *Beyond the Melting Pot*. Cambridge, MA: MIT Press.

Gleckman, Howard. 2001. Whose Tax Plan Will Save You More? *Business Week* February 20, 2001.

Glick, P. C. 1997. Demographic Pictures of African American Families. In *Black Families*, ed. H.P. McAdoo. Thousand Oaks, CA: Sage Publications, 118–39.

GlobalNation. 2003. Washington, DC. www.inq7.net/globalnation/sec_rec/2003/dec/index.htm, accessed November 24, 2003.

Gokhale, Jagadeesh, and Laurence J. Kotlikoff. 2000. The Baby Boomers' Mega-Inheritance—Myth or Reality? Federal Reserve Bank of Cleveland, Economic Commentary. people.bu.edu/kotlikoff/Baby%20Boomer%20Inheritances.pdf.

Goldscheider, Frances K., and Leora Lawton. 1998. Family Experiences and the Erosion of Support for Intergenerational Coresidence. *Journal of Marriage and the Family* 60, no. 3: 623–32.

Goldscheider, Frances, and Calvin Goldscheider. 1994. Leaving and Returning Home in 20th-Century America. *Population Reference Bureau Bulletin* 48: 1–35.

Goldscheider, Frances, Calvin Goldscheider, Patricia St. Clair, and James Hodges. 1999. Changes in Returning Home in the United States, 1925–1985. *Social Forces* 78, no. 2: 695–720.

Goode, William J. 2005. The Theoretical Importance of the Family. In *Family in Transition*, 13th ed., ed. Arlene S. Skolnick and Jerome H. Skolnick. New York: Pearson, 14–26.

Goodin, Robert. 1999. *The Real Worlds of Welfare Capitalism*. New York: Cambridge University Press.

Goodin, Robert, James M. Rice, and Antti Parpo. 2005. The Temporal Welfare State: A Cross-National Comparison. Paper presented at Time Use and Economic Well-Being conference, October 2005. Levy Economics Institute of Bard College.

Goodin, Robert E. 1988. *Reasons for Welfare: The Political Theory of the Welfare State*. Princeton University Press.

Granovetter, Mark. 1983. The Strength of Weak Ties: A Network Theory Revisited. *Sociological Theory* 1: 201–33.

Gratton, B. 1987. Familism Among Black and Mexican American Elderly: Myth or Reality? *Journal of Aging Studies* 1.

Greenhouse, Steven. 2005. Are Unions Still Relevant? *New York Times*, Business Day, July 30, 2005, C1, C13.

Greenspan, Alan. 2005. Federal Reserve Board's Semiannual Monetary Policy Report to the Congress, before the Committee on Banking, Housing, and Urban Affairs, U.S. Senate. February 16, 2005.

———. 2000. The Federal Reserve's Semiannual Report on the Economy and Monetary Policy, before the Committee on Banking and Financial Services, U.S. House of Representatives. February 17, 2000.

Grusky, David B., and Jesper B. Sorensen. 1998. Can Class Analysis Be Salvaged? *American Journal of Sociology* 103, no. 5: 1187–1234.

Gulbrandsen Lars, and Asmund Langsether. 2000. Wealth Distribution Between Generation: A Source of Conflict or Cohesion? In *The Myth of Generational Conflict: The Family and State in Ageing Societies*, ed. Sara Arber and Claudine Attias-Donfut. London: Routledge: 69–88.

Habermas, Jürgen. 1989. What Does a Crisis Mean Today? Legitimation Problems in Late Capitalism. In *On Society and Politics*, ed. S. Seidman. Boston: Beacon Press, 266–84.

Hackstaff, Karla B. 2005. Divorce Culture: A Quest for Relational Equality in Marriage. In Family in Transition. Skolnick Arlene S. and Jerome H. Skolnick. Pearson Education Inc. pp 197-209.

Hall Peter D., and George E. Marcus. 1998. Why Should Men Leave Great Fortunes to Their Children? Dynasty and Inheritance in America. In *Inheritance and Wealth in America*, ed. Robert K. Miller and Stephen J. McNamee. New York: Plenum Press, 173–93.

Hamnett, Chris. 2004. Trend to Greater Equality Reversed by the 'Winner-Take-All' Society. *The Independent* (London), August 3, 2004, 41.

———. 1999. *Winners and Losers: Homeownership in Modern Britain*. New York: Routledge.

———. 1991. A Nation of Inheritors? Housing Inheritance, Wealth and Inequality in Britain. *Journal of Social Policy* 20, no. 4: 509–36.

Hamnett, Chris, M. Harmer, and P. Williams. 1991. *Safe as Houses: Housing Inheritance in Britain*. London: Paul Chapman.

Hao, Lingxin. 2004. Wealth of Immigrant and Native-Born Americans. *International Migration Review* 38: 518–46.

———. 1996. Family Structure, Private Transfers, and the Economic Well-Being of Families with Children. *Social Forces* 7, no. 1: 269–92.

Haslett, D. W. 1986. Is Inheritance Justified? *Philosophy and Public Affairs* 15, no. 2: 122–55.

Hauser, Robert M. 1998. Intergenerational Economic Mobility in the United States: Measures, Differentials and Trends. CDE Working Paper No. 98–12. Madison, WI: Center for Demography and Ecology, University of Wisconsin, Madison.

Hauser, Robert M., and David L. Featherman. 1977. *The Process of Stratification: Trends and Analyses*. New York: Academic Press.

Haveman, Robert, and Barbara Wolfe. 1995. The Determinants of Children's Attainments: A Review of Methods and Findings. *Journal of Economic Literature* 33, no. 4: 1829–78.

Havens, John J., and Paul G. Schervish. 2003. Why the $41 Trillion Wealth Transfer Estimate Is Still Valid: A Review of Challenges and Questions. Social Welfare Research Institute, Boston College, Boston, MA. www.bc.edu/research/cwp/meta-elements/pdf/41trillionreview.pdf.

———. 1999. Millionaires and the Millennium: New Estimates of the Forthcoming. Social Welfare Research Institute, Boston College, Boston, MA. www.bc.edu/bc_org/avp/gsas/swri/swri_features_wealth_transfer_report.htm.

Hearing before the Subcommittee on Financial Institutions and Consumer Credit of the Committee on Financial Services US House of Representatives. 2006. 109th Congress Second Session. June 13, serial number 109-99. Washington, DC: U.S. Government Printing Office.

Heflin, Colleen M., and Mary Patillo-McCoy. 2002. Kin Effects on Black-White Account and Home Ownership. *Sociological Inquiry* 72, no. 2: 220–39.

Heller, Peter L. 1976. Familism Scale: Revalidation and Revision. *Journal of Marriage and the Family* 38, no. 3: 423–29.

Henretta John C. 1984. Parental Status and Child's Home Ownership. *American Sociological Review* 49, no. 1: 131–40.

———. 1979. Race Differences in Middle Class Lifestyle: The Role of Home Ownership. *Social Science Research* 8, no. 1: 63–78.

Henretta, John C., and Richard T. Campbell. 1978. Net Worth as an Aspect of Status *The American Journal of Sociology* 83, no. 5: 1204–23.

Hernandez, Donald. 2004. Demographic Change and the Life Circumstances of Immigrant Families. *The Future of Children* 14, no. 2: 17-47.

———., ed. 1999. *Children of Immigrants: Health, Adjustment, and Public Assistance.* Washington, DC: National Academy Press.

Hernandez, Donald J, and David E. Myers. 1995. *America's Children: Resources from Family, Government, and the Economy.* New York: Russell Sage.

Hertz, Tom. 2006. Understanding Mobility in America. Center for American Progress. www.americanprogress.org/kf/hertz_mobility_analysis.pdf.

Hill, Martha S., and Greg J. Duncan. 1987. Parental Family Income and the Socioeconomic Attainment of Children. *Social Science Research* 16: 39–73.

Hobbs, Frank, and Nicole Stoops. 2002. Demographic Trends in the 20th Century. U.S. Department of Commerce.

Holden, K. C., and H. H. Kuo. 1996. Complex Marital Histories and Economic Well-Being: The Continuing Legacy of Divorce and Widowhood as the HRS Cohort Approaches Retirement. *Gerontologist* 36, no. 3: 383–90.

Holtz-Eakin, Douglass, David Joulfaian, and Harvey S. Rosen. 1994. Entrepreneurial Decisions and Liquidity Constraints. *The RAND Journal of Economics* 25, no. 2: 334–47.

Horan, Patrick M. 1978. Is Status Attainment Research Atheoretical? *American Sociological Review* 43: 534–41.

Hoyert, D. L., H. C. King, and B. L. Smith. 2005. Deaths: Preliminary Data for 2003. *National Vital Statistics Reports* 53, no. 15. Hyattsville, MD: National Center for Health Statistics.

Hurst, Erik, Ming Ching Luoh, and Frank P. Stafford. 1998. Wealth Dynamics of American Families, 1984–1994. *Brookings Papers on Economic Activity* no. 1: 276–337.

Iceland, John. 2003a. *Poverty in America: A Handbook.* Berkeley: University of California Press.

———. 2003b. Why Poverty Remains High: The Role of Income Growth, Economic Inequality, and Changes in Family Structure, 1949–1999. *Demography* 40, no. 3: 499–519.

Inhaber, Herbert, and Sidney L. Carroll. 1992. *How Rich is Too Rich? Income and Wealth in America.* New York: Praeger.

Jackman, Mary R., and Robert W. Jackman. 1980. Racial Inequalities in Home Ownership. *Social Forces* 58, no. 4: 1221–34.

Jackson, James S., Rukmalie Jayakody, and Toni C. Antonucci. 1997. Exchanges within Black American Three-Generation Families: The Family Environment Context Model. In *Aging and Generational Relations: Life Course and Cross Cultural Perspectives*, ed. Tamara Hareven. New York: Aldine de Gruyter, 83–115.

Jacobs, Jerry A., and Teresa G. Labov. 2002. Gender Differentials in Intermarriage among Sixteen Race and Ethnic Groups. *Sociological Forum* 17, no. 4: 621–46.

Jaffe, Abram J., Ruth M. Cullen, and Thomas D. Boswell. 1980. *The Changing Demography of Spanish Americans.* New York: Academic Press.

Jaher, Frederick. 1980. The Gilded Elite: American Multimillionaires, 1865 to the Present. In *Wealth and the Wealthy in the Modern World*, ed. W. D. Rubinstein. London: Croom Helm, 189–277.

Jarrett, Robin L. 1994. Living Poor: Family Life among Single-Parent, African American Women. *Social Problems* 41: 30-49.

Jencks, Christopher. 1979. *Who Gets Ahead? The Determinants of Economic Success in America.* New York: Basic Books, 397.

Johnson, Richard W., and Simone G. Schaner. 2005. Many Older Americans Engage in Caregiving Activities. Policy Briefs, Perspectives on Productive Aging. The Urban Institute, July 28, www.urban.org.

Joulfaian, David, and Mark O. Wilhelm. 1994. Inheritance and Labor Supply. *Journal of Human Resources* 92, no. 4: 1205–34.

Kain, John F., and John M. Quigley. 1975. *Housing Market and Racial Discrimination: A Microeconomic Analysis.* New York: National Bureau of Economic Research.

Kalmijn, Matthijs. 1998. Intermarriage and Homogamy: Causes, Patterns, Trends. *Annual Review of Sociology* 24: 395–421.

———. 1996. The Socioeconomic Assimilation of Caribbean American Blacks. *Social Forces* 74, no. 3: 911–30.

———. 1994. Assortative Mating By Cultural and Economic Occupational Status. *American Journal of Sociology* 100, no. 2: 422–52.

———. 1993. Trends in Black/White Intermarriage. *Social Forces* 72, no. 1: 119–46.

Kaplan, H. Roy. 1978. *Lottery Winners: How They Won and How Winning Changed Their Lives.* New York: Harper and Row.

Karoly, Lynn A. 1994. Trends in Income Inequality: The Impact of, and Implications for, Tax Policy. In *Tax Progressivity*, ed. Joel B. Slemrod. New York: Cambridge University Press, 95–129.

Kasarda, John D. 1995. Industrial Restructuring and the Changing Location of Jobs. In *State of the Union*, ed. R. Farley, vol. 1. New York: Russell Sage, 215–68.

Katz, Stanley. 1976. Thomas Jefferson and the Right to Property in Revolutionary America. *Journal of Law and Economics* 19, no. 3: 467–88.

Katznelson, Ira, 1992. *Marxism and the City*. Oxford: Clarendon Press.

Kearl, James R., and Clayne L. Pope. 1983. The Life Cycle in American Economic History. *Journal of Economic History* (March): 149–58.

Keister Lisa A. 2000. *Wealth in America: Trends in Wealth Inequality*. Cambridge University Press.

Keister, Lisa A. 2005. *Getting Rich: America's New Rich and How They Got That Way*. Cambridge, UK: Cambridge University Press.

Keister, Lisa A., and Stephanie Moller. 2000. Wealth Inequality in the United States. *Annual Review of Sociology* 26, no. 26: 63–81.

Keith, Verna M., and Cedric Herring. 1991. Skin Tone and Stratification in the Black Community. *The American Journal of Sociology* 97, no. 3: 760–78.

Kennickell, Arthur B. 2003. A Rolling Tide: Changes in the Distribution of Wealth in the U.S., 1989–2001. Federal Reserve Board. www.federalreserve.gov/Pubs/Feds/2003/200324/200324pap.pdf.

Kennickell, Arthur B., and Martha Starr-McCluer. 1997. Household Saving and Portfolio Change: Evidence from the 1983–1989 SCF Panel. *Review of Income and Wealth* 43, no. 4: 381–99.

Kennickell, Arthur B., Martha Starr-McCluer, and Annika E. Sunden. 1997. Family Finances in the U.S.: Recent Evidence from the Survey of Consumer Finances. *Federal Reserve Bulletin*, January.

Kerbo, Harold R. 2000. *Social Stratification and Inequality: Class Conflict in Historical, Comparative, and Global Perspective*. Boston: McGraw-Hill.

King, Gary, and Langche Zeng. 2001. Logistic Regression in Rare Events Data. *Political Analysis* 9, no. 2: 137–63.

King, Wilford Isbell. 1969. *The Wealth and Income of the People of the United States*. New York: Johnson Reprint Corp. [1915].

Kingston, Paul W. 2000. *The Classless Society*. Stanford, CA: Stanford University Press.

Kinsella, Kevin, and Yvonne J. Gist. 1995. Older Workers, Retirement, and Pensions: A Comparative International Chartbook. U.S. Department of Commerce, IPC/95–2.

Kluegel, James R., and Smith, Elliot R. 1986. *Beliefs about Inequality: American's Views of What is and What Ought to Be*. New York: Aldine de Gruyter.

Knight, Frank. 1997 [1923]. *The Ethics of Competition*. Edison, NJ: Transaction Publishers.

Kohli, Martin. 1999. Private and Public Transfers Between Generations: Linking the Family and the State. *European Societies* 1: 81–104.

Kohli, Martin, and Harald Künemund. 2003. Intergenerational Transfers in the Family: What Motives for Giving? In *Global Aging and Challenges to Families*, ed.

Vern L. Bengtson and Ariela Lowenstein. Hawthorne, NY: Aldine de Gruyter, 123–42.

Kolko, Gabriel. 1962. *Wealth and Power in America: An Analysis of Social Class and Income Distribution.* New York: Praeger.

Kotlikoff, Laurence J., ed. 1989. *What Determines Savings?* Cambridge, MA: MIT Press.

Kotlikoff, Laurence J., and Lawrence H. Summers. 1989. The Role of Intergenerational Transfers in Aggregate Capital Accumulation. In *What Determines Savings?*, ed. Laurence J. Kotlikoff. Cambridge, MA: MIT Press, 43–68.

———. 1988. The Concentration of Intergenerational Transfers to Total Wealth: A Reply. In *Modelling the Accumulation and Distribution of Wealth*, ed. D. Kessler and A. Masson. Oxford: Clarendon Press, 53–68.

Kotlikoff, Laurence J. and John N. Morris. 1989. How Much Care Do the Aged Receive from their Children? A Bimodal Picture of Contact and Assistance. In *The Economics of Aging*, ed. D. A. Wise. Chicago: University of Chicago Press. 149–172.

Kozol, Jonathan. 1991. *Savage Inequalities.* New York: Crown Publishers.

Kreider, Rose, and Jason Fields. 2005. Living Arrangements of Children: 2001. Household Economic Studies, P70–104. Issued in July. Current Population Reports, U.S. Department of Commerce. www.census.gov/prod/2005pubs/p70–104.pdf.

Krivo, Lauren J. 1995. Immigrant Characteristics and Hispanic-Anglo Housing Inequality. *Demography* 32, no. 4: 599–615.

Krivo, Lauren J., and Robert L. Kaufman. 2004. Housing and Wealth Inequality: Race/Ethnic Differences in Home Equity in the United States. *Demography* 41: 585–605.

Krumm, Ronald, and Austin Kelly. 1989. Effects of Home Ownership on Household Savings. *Journal of Urban Economics* 26, no. 3: 281–94.

Lamm, Richard D. 1999. Care for the Elderly: What about Our Children? In *The Generational Equity Debate*, ed. J. Williamson, D. M. Watts-Roy, and E. R. Kingson. New York: Columbia University Press, 87–101.

Lampman, Robert J. 1967. Changes in the Concentration of Wealth. In *Inequality and Poverty*, ed. Edward C. Budd. New York: W.W. Norton, 80–86.

Land, Kenneth C., and Stephen Russell. 1996. Wealth Accumulation Across the Adult Life Course: Stability and Change in Sociodemographic Covariate Structures of Net Worth Data in the Survey of Income and Program Participation, 1984–1991. *Social Science Research* 25, no. 4: 423–62.

Landry, Bart. 1987. *The New Black Middle Class.* Berkeley: University of California Press.

Langbein, John H. 1991. The Inheritance Revolution. *The Public Interest* 102: 15–31.

Laslett, Peter. 1994. The Third Age, the Fourth Age, and the Future. *Ageing and Society* 14: 436–47.

———. 1991. *A Fresh Map of Life: The Emergence of the Third Age*. Cambridge, MA: Harvard University Press.

———. 1987. The Emergence of the Third Age. *Ageing and Society* 7: 133–60.

Lebergott, Stanley. 1975. *Wealth and Want*. Princeton, NJ: Princeton University Press.

Lee, Gary R., Julie K. Netzer, and Raymond T. Coward. 1994. Filial Responsibility Expectations and Patterns of Intergenerational Assistance. *Journal of Marriage and the Family* 56, no. 3: 559–65.

Lee, Gary R., Chuck W. Peek, and Raymond T. Coward. 1998. Race Differences in Filial Responsibility Expectations among Older Parents. *Journal of Marriage and the Family* 60, no. 2: 404–12.

Lee, Ronald D. 1994. Population Age Structure, Intergenerational Transfers and Wealth: A New Approach, with Applications to the United States. *The Journal of Human Resources* 29, no. 4: 1027–63.

Lee, Yean-Ju, and Isik A. Aytac. 1998. Intergenerational Financial Support Among Whites, African-Americans, and Latinos. *Journal of Marriage and the Family* 60, no. 2: 426–41.

Lenski, Gerhardt E. 1984. Income Stratification In the United States: Toward a Revised Model of the System. *Research in Social Stratification and Mobility* 3: 173–205.

Levin, Laurence. 1998. Are Assets Fungible? Testing the Behavioral Theory of Life-Cycle Savings. *Journal of Economic Behavior and Organization* 36: 59–83.

Levine, Daniel. 1988. *Poverty and Society: The Growth of the American Welfare State in International Comparison*. New Brunswick, NJ: Rutgers University Press.

Levine, Ross. 1997. Financial Development and Economic Growth: Views and Agenda. *Journal of Economic Literature* 35, no. 2 (June): 688–726.

Levine, Ross, and Sara Zervos. 1996. Stock Markets, Banks, and Economic Growth, Policy Research Working Paper Series 1690, Washington, DC: The World Bank.

Levy, Frank. 1995. Incomes and Income Inequality. In *State of the Union*, ed. Reynolds Farley, vol. 1. New York: Russell Sage, 1–59.

Lewin-Epstein, Noah, Yuval Elmelech, and Moshe Semyonov. 1997. Ethnic Inequality in Home Ownership and the Value of Housing: The Case of Immigrants in Israel. *Social Forces* 75, no. 4: 1439–62.

Light, Ivan H., and Steven J. Gold. 2000. *Ethnic Economies*. San Diego: Academic Press.

Light, Ivan H., and Carolyn Rosenstein. 1995. *Race Ethnicity and Entrepreneurship in Urban America*. Piscataway, NJ: Aldine Transactions.

Loftus, Jeni. 2001. America's Liberalization in Attitudes Toward Homosexuality, 1973–1998. *American Sociological Review* 66, no. 5: 762–82.

Logan, John R., and Richard D. Alba. 1993. Locational Returns to Human Capital: Minority Access to Suburban Community Resources. *Demography* 30, no. 2: 243–68.

Logan, John R., and Glenna D. Spitze. 1996. *Family Ties: Enduring Relations Between Parents and Their Grown Children*. Philadelphia: Temple University Press.

Long, J. Scott. 1997. *Regression Models for Categorical and Limited Dependent Variables*. Thousand Oaks, CA: Sage Publications.

Lowe, S. 1988. New Patterns of Wealth: The Growth of Owner Occupation. In *Money Matters: Income, Wealth and Financial Welfare*, ed. R. Walker and G. Parker. London: Sage Publications, 149–66.

Lowenstein, Ariela, and Vern L. Bengtson. 2003. Challenges of Global Aging to Families in the Twenty-First Century. In *Global Aging and Challenges to Families*, ed. V. L. Bengtson and A. Lowenstein. New York: Aldine de Gruyter, 371–79.

Lu, Hsien-Hen, Julian Palmer, Younghwan Song, Mary Clare Lennon, and Larry J. Aber. 2004. Children Facing Economic Hardship in the United States: Differentials and Changes in the 1990s. *Demographic Research* 10: 285–338.

Macpherson, C. B. 1973. *Democratic Theory: Essays in Retrieval*. Oxford, UK: Clarendon Press.

———. 1962. *The Political Theory of Possessive Individualism: Hobbes to Locke*. Oxford: Clarendon Press.

Madison, James. 1787. *The Federalist*, no. 10.

Madison, James. 1792 (March 29). Property. *National Gazette*.

Manstead, Antony S. R. 1996. Attitudes and Behavior. In *Applied Social Psychology*, ed. G. R. Semin and K. Fiedler. London: Sage, 3–30.

Marcuse, Peter. 1987. The Other Side of Housing: Oppression and Liberation. In Turner, Bengt, Jim Kemeny, and Lennart J. Lundqvist, ed. *Between State and Market: Housing in the Post-Industrial Era*. Sweden: The National Swedish Institute for Building Research.

Mare, Robert D. 1991. Five Decades of Educational Assortative Mating. *American Sociological Review* 56, no. 1: 15–32.

Marks, Carole. 1991. The Urban Underclass. *Annual Review of Sociology* 17: 445–66.

Martin, Claude. 1997. Social Welfare and the Family in Southern Europe. In *Southern European Welfare States: Between Crisis and Reform*, ed. Martin Rhodes. London: Frank Cass.

Martin, Rhodes, ed. 1997. *Southern European Welfare States: Between Crisis and Reform*. London: Frank Cass.

Marx, Karl, and Friedrich Engels. 1962. *Capital*, vol. 3. Moscow: Foreign Languages Publishing House.

Marx, Karl and Engels, Friedrich. [1848] 1962. *The Communist Manifesto.*, in K. Marx and F. Engels, *Selected Works*, Volume 1, Moscow: Foreign Languages Publishing House.

———. [nd]. *Manifesto of the Communist Party*. In *Selected Works*, vol. 1. Moscow: Foreign Languages Publishing House.

Mason, Patrick L. 1996. Race, Culture and the Market. *Journal of Black Studies* 26, no. 6: 782–808.

Massey, Douglas S. 1995. The New Immigration and Ethnicity in the United States. *Population and Development Review* 21, no. 3: 631–52.

Massey, Douglas S., and L. C. Basem. 1992. Determinants of Savings, Remittances, and Spending Patterns among U.S. Migrants in Four Mexican Communities. *Sociological Inquiry* 62: 185–207.

Massey, Douglas S., Andrew B. Gross, and Kumiko Shibuya. 1994. Migration, Segregation, and the Geographic Concentration of Poverty. *American Sociological Review* 59, no. 3: 425–45.

McAdoo, P. Harriette. 1997. Upward Mobility Across Generations in African American Families. In *Black Families*, ed. H. P. McAdoo. Thousand Oaks, CA: Sage Publications, 139–62.

McCall, Leslie. 2003. Do They Know and Do They Care? Americans' Awareness of Rising Inequality. Working paper. Social Science Research Council. www.ssrc.org.

McDermott, John. 1991. *Corporate Society: Class, Property and Contemporary Capitalism*. Boulder, CO: Westview Press.

McDonald, John F., and Robert M. Moffit. 1980. The Use of TOBIT Analysis. *Review of Economics and Statistics* 62: 18–21.

McGarry, Kathleen, and Robert F. Schoeni. 1995. Transfer Behavior in the Health and Retirement Study: Measurement and the Redistribution of Resources within the Family. *Journal of Human Resources* 30, no. 5: S184–S226.

McLanahan, Sara. 2004. Diverging Destinies: How Children Are Faring under the Second Demographic Transition. *Demography* 41: 607–27.

McNamee, Stephen J., Robert K. Miller Jr. 1998. Inheritance and Stratification. In *Inheritance and Wealth in America*, ed. R. K. Miller Jr. and S. J. McNamee. New York: Plenum Press, 193–215.

McPherson, Miller, Lynn Smith-Lovin, and Matthew E. Brashears. 2006. Social Isolation in America: Changes in Core Discussion Networks over Two Decades. *American Sociological Review* 71: 353–75.

Meade, J. E. 1980. The Inheritance of Inequalities. In *Wealth, Income and Inequality*, ed. A. B. Atkinson. New York: Oxford University Press, 253–69.

Meisenheimer II, Joseph R. 1998. The Services Industry in the 'Good' Versus 'Bad' Jobs Debate. *Monthly Labor Review*: 22–47.

Menchik, Paul L. 1988. Unequal Estate Division: Is it Altruism, Reverse Bequests, or Simply Noise? In *Modelling the Accumulation and Distribution of Wealth*, ed. D. Kessler and A. Masson. Oxford, UK: Clarendon Press, 105–16.

Menchik, Paul L., and Nancy A. Jianakopolos. 1998. Economics of Inheritance. In *Inheritance and Wealth in America*, ed. R. K. Miller Jr. and J. S. McNamee. New York: Plenum Press, 45–57.

———. 1997. Black-White Wealth Inequality: Is Inheritance the Reason? *Economic Inquiry* 35, no. 2: 428–42.

Merton, Robert K. 1941. Intermarriage and the Social Structure: Fact and Theory. *Psychiatry* 4: 361–74.

Michalski, Joseph H. 2003. Financial Altruism or Unilateral Resource Exchanges? Toward a Pure Sociology of Welfare. *Sociological Theory* 21, no. 4: 341–58.

Midgley, James. 2005. Asset-Based Policy in Historical and International Perspective. In *Inclusion in the American Dream: Assets, Poverty and Public Policy*, ed. Michael Sherraden. Oxford: Oxford University Press, 42–58.

Miller Jr., Robert K., and Stephan J. McNamee. 1998. *Inheritance and Wealth in America*. New York: Plenum Press.

Mills, C. Wright. 1956. *The Power Elite*. New York: Oxford University Press.

Mishel, L., J. Bernstein, and J. Schmitt. 1999. *The State of Working America, 1998–1999*. Ithaca, NY: Economic Policy Institute and Cornell University Press.

Modigliani, Franco. 1988. The Role of Intergenerational Transfers and Life Cycle Saving in the Accumulation of Wealth. *Journal of Economic Perspectives* 2: 15–40.

Monnier, A., and C. de Guilbert-Lantoine. 1996. The Demographic Situation of Europe and the Developed Countries Overseas: An Annual Report. Population: English Selection, 235–50.

Morris, Martina, and Bruce Western. 1999. Inequality in Earnings at the Close of the Twentieth Century. *Annual Review of Sociology* 25: 623–57.

Mulder, Clara H., and Jeroen Smits. 1999. First Time Home-Ownership of Couples: The Effect of Inter-Generational Transmission. *European Sociological Review* 15, no. 3: 323–37.

Munnell, Alicia H., Kevin E. Cahill, and Natalia A. Jivan. 2003. How Has the Shift to 401(k)s Affected the Retirement Age? An Issue in Brief. (September, no. 13). Center for Retirement Research at Boston College.

Munro, M. 1988. Housing Wealth and Inheritance. *Journal of Social Policy* 17: 417–36.

Murie, Alan, and Ray Forrest. 1980. Wealth, Inheritance and Housing Policies. *Policy and Politics* 8, no. 1: 1–19.

Murray, Charles A. 1984. *Losing Ground: American Social Policy, 1950–80*. New York: Basic Books.

Mutran, Elizabeth. 1985. Intergenerational Family Support Among Blacks and Whites: Response to Culture or to Socioeconomic Differences. *Journal of Gerontology* 40: 382–89.

National Committee on Pay Equity. 2001. The Wage Gap: Myths and Facts. In *Gender and Work in Today's World*. Bounder, CO: Westview Press, 213–21, esp. figure 14.4, p. 214.

NCHS (National Center for Health Statistics). 2002. Women Are Having More Children, New Report Shows Teen Births Continue to Decline. *HHS News*. U.S. Department of Health and Human Services. www.cdc.gov/nchs/pressroom/02news/womenbirths.htm.

NCHS (National Center for Health Statistics). 2004. Births, Marriages, Divorces, and Deaths: Provisional Data for 2005 National Vital Statistics Reports. Volume 53, number 21.

Nedelsky, Jennifer. 1990. *Private Property and the Limits of American Constitutionalism: The Madisonian Framework and Its Legacy*. Chicago: University of Chicago Press.

Nembhard, Jessica Gordon, and Ngina Chiteji. 2006. Introduction and Overview to *Wealth Accumulation in Communities of Color in the United States: Current Issues*, ed. Nembhard and Chiteji. Ann Arbor: University of Michigan Press.

Nembhard, Jessica Gordon, Steven C. Pitts, and Patrick L. Mason. 2005. African-American Intra-Group Inequality and Corporate Globalization. In *African Americans in the United States Economy*, ed. Cecilia Conrad, John Whitehead, Patrick Mason, and James Stewart. Lanham, MD: Rowman & Littlefield.

Newman, Katherine S. 1993. *Declining Fortunes: The Withering of the American Dream*. New York: Basic Books.

New York Times, July 3, 2005. Were the Old Days Really That Good? Sunday Business, Louise Uchitelle.

———, February 24, 2000. Tracking the Wealth Effect. Business Day, p. C1, Richard W. Stevenson.

OECD. 1988. Taxation of Net Wealth, Capital Transfers and Capital Gains of Individuals. Paris: Organization for Economic Cooperation & Development.

Ogbu, John U. 1987. African American Education: A Cultural-Ecological Perspective. In *Black Families*, 3rd ed., ed. Harriette Pipes McAdoo. Thousand Oaks, CA: Sage Publications, 234–51.

Oliver, Melvin L., and Thomas M. Shapiro. 1995. *Black Wealth/White Wealth: A New Perspective on Racial Inequality*. New York: Routledge.

Oliver, Melvin L., and Thomas M. Shapiro. 1989. Race and wealth. *Review of Black Political Economy*. 17 (4): 5– 25.

———. [nd]. Race and Wealth. *The Review of Black Political Economy* 17, no. 4: 5–25.

Orr, Amy J. 2003. Black-White Differences in Achievement: The Importance of Wealth. *Sociology of Education* 76, no. 4: 281–304.

Orzechowski, Shawna, and Peter Sepielli. 2003. Net Worth and Asset Ownership of Households: 1998 and 2000. Household Economics Studies, P70–88. U.S. Department of Commerce and U.S. Census Bureau www.census.gov/prod/2003pubs/p70–88.pdf.

Ove, Moene K., and M. Wallerstein. 1996. Redistribution of Assets Versus Redistribution of Income. *Politics and Society* 24, no. 4: 369–83.

Page, Marianne. 1995. Racial and Ethnic Discrimination in Urban Housing Markets—Evidence from a Recent Audit Study. *Journal of Urban Economics* 38, no. 2: 183–206.

Pagnini, Deanna L., and Morgan S. Philip. 1990. Intermarriage and Social Distance Among U.S. Immigrants at the Turn of the Century. *American Journal of Sociology* 96, no. 2: 405–32.

Pahl, Ray. 1975. *Whose City?* 2nd ed. Harmondsworth, UK: Penguin.

Palley, Thomas I. 2007. Financialization: What It Is and Why It Matters. Levy Economics Institute, Working Paper 525.

Parcel, Toby L. 1982. Wealth Accumulation of Black and White Men: The Case of Housing Equity. *Social Problems* 30, no. 2: 199–211.

Parkin, Frank. 1978. Social Stratification. In *A History of Sociological Analysis*, ed. T. Bottomore and R. Nisbet. New York: Basic Books, 599–632.

———. 1974. Strategies of Social Closure in Class Formation. In *The Social Analysis of Class Structure*, ed. F. Parking. London: Tavistock Publications.

———. 1973. *Marxism and Class Theory: A Bourgeois Critique*. New York: Taylor and Francis Books.

———. 1971. *Class Inequality and Political Order: Social Stratification in Capitalist and Communist Societies*. London: Holt, Rinehart and Winston.

Parl, Robert E. 1928. The Basis of Race Prejudice. *Annals of the American Academy of Political and Social Science* 140: 11–20.

Parsons, Talcott. 1970. Equality and Inequality in Modern Society, or Social Stratification Revised. *Sociological Inquiry* 40, no. 2: 13–72.

Patillo-McCoy, Mary. 1999. *Black Picket Fences: Privilege and Peril among the Black Middle Class*. Chicago: University of Chicago Press.

Pearce, Diana. 1978. The Feminization of Poverty: Women, Work, and Welfare. *Urban and Social Change Review* 11: 28–36.

Penalver, Eduardo M. 2005. Property as Entrance. *Virginia Law Review* 91: 1889–1972.

Peng, Ito. 2000. A Fresh Look at the Japanese Welfare State. *Social Policy and Administration* 34, no. 1: 87–114.

Perlmann, Joel, and Roger Waldinger. 1997. Second Generation Decline? Children of Immigrants, Past and Present—A Reconsideration. *International Migration Review* 31, no. 4: 893–922.

Perlmann, Joel, and Mary C. Waters. 2007. Assimilation and Intermarriage. In *The New Americans*, ed. Reed Ueda and Mary Waters. Cambridge, MA: Harvard University Press.

———. 2004. Intermarriage Then and Now: Race, Generation and the Changing Meaning of Marriage. In *Not Just Black and White: Historical and Contemporary Perspectives on Immigration, Race and Ethnicity in the United States*, ed. Nancy Foner and George M. Fredrickson. New York: Russell Sage: 262–77.

Perrucci, Robert, and Earl Wysong. 2003. *The New Class Society*. Lanham, MD: Rowman & Littlefield.

Pew Charitable Trusts. 2003. Immigrants Send Billions to Families Back Home in Latin America and Caribbean. Washington, DC, www.pewtrusts.com/news/news_subpage.cfm?content_item_id=1951&content_type_id=7&page=nr1.

Pezzin, Liliana E., and Barbara Steinberg Schone. 1999. Intergenerational Household Formation, Female Labor Supply, and Informal Caregiving: A Bargaining Approach. *Journal of Human Resources* 34, no. 3: 475–503.

Phillips, Julie A., and Douglas S. Massey. 1999. The New Labor Market: Immigrants and Wages After IRCA. *Demography* 36, no. 2: 233–46.

Plamenatz, John. 1975. *Karl Marx's Philosophy of Man*. Oxford: Clarendon Press.

Popenoe, David. 1996. *Life Without Father: Compelling New Evidence that Fatherhood and Marriage Are Indispensable for the Good of Children and Society*. New York: Martin Kessler Books.

———. 1993. American Family Decline, 1960–1990: A Review and Appraisal. *Journal of Marriage and the Family* 55, no. 3: 527–42.

Portes, Alejandro, and Min Zhou. 1995. Divergent Destinies: Immigration, Poverty, and Entrepreneurship in the United States. In *Poverty, Inequality, and the Future of Social Policy*, ed. K. McFate, B. Lawson, and W. J. Wilson. New York: Russell Sage, 489–520.

Preston, Samuel H. 1984. Children and the Elderly: Divergent Paths for America's Dependents. *Demography* 21, no. 4: 435–57.

Price, Polly J. 2003. Property Rights: Rights and Liberties Under the Law. (ABC-CLIO 2003).

Pryor, Frederick L. 2007. The Anatomy of Increasing Inequality of U.S. Family Income. *Journal of Socio-Economics* 36, no. 4: 595–618.

———. 1973. *Property and Industrial Organization in Communist and Capitalist Nations*. Bloomington: Indiana University Press.

Pyke, Karen. 1999. The Micropolitics of Care in Relationships between Aging Parents and Adult Children: Individualism, Collectivism and Power. *Journal of Marriage and the Family* 61, no. 3: 661–72.

Qian, Zenchao. 1997. Breaking the Racial Barriers: Variation in Interracial Marriage between 1980 and 1990. *Demography* 34, no. 2: 263–76.

Quadagno, Jill. 1987. Theories of the Welfare State. *Annual Review of Sociology* 13: 109–28.

Quillian, Lincoln, and Mary E. Campbell. 2003. Beyond Black and White: The Present and Future of Multiracial Friendship Segregation. *American Sociological Review* 68, no. 4: 540–66.

Radner, Daniel B., and Denton R. Vaughan. 1987. Wealth, Income and the Economic Status of Aged Households. In *International Comparisons of the Distribution of Household Wealth*, ed. E. Wolff. Oxford: Clarendon Press, 93–121.

Randolph, B. 1991. Housing Markets Labor Markets and Discontinuity Theory. In *Housing and Labor Markets: Building the Connections*, ed. J. Allen and C. Hamnett. London: Unwin Hayman, 17–51.

Reeve, Andrew. 1986. *Property*. Atlantic Highlands, NJ: Humanities Press International Inc.

Reich, Charles A. 1964. The New Property. *The Yale Law Journal* 73, no. 5: 733–87.

Rex, John, and Robert S. Moore. 1967. *Race, Community and Conflict: A Study of Sparkbrook*. London: Institute of Race Relations, Oxford University Press.

Rice, James Mahmud, Robert E. Goodin, and Antti Parpo. 2006. The Temporal Welfare State: A Cross-National Comparison. Levy Economics Institute, Working Paper 449.

Riley, Matilda W., and John W. Riley. 1996. Generational relations: a future perspective. In *Aging and Generational Relations: A Historical and Cross-cultural Perspective*, ed. Tamara K. Hareven. Berlin: Walter de Gruyter: 526-533.

Robb, Alicia M., and Robert W. Fairlie. 2007. *The Annals of the American Academy of Political and Social Science* 613, no. 1: 47–72.

Robinson, Robert V., and Jonathan Kelley. 1979. Class as Conceived by Marx and Dahrendorf: Effects on Income Inequality and Politics in the United States and Great Britain. *American Sociological Review* 44, no. 1: 38–58.

Rockquemore, Kerry Ann. 2002. Negotiating the Color Line: The Gendered Process of Racial Identity Construction among Black/White Biracial Women. *Gender and Society* 16, no. 4: 485–503.

Rodgers, Harrell R., Jr. 1987. Black Americans and the Feminization of Poverty: The Intervening Effects of Unemployment. *Journal of Black Studies* 17, no. 4: 402–17.

Rohe, W. M., and M. A. Stegman. 1994. The Effects of Home-Ownership on the Self-Esteem, Perceived Control and Life Satisfaction of Low-Income People. *Journal of the American Planning Society* 60: 173–84.

Roncek, Dennis, W. 1992. Learning More from Tobit Coefficients: Extending a Comparative Analysis of Political Protest. *American Sociological Review* 57, no. 4: 503–7.

Rosenbaum, Emily. 1996. Racial/Ethnic Differences in Home Ownership and Housing Quality. *Social Problems* 43, no. 4: 403–26.

Rossi, Alice S., and Peter H. Rossi. 1990. *Human Bonding of Parent-Child Relations Across the Life Course*. New York: Aldine de Gruyter.

Rothman, Robert A. 2002. *Inequality and Stratification: Race, Class and Gender*, 4th ed. Upper Saddle River, NJ: Prentice Hall.

Ruggles, Steven. 2007. The Decline of Intergenerational Co-residence in the United States, 1850–2000. *American Sociological Review* 72: 964–89.

———. 2006. Multigenerational Families in Nineteenth-Century America. In *American Families Past and Present: Social Perspectives on Transformations*, ed. Susan M. Ross. New Brunswick, NJ: Rutgers University Press, 101–19.

Ruggles, Steven, and Ron Goeken. 1992. Race and Multigenerational Family Structure, 1900–1980. In *The Changing American Family: Sociological and Demographic Perspectives*, ed. S. J. South and S. E. Tolnay. Boulder, CO: Westview Press, 15–43.

Ryan, Mary P. 1983. *Cradle of the Middle Class*. Cambridge, UK: Cambridge University Press.

Ryder, Norman B. 1965. The Cohort as a Concept in the Study of Social Change. *American Sociological Review* 30: 843–61.

Sakamoto, Arthur, Huei-Hsia Wu, and Jessie M Tzeng. 2000. The Declining Significance of Race Among American Men During the Latter Half of the Twentieth Century. *Demography* 37, no. 1: 41–51.

Samuelson, Robert. 2001. Indifferent to Inequality? *Newsweek*, May 7.

———. 2000. Darling, It'll All Be Yours—Soon. *Newsweek*, April 3.

Sandberg, John F., and Sandra L. Hofferth. 2001. Changes in Children's Time with Parents, U.S. 1981-1997. *Demography* 38, no. 3 (August): 423–36.

Sandefur, Gary D., and Arthur Sakamoto. 1988. American Indian Household Structure and Income. *Demography* 25, no. 1: 71–80.

Sassen, Saskia. 1996. Service Employment Regimes and the New Inequality. In *Urban Poverty and the Underclass*, ed. Enzo Mingione. Oxford: Blackwell, 64–83.

Saunders, Peter. 1990. *A Nation of Home Owners*. London: Unwin Hyman.

———. 1984. Beyond Housing Classes: The Sociological Significance of Private Property Rights in Means of Consumption. *International Journal of Urban and Regional Research* 8, no. 2: 202–27.

———. 1978. Domestic Property and Social Class. *International Journal of Urban and Regional Research* 2: 233–51.

Savage, Mike, Paul Watt, and Sara Arber. 1992. Social Class, Consumption Divisions and Housing Mobility. In *Consumption and Class: Divisions and Change*, ed. R. Burrows and C. Marsh. London: Macmillan, 52–71.

Schick, Frank L., and Renee Schick 1991. *Statistical Handbook on U.S. Hispanics*. Phoenix, AZ: Oryx.

Schlatter, Richard. 1951. *Private Property: The History of an Idea*. New Brunswick, NJ: Rutgers University Press.

Schreiner, M. (2004). Match Rates, Individual Development Accounts, and Saving by the Poor (CSD Working Paper 04-02). St. Louis: Washington University, Center for Social Development.

Schultz, J. H. 1988. *The Economics of Aging*. Boston: Auburn House Publishing Company.

Schuman, Howard, and Jacqueline Scott. 1989. Generations and Collective Memories. *American Sociological Review* 54, no. 3: 359–81.

Schumpeter, Joseph. 1966. The Problems of Classes. In *Class, Status and Power*, ed. R. Bendix and S. M. Lipset. Toronto: The Free Press.

Schwartz, Christine R., and Robert D. Mare. 2005. Trends in Educational Assortative Marriage from 1940 to 2003. *Demography* 42: 621–46.

Sewell, William H., and Robert M. Hauser. 1975. *Education, Occupation and Earnings: Achievement in the Early Career*. New York: Academic Press.

Shammas, Carole. 1993. A New Look at Long-Term Trends in Wealth Inequality in the United States. *The American Historical Review* 98, no. 2: 412–31.

Shammas, Carole, Marylynn Salmon, and Michel Dahlin. 1997. *Inheritance in America: From Colonial Times to the Present*. New Brunswick, NJ: Rutgers University Press.

Shanks, Trina Williams. 2005. The Homestead Act: A Major Asset-Building Policy in the American History. In *Inclusion in the American Dream: Assets, Poverty and Public Policy*, ed. Michael Sherraden. Oxford: Oxford University Press, 20–42.

Shapiro, H. D. 1994. The Coming Inheritance Bonanza. *Institutional Investor* 28: 143–48.

Shapiro, Thomas M. 2006. Race, Homeownership and Wealth. *Washington University Journal of Law and Policy*.

———. 2004. *The Hidden Cost of Being African American: How Wealth Perpetuates Inequality*. Oxford: Oxford University Press.

Sherraden, Margaret S., A. M. McBride, E. Johnson, S. Hanson, F. Sewamala, and T. Shanks. 2005. Saving in Low-Income Households: Evidence from Interviews with Participants in the American Dream Demonstration. St. Louis, MO: Washington University, Center for Social Development. gwbweb.wustl.edu/csd/Publications/2005/IDIPResearchReport2005.pdf.

Sherraden, Michael, ed. 2005. *Inclusion in the American Dream: Assets, Poverty and Public Policy*. Oxford: Oxford University Press.

——. 1991. *Assets and the Poor: A New American Welfare Policy*. Armonk, NY: M. E. Sharpe, Inc.

——. 1990. Stakeholding: Notes on a Theory of Welfare Based on Assets. *Social Service Review* 64: 580–601.

——. 1988. Rethinking Social Welfare: Toward Assets. *Social Policy* 18, no. 3: 37–43.

Sherraden, Michael, Deborah Page-Adams, and Gautam Yamada. 1995. Assets and the Welfare State: Policies, Proposals, Politics and Research. *Research in Politics and Society* 5: 241–68.

Silver, Catherine B., and Charlotte Muller. 1997. Effect of Ascribed and Achieved Characteristics on Social Values in Japan and the United States. *Research in Stratification and Mobility* 15: 153–76.

Skolnick, Arlene. 2005. The Life Course Revolution. In *Family in Transition*, ed. Arlene S. Skolnick and Jerome H. Skolnick, 13th ed. New York: Pearson, 32–40.

Smeeding, T. M., L. Rainwater, and G. Burtless. 2001. United States Poverty in a Cross-National Context. In *Understanding Poverty*, ed. S. H. Danziger and R. H. Haveman. New York: Russell Sage, 162–89.

Smith, Ada. 1976. *An Inquiry into the Nature and Causes of the Wealth of Nations*. New York: Clarendon Press.

Smith, James P. 1997. Wealth Inequality among Older Americans. *Journal of Gerontology*, Series B—Psychological Sciences and Social Sciences 52: 74–81.

——. 1995. Racial and Ethnic Differences in Wealth in the Health and Retirement Study. *The Journal of Human Resources* 30, no. 0: S158–S183.

Smith, James P., and Michael Ward. 1980. Asset Accumulation and Family Size. *Demography* 17, no. 3: 243–60.

Sobol, Marion Gross. 1979. Factors Influencing Private Capital Accumulation on the 'Eve of Retirement.' *The Review of Economics and Statistics* 61, no. 4: 585–93.

Social Security Online. 2002. Income of the Population 55 or Older, 2000. www.ssa.gov/policy/docs/statcomps/income_pop55/2000/sect1.html#t1_3.

Soltow, Lee. 1976. Comment on Paper by Lebergott. *The Journal of Economic History* 36, no. 1: 163–65.

Sorensen, Aage B. 2000. Toward a Sounder Basis for Class Analysis. *American Journal of Sociology* 105, no. 6: 1523–58.

——. 1991. On the Usefulness of Class Analysis in Research on Social Mobility and Socioeconomic Inequality. *Acta Socoiologica* 34, no. 2: 71–87.

Sorokin, Pitirim. 1925. American Millionaires and Multi-Millionaires. *Journal of Social Forces* 3, no. 4: 627–40.

South, Scott J., and Stewart E. Tolnay, eds. 1992. *The Changing American Family: Sociological and Demographic Perspectives*. Boulder, CO: Westview Press.

Sowell, Thomas. 1981. *Ethnic America: A History*. New York: Basic Books.

——. 1975. *Race and Economics*. New York: David McKay Co.

Spilerman, Seymour. 2000. Wealth and Stratification Processes. *Annual Review of Sociology* 26: 497–524.

Spilerman, Seymour, and Yuval Elmelech. 2003. Israeli Attitudes about Inter vivos Transfers. In *International Perspectives on Families, Aging and Social Support*, ed. V. L. Bengston and A. Lowenstein. Hawthorne, NY: Aldine de Gruyter.

Spilerman, Seymour, Noah Lewin-Epstein, and Moshe Semyonov. 1993. Wealth, Intergenerational Transfers and Life Chances. In *Social Theory and Social Policy: Essays in Honor of James S. Coleman*, ed. A. Sorensen and S. Spilerman. Westport, CT: Praeger, 165–85.

Stark, Oded. 1995. *Altruism and Beyond: An Economic Analysis of Transfers and Exchanges within Families and Groups*. Cambridge, UK: Cambridge University Press.

Stearns, Linda B., and Kenneth D. Allan. 1996. Economic Behavior in Institutional Environment: The Corporate Merger Wave of the 1980s. *American Sociological Review* 61, no. 4: 699–718.

Steelman, Lala Carr, and Brian Powell. 1993. Doing the Right Thing: Race and Parental Locus of Responsibilities for Funding College. *Sociology of Education* 66, no. 4: 223–44.

Steinberg, Stephen. 1989. *The Ethnic Myth: Race, Ethnicity and Class in America*. Boston: Beacon Press.

Steinmo, Sven. 1989. Political Institutions and Tax Policy in the United States, Sweden and Britain. *World Politics* 61, no. 4: 500–35.

Stone, Michael. 1980. Housing and the American Economy: A Marxist Analysis. In *Urban and Regional Planning in an Age of Austerity*, ed. Pierre Clavel, John Forrester, and William Goldsmith. Pergamon Press.

Stone Michael E. 1993. *Shelter Poverty*. Temple University Press.

Stevenson, Richard W. 2000. *New York Times*. Tracking the Wealth Effect. Business Day, p. C1, February 24.

Svallfors, Stefan. 1997. Worlds of Welfare and Attitudes to Redistribution: A Comparison of Eight Western Nations. *European Sociological Review* 13 (3): 283–304.

Sweeney, Megan M., and Maria Cancian. 2004. The Changing Importance of White Women's Economic Prospects for Assortative Mating. *Journal of Marriage and the Family* 66: 1015–28.

Taylor, Ronald L. 2005a. Diversity within African American Families. *Handbook of Family Diversity*, ed. David H. Demo, Katherine R. Allen, and Mark A. Fine. Oxford: Oxford University Press.

———. 2005b. *Black American Families*. New York: HarperCollins.

Taylor, Ronald, ed. 2002. Minority Families in Amerca: An Introduction. In *Minority families in the United States: A Multicultural Perspective*, ed. Ronald Taylor. New Jersey: Prentice Hall, 1–17.

Teplin, Albert M. 2001. The U.S. Flow of Funds Accounts and Their Uses. *Federal Reserve Bulletin*, July.

Terrell, Henry S. 1971. Wealth Accumulation of Black and White Families: The Empirical Evidence. *Journal of Finance* 26, no. 2: 363–77.

Thernstrom, S. 1973. *The Other Bostonians*. Cambridge, MA: Harvard University Press.

Thomas, Adam, and Isabel Sawhill. 2005. For Love and Money? The Impact of Family Structure on Family Income. *The Future of Children* 15, no. 2: 57–74.

Thorns, D. C. 1981. Owner Occupation: Its Significance for Wealth Transfer and Class Formation. *Sociological Review* 29, no. 4: 705–28.

Thurow, Lester C. 1999. Generational Equity and the Birth of a Revolutionary Class. In *The Generational Equity Debate*, ed. John B. Williamson, Diane M. Watts-Roy, and Eric R. Kingson. New York: Columbia University Press, 58–75.

———. 1996. *The Future of Capitalism: How Today's Economic Forces Shape Tomorrow's World*. New York: William Morrow.

———. 1981. *The Zero-Sum Society: Distribution and the Possibilities for Economic Change*. New York: Penguin.

———. 1976. Tax Wealth, Not Income. *New York Times Magazine*, April 11.

———. 1975. *Generating Inequality: Mechanisms of Distribution in the U.S. Economy*. New York: Basic Books.

Tidwell, Billy J. 1997. *The Black Report: Charting the Changing Status of African Americans*. Lanham, MD: University Press of America.

Tilly, Charles. 2000. Past and Future Inequalities. *Hagar* 2: 5–18.

———. 1998. *Durable Inequality*. Berkeley: University of California Press.

———. 1996. *Half a Job: Bad and Good Part-Time Jobs in a Changing Labor Market*. Philadelphia: Temple University Press.

Tilly, Louise A., and Joan W. Scott. 1978. *Women, Work, and the Family*. New York: Holt, Rinehart and Winston.

Titmuss, Richard M. 1974. *Social Policy: An Introduction*. London: Allen and Unwin.

———. 1962. *Income Distribution and Social Change: A Study in Criticism*. London: Allen and Unwin.

Torrey, Barbara B., and Cynthia Taeuber. 1986. The Importance of Asset Income among the Elderly. *Review of Income and Wealth* 4: 443–49.

Townsand, Robert A. 2005. Networks and Finance in Ethnic Neighborhoods. In *Credit Markets for the Poor*, ed. Patrick Bolton and Howard Rosenthal. New York: Russell Sage, 179–98.

Tracy, Joseph, Henry Schneider, and Sewin Chan. 1999. Are Stocks Overtaking Real Estate in Household Portfolios? Current Issues in Economics and Finance, Federal Reserve Bank of New York, 5, no. 5.

Treas, Judith. 1993. Money in the Bank: Transaction Costs and the Economic Organization of Marriage. *American Sociological Review* 58, no. 5: 723–34.

Turner, Jonathan H., and Charles E. Starnes. 1976. *Inequality: Privilege and Poverty in America*. Santa Monica, CA: Goodyear.

Uhlenberg, Peter. 1996. Mortality Decline in the Twentieth Century and Supply of Kin over the Life Course. *The Gerontologist* 36, no. 5: 681–85.

———. 1980. Death and the Family. *Journal of Family History* 5 (Fall): 313–20.

U.S. Census Bureau. 2005. Statistical Abstract of the US, 2000. www.census.gov/prod/www/statistical-abstract-1995_2000.html. Last Revised: Wednesday, 21-Dec-2005 10:13:50 EST.

U.S. Census Bureau. 2006a. Statistical Abstract of the United States. Section 13. Income, Expenditures and Wealth. www.census.gov/prod/2005pubs/06statab/income.pdf.

———. 2006b. Current Population Survey, Annual Social and Economic Supplements 2006. Table HH-1: Households by Type: 1940 to Present. www.census.gov /population/socdemo/hh-fam/hh1.xls

———. 2004a. Current Population Survey, Selected Years 1976-2004. Table H-1. www.census.gov/population/socdemo/fertility/tabH1.xls

———. 2004b. America's Families and Living Arrangements: 2003. Population Division, Fertility & Family Statistics Branch. www.census.gov/population/www/ socdemo/hh-fam/cps2003.html

———. 2004c. U.S. Interim Projections by Age, Sex, Race and Hispanic origin. www.census.gov/ipc/www/usinterimproj. Internet release date: March 18, 2004.

———. 2003. Marital Status and Living Arrangements. Historical Time Series, Tables CH-3. Internet release date June 12, www.census.gov/population/ socdemo/ hh-fam/tabCH-3.pdf.

———. 2002a. Global Population Profile. www.census.gov/ipc/prod/wp02/tabA-09 .pdf. Internet Release date: March 22, 2004.

———. 2002b. Current Population Survey. Annual Demographic Supplement, poverty and health statistics branch/HHES Division. www.census.gov/hhes/ poverty/histpov/hstpov3.html.

———. 2001. Current Population Survey. Poverty and Health Statistics Branch, NHES Division. U.S. Department of Commerce, Washington, DC. Table 7: Poverty of People, by Sex: 1966 to 2000. www.census.gov/hhes/ poverty/histpov/ hstpov7.html.

———. 1999. International Data Base. www.census.gov/ipc/www/idbnew.html, accessed November 25, 2006.

———. 1997. Current Population Reports. Series P20–509, Household and Family Characteristics, March.

———. 1992. Housing in America. F. J. Devaney, Current Housing Reports, Series H123.

U.S. Department of Commerce. 2006. Earnings Gap Highlighted by Census Bureau Data on Educational Attainment. Released October 26. www.census.gov/PressRelease/www/releases/archives/education/007660.html.

———. 1995a. What We're Worth—Asset Ownership of Households: 1993. Bureau of Census SB/95–26.

———. 1995b. Assets Ownership of Households: 1993. Current Population Reports, Household Economic Studies, P70–47, Bureau of the Census.

U.S. Department of Housing and Urban Development. 1996. U.S. Housing Market Conditions. Office of Policy Development and Research.

U.S. Department of the Interior, National Park Service. The Homestead Act. www.nps.gov/home/homestead_act.html.

U.S. Office of the Press Secretary. 2005. President Discusses Education, Entrepreneurship & Home Ownership at Indiana Black Expo, Press Release. Office of the Press Secretary. www.whitehouse.gov/news/releases/2005/07/20050714–4.html.

Van Voorhis, Rebecca A. 2002. Different Types of Welfare States? A Methodological Deconstruction of Comparative Research. *Journal of Sociology and Social Welfare* 29: 3–18.

Vinovskis, M. A. 1987. Historical Perspectives on Parent-Child Interactions. In *Parenting Across the Lifespan: Biosocial Dimensions*, ed. Lonnie Sherrod, Alice Rossi, and Jane Beckman Lancaster. Hawthorne, NY: Aldine de Gruyter.

Waite, Linda, and Maggie Gallagher. 2000. *The Case for Marriage: Why Married People Are Happier, Healthier, and Better off Financially*. New York: Doubleday.

Waldinger, Roger. 1996. *Still the Promised City? African-Americans and New Immigrants in Postindustrial New York*. Cambridge, MA: Harvard University Press.

Waldinger, Roger, and Mehdi Bozorgmehr, eds. 1996. *Ethnic Los Angeles*. New York: Russel Sage.

Walker, Alan. 1996. *The New Generational Contract: Intergenerational Relations and the Welfare State*. London: UCL Press.

Warren, John Robert, and Robert M. Hauser. 1997. Social Stratification across Three Generations: New Evidence from the Wisconsin Longitudinal Study. *American Sociological Review* 62, no. 4: 561–72.

Waters, Mary C., and Karl Eschbach. 1995. Immigration and Ethnic and Racial Inequality in the United States. *Annual Review of Sociology* 21: 419–46.

Weber, Max. 1981. *General Economic History*. New Brunswick, NJ: Transaction Books.

———. 1978. The Market: Its Impersonality and Ethic. In *Economy and Society: An Outline of Interpretive Sociology*, ed. M. Weber, Guenther Roth, and Claus Wittich. Berkeley: University of California Press.

———. 1964. Social Stratification and Class Structure. In *The Theory of Social and Economic Organization*, ed. Talcott Parsons. New York: Oxford University Press, 424–30.

———. 1958. Class, Status, Party. In *From Max Weber: Essays in Sociology*, ed. H. H. Gerth and C. Wright Mills. New York: Oxford University Press, 180–95.

Wedgwood, Josiah. 1929. *The Economics of Inheritance*. London: Routledge.

Weil, David N. 1994. The Saving of the Elderly in Micro and Macro Data. *The Quarterly Journal of Economics* 109, no. 1: 55–81.

Weitzman, Lenore J. 1985. *The Divorce Revolution*. New York: Free Press.

Wenglinsky, Harold. 1997. How Money Matters: The Effect of School District Spending on Academic Achievement. *Sociology of Education* 70, no. 3: 221–37.

Wilhelm, Mark O. 2001. The Role of Intergenerational Transfers in Spreading Asset Ownership. In *Assets for the Poor: The Benefits of Spreading Asset Ownership*, eds. Thomas Shapiro and Edward Wolff. New York: Russell Sage, 132–65.

———. 1996. Bequest Behavior and the Effect of Heirs' Earnings: Testing the Altruistic Model of Bequests. *American Economic Review* 86, no. 4: 874–92.

Willer, David. 1999. Network Exchange Theory: Issues and Directions. In *Network Exchange Theory*, ed. David Willer. Westport, CT: Praeger, 1–22.

Williamson, John B., Tay K. McNamara, and Stephanie A. Howling. 2003. Generational Equity, Generational Interdependence, and the Framing of the Debate over Social Security Reform. *Journal of Sociology and Social Welfare* 30, no. 3: 3–14.

Wilmoth, Janet, and Gregor Koso. 2002. Does Marital History Matter? Marital Status and Wealth Outcomes among Pre-retirement Adults. *Journal of Marriage and Family* 64: 254–68.

Wilson, William J. 1987. *The Truly Disadvantaged: The Inner City, the Underclass, and Public Policy*. Chicago: University of Chicago Press.

———. 1980. *The Declining Significance of Race: Blacks and Changing American Institutions*. Chicago: University of Chicago Press.

Wolff, Edward N. 2007. Recent Trends in Households Wealth in the United States: Rising Debt and the Middle-Class Squeeze. Levy Economics Institute, Working Papers, 502.

———. 2004. Changes in Household Wealth in the 1980s and 1990s. Levy Economics Institute, working paper series, 407.

———. 1996. International Comparisons of Wealth Inequality. *Review of Income and Wealth* 42, no. 4: 433–51.

———. 1995. *Top Heavy: A Study of Increasing Inequality of Wealth in America*. New York: Twentieth Century Fund Press.

———. 1994. Trends in Household Wealth in the United States, 1962–83 and 1983–89. *Review of Income and Wealth* 40, no. 2: 143–75.

Wolff, Edward N., and Ajit Zacharias. 2006. Wealth and Economic Inequality: Who's at the Top of the Economic Ladder? Levy Institute Measure of Economic Well-Being. www.levy.org/pubs/limew1206.pdf.

Woo, Lilian, and David Buchholz. 2007. Subsidies for Assets: A New Look at the Federal Budget. CFED. www.cfed.org/imageManager/assets/subsidiesforassets.pdf.

Woodward, Jeanne, and Bonnie Damon. 2001. Housing Characteristics 2000. U.S. Census Bureau 2000 Brief. U.S. Department of Commerce, Economics and Statistics Administration. Issued in October.

Wray, L. Randall. 2005. *The Ownership Society*. Levy Economics Institute, Public Policy Brief 82.

Wright, Erik Olin. 1997. *Class Counts: Comparative Studies in Class Analysis*. Cambridge, UK: Cambridge University Press.

Wyllie, Irvin G. 1954. *The Self-Made Man in America: The Myth of Rags to Riches*. New Brunswick, NJ: Rutgers University Press.

Yamokoski, Alexis, and Lisa A. Keister. 2006. The Wealth of Single Women: Marital Status and Parenthood in the Asset Accumulation of Young Baby Boomers in the United States. *Feminist Economics* 12: 167–94.

Yinger, John. 1995. *Closed Doors, Opportunities Lost: The Continuing Costs of Housing Discrimination*. New York: Russell Sage Foundation.

Zedlewski, Sheila R., and Simone G. Schaner. 2006. Older Adults' Engagement Should Be Recognized and Encouraged. The Retirement Project: Perspectives on Productive Aging, 5: www.urban.org/url.cfm?ID=311325.

Zeitlin, Maurice. 1974. Corporate Ownership and Control: The Large Corporation and the Capitalist Class. *The American Journal of Sociology* 79, no. 5: 1073–1119.

Zepezauer, Mark, and Arthur Naiman. 1996. *Take the Rich off Welfare*. Tucson, AZ: Odonian Press.

Zhan, Min. 2006. Assets, Parental Expectations and Involvement, and Children's Educational Performance. *Children and Youth Services* 28, no. 8: 961–75.

———. 1997. Segmented Assimilation: Issues, Controversies, and Recent Research on the New Second Generation. *International Migration Review* 31, no. 4: 975–1008.

Zinn, Maxine Baca, and Angela Y. H. Pok. 2002. Tradition and Transition in Mexican Origin Families. In *Minority Families in the United States*, ed. R. L. Taylor. Upper Saddle River, NJ: Prentice Hall, 79–100.

Zinn, Maxine Baca, and Barbara Wells. 2005. Diversity within Latino Families: New Lessons for Family Social Science. In *Family in Transition: Dimensions of Diversity*, ed. Arlene Skolnick and Jerome H. Skolnick. Boston: Allyn and Bacon.

Zweigenhaft, Richard L., and G. William. Domhoff. 2003. *Blacks in the White Elite: Will the Progress Continue?* Lanham, MD: Rowman & Littlefield.

~

Index

~

About the Author

Yuval Elmelech is associate professor of sociology at Bard College and a research associate at the levy economics institute of Bard College. He earned his Ph.D. in sociology from Columbia University in 2002. His research focuses on social stratification, poverty, wealth, housing inequality and issues related to race, and immigration. His published articles have appeared in academic journals such as *Social Science Research*, *Sociological Inquiry*, *Social Forces*, and *Housing Theory and Society* and he has contributed chapters to several edited volumes including *Global Aging and Challenges to Families* and *Wealth Accumulation and Communities of Color in the United States*.